The Vietnam Lobby

The American Friends of Vietnam,

The Vietnam Lobby

1955–1975

Joseph G. Morgan

The
University
of North
Carolina
Press

Chapel Hill
& London

© 1997 The University of North Carolina Press
All rights reserved
Manufactured in the United States of America

The paper in this book meets the guidelines for permanence and durability of the Committee on Production Guidelines for Book Longevity of the Council on Library Resources.

Library of Congress Cataloging-in-Publication Data
Morgan, Joseph G.   The Vietnam lobby : the American Friends of Vietnam, 1955–1975 / by Joseph G. Morgan.
p. cm.   Includes bibliographical references and index. ISBN 0-8078-6571-0 (alk. paper)
1. American Friends of Vietnam — History.
2. United States — Foreign relations — Vietnam.
3. Vietnam — Foreign relations — United States.
4. Vietnamese Conflict, 1961–1975 — Diplomatic history.   5. Lobbying — United States.   I. Title.
E183.8.V5M58   1997   96-32708
327.730597 — dc20   CIP

01 00 99 98 97   5 4 3 2 1

To James and Joan Morgan

contents

Preface ix

Acknowledgments xv

Abbreviations xvii

1 Ngo Dinh Diem's Early American Supporters, 1950–1954 1

2 The Founding of the AFV, 1954–1955 15

3 The Early Activities of the AFV, 1955–1956 31

4 Promoting the Diem Regime, 1956–1959 46

5 Losing Faith in Diem, 1959–1961 62

6 AFV Policy Disputes and American Escalation, 1961–1962 77

7 The AFV and the Fall of Diem, 1963 91

8 The AFV and the Escalation of the War in Vietnam, 1964–1965 104

9 The AFV and the American War in Vietnam, 1966–1968 122

10 The Last Years of the AFV, 1969–1975 137

11 Conclusion 153

Appendix: Officers of the AFV 161

Notes 165

Bibliography 209

Index 221

preface

When the United States tried to shape Vietnam's destiny in the mid-twentieth century, millions of American citizens became participants in this massive, and ultimately fruitless, effort. Elected and appointed officials formulated and implemented plans designed to prevent a communist victory in Vietnam. Thousands of soldiers, pilots, and marines risked, and often lost, their lives on Vietnam's battlefields in order to ensure the success of this policy. Journalists assigned to Vietnam and their editors in America reported and assessed the effectiveness of their government's course of action. The conflict in Vietnam also became a focus of concern for tens of thousands of private citizens who heatedly debated the wisdom of their nation's involvement. They debated on speaking platforms, in street demonstrations, in the pages of the press, and on radio and television networks. As American casualties steadily rose in an apparently endless struggle, a growing number of people concluded that America's intervention in Vietnam's affairs had been a mistaken, or even immoral, enterprise, and they called for a rapid end to their country's role in the fighting. Other Americans, however, argued that the United States had the right, and even the duty, to oppose communism in Vietnam and to aid the Vietnamese who sought America's assistance.

Some of the strongest supporters of the war effort belonged to the American Friends of Vietnam (AFV), one of the earliest, and perhaps the first, of the private associations concerned with Vietnam. Founded in 1955, the AFV could trace its roots to 1950, when some of the individuals who became its first members met Ngo Dinh Diem, a Vietnamese nationalist who claimed that his country needed America's help not only in freeing itself from French colonial rule, but in preventing a communist-led independence movement from winning power. Impressed by Diem's fervent patriotism and convinced that he was the best candidate for defeating the forces of colonialism and communism in Vietnam, these Americans became Diem's partisans and promoted his cause by introducing him to prominent figures such as Francis Cardinal Spellman, Justice William O. Douglas, and Senators Mike Mansfield and John F. Kennedy. When Diem became the Vietnamese premier in

1954, they tried to convince the government, the press, and the public that he deserved solid American backing. They decided to organize their work on a more formal basis by establishing the AFV at the end of 1955.

The AFV's early membership reflected the broad spectrum of Americans who believed that the United States had an obligation to help Diem in his struggle against the French and the communists. Well-known figures such as Kennedy, Douglas, Mansfield, General William J. Donovan, and Norman Thomas, the American socialist leader, joined the AFV, but the group's most influential members were on its executive committee. These officers included the economist Leo Cherne, political activists such as Joseph Buttinger and Christopher Emmet, General John W. O'Daniel, academics such as Wesley Fishel and William Henderson, and Harold Oram and Gilbert Jonas, two public relations executives who worked for the Diem regime. Many of these people had been Diem's earliest admirers and would support him for years. Nevertheless, when it became evident that Diem's idea of national independence amounted to little more than establishing a dictatorship to benefit his own family, most of them turned against the Vietnamese leader and called for his ouster. Few of them, however, doubted that an anticommunist state in South Vietnam could be established; after Diem was overthrown in 1963, they supported repeated American efforts to help his successors in the 1960s and 1970s.

As the conflict in Vietnam and the controversy that surrounded it intensified in the 1960s, the AFV became a target for Americans who opposed the war. These critics called the AFV and its membership "the Vietnam Lobby" and they charged that the individuals who had formed the group had "maneuvered the Eisenhower administration and the American press into supporting the rootless, unpopular, and hopeless regime of a despot."[1] Once this had been done, Diem's partisans used the AFV to stage "a massive pro-Diem lobbying campaign that had a great deal to do with getting the U.S. into the Vietnam War."[2] They did this by drawing an excessively optimistic picture of Diem's accomplishments and by suppressing or ridiculing reports that criticized Diem. Moreover, the AFV's members created an "ideological framework" justifying America's intervention in Vietnam and the Saigon government's harsh treatment of political opponents "as 'a necessary reaction to the Communist menace.'"[3]

Numerous accounts of the Vietnam War have repeated many of the charges leveled against the AFV and also have raised new questions about its influence.[4] Some writers have speculated on the role Diem's American backers may have played in securing his appointment as South Vietnam's leader, while others have discussed the ties the AFV may have had with officials in Washington.[5] In his examination of the activities of the executive and legislative branches in the Vietnam War, William Conrad Gibbons said "it is reasonable to assume" that the United States government had a hand in the AFV's creation, and recent studies by Gibbons, George McT. Kahin, and Melvin Small have established that the AFV worked closely with the Johnson administration in 1965 and received indirect financial assistance from the White House in carrying out its work.[6]

Other discussions of the AFV express an interest in its activities, but tend to discount claims about its influence. While some accounts have implied that Diem's American supporters played a major part in his accession to power, others have expressed doubts that these people "catapulted Diem from the cloister to the palace."[7] The AFV's ability to affect public opinion and government policy also has been disputed. Reflecting on his own experiences in the AFV, Joseph Buttinger contended that the association's effectiveness had been "highly overestimated by its critics" because the AFV became "a deeply divided" organization plagued with misgivings about the Diem regime.[8] The diplomatic historian George Herring also questions assertions about the strength of the AFV. "Already deeply committed to South Vietnam," he writes, "the Eisenhower administration needed no urging from private lobby groups" to throw its support behind the Diem regime.[9] Some AFV members challenged allegations not only about the AFV's influence but also about the nature of its work. At one point, Buttinger told a friend, "There is no Vietnamese lobby of the American Friends of Vietnam, unless you call, mistakenly, the writings of members of our committee and occasional talks with officials interested in Vietnam a lobby."[10]

Although there is an element of truth in Buttinger's denial, the AFV nevertheless acted as a pressure group in a number of ways. It did not, as did most lobbying associations, directly influence the passage of legislation, because such behavior would have jeopardized its attempt to win tax-exempt status. The AFV's activities, however, represented a lobbying effort because they were intended to convince the American government and public that the South Vietnamese regime, the Republic of Vietnam (RVN), needed the help of the United States. The AFV sponsored conferences and relief projects in order to attract sympathy for the RVN, and its members composed articles and letters arguing that South Vietnam deserved American support. On one occasion, Buttinger himself implicitly acknowledged that the AFV had the character of a pressure group. "The American Friends of Vietnam was formed for an essentially political reason—to help save South Vietnam from Communist rule," he wrote.[11]

Besides making repeated attempts to shape American opinion, the AFV had other attributes of lobbying associations. As in several other private organizations, a relatively small leadership group took an active part in its affairs. These individuals, usually the fifteen to twenty officers who sat on the AFV's executive committee, tried to attract figures from all shades of the political spectrum in order to give the impression that the AFV was nonpartisan and enjoyed broad support. The AFV's leaders also set the group's policies and programs and informed national committee members of these decisions, as well as of developments in Vietnam, through letters and reprinted articles. Finally, the AFV's officers tried to influence American attitudes toward Vietnam by contacting officials, journalists, and private citizens concerned with Vietnam and by expressing their opinions in the press and in public forums such as conferences, debates, and radio and television interviews.[12]

In promoting American support for the Saigon regime, the AFV enjoyed success on a number of occasions, especially in its early years. It had little trouble in drawing an optimistic picture of developments in Vietnam or in fostering the notion that the RVN would prosper under Ngo Dinh Diem's leadership. By doing this, Buttinger later wrote, the AFV performed a valuable service for Diem because its members "were in a better position than any Vietnamese agent to convince the American public and government that Diem's achievements were real."[13] The AFV also encountered few difficulties in getting its views across to officials or politicians in Washington, who gave the association friendly hearings and frequently assisted it in its work. The executive branch, in particular, regarded the AFV as a "useful ally" in its own efforts to bolster an anticommunist state in Vietnam, and it aided the organization by meeting with its officers, providing it with information, and sending speakers to AFV conferences.[14] It collaborated closely with the AFV on several occasions, and, in 1965, the White House helped the AFV obtain funds to counteract growing criticisms of U.S. policy.

Although able to reach a wide and often sympathetic audience, the American Friends of Vietnam exerted, at the most, a marginal influence over America's Vietnam policy. Its activity on behalf of the RVN in the 1950s was largely superfluous because Washington had committed itself to anticommunist governments in Vietnam since 1950, and few Americans in public life seriously questioned this decision. When escalating violence in the early 1960s prompted the Kennedy administration to send a large advisory contingent to Vietnam, an action that significantly deepened the level of American involvement in Vietnam's affairs, the AFV said virtually nothing because its own internal policy disputes had paralyzed the group. This deadlock came to an end after Diem, whose conduct had been the primary focus of disagreement, was overthrown in 1963, and the AFV was once again able to call for strong measures to aid the RVN, but the growing controversy over the war made its voice simply one of many engaged in the Vietnam debate. Moreover, the AFV's ability to reach the public was seriously undermined by financial and administrative problems that troubled the association throughout its existence. By the time the fighting ended in 1975, the AFV had become a shell of an organization that could barely function.

Despite its ineffectiveness, the American Friends of Vietnam is a group that merits attention. An examination of its work provides an insight into the problems a private association faces in persuading the government, press, and public to accept its views. It also can answer questions about the ties the organization established with its own government and with a foreign regime and the influence these parties exercised over one another. Moreover, a study of the AFV sheds light on the activities of citizens who supported the American intervention in Vietnam, individuals who frequently are neglected in many discussions of the Vietnam War.

Finally, the AFV's story gives one an opportunity to examine assumptions that guided America's Vietnam policy for several years. These beliefs rested on the conviction that the United States had a unique ability, even an obligation, to lead the peoples of Asia into a modern democratic world. Moreover, they reflected the notion that America's involvement in Asian affairs would benefit not only the societies of that continent, but the United States itself by providing the nation with a chance to renew its own sense of purpose as it faced the challenge of shaping Asia's future. These attitudes had influenced American views of Asia since the nineteenth century, and they continued to exercise a strong hold over American thinking as the United States became involved in Vietnam in the mid-twentieth century. The flaws of these opinions would become painfully clear during the course of the Vietnam conflict, but by then America had embroiled itself in a savage war that devastated Vietnam and ravaged its own spirit.

acknowledgments

This work could not have been completed without the help of many individuals who generously assisted me in my research and writing. Several former members of the American Friends of Vietnam set aside valuable time to answer questions I had about the organization and their participation in it. These included Leo Cherne, Gilbert Jonas, Murray Baron, Sol Sanders, William Ward, William Brownell, Ralph Smuckler, Gary MacEoin, Peter White, and the late David Martin, Harold Oram, and Angier Biddle Duke. I am particularly grateful to Hugh O'Neill not only for consenting to an interview, but for assisting me in finding the AFV's records, a collection of documents that was essential to this study. Former American and Vietnamese officials who dealt with the AFV were also very helpful, and I would like to thank Chester L. Cooper, Paul Kattenburg, Bui Diem, and the late Vu Van Thai for their cooperation.

I also received valuable aid in gaining access to the documentary sources needed for this work. When I began this project, the AFV's records were deposited at Temple University, and Professor Charles A. Joiner and the staff of Temple's political science department acted as very gracious hosts while I examined the records. Moreover, I am indebted to the archivists and staffs of the following institutions for their generous help: the University Archives and Historical Collections of Michigan State University, the Harvard-Yenching Library, the Diplomatic Branch and Nixon Materials Project of the National Archives, the United States Army Military History and Historical Institute, the Hoover Institution Archives, the Seeley Mudd Manuscript Library at Princeton University, the National Security Archive, the University of Notre Dame Archives, the Public Record Office, Brooklyn College Library, the Center for the Study of the Vietnam Conflict at Texas Tech University, the Indiana University and Purdue University special collections and archives, the manuscript divisions of the Library of Congress and the New York Public Libraries, and the Eisenhower, Kennedy, Johnson, and Ford presidential libraries. I would also like to thank the information staffs of the Central Intelligence Agency, Internal Revenue Service, and Defense and State Departments for responding to my Freedom of Information Act requests.

There are others who gave me useful advice either on how to proceed with my research or on the publication of the manuscript. I am grateful to George McT. Kahin, Helen Chauncey, Francis X. Winter, David Painter, Emmet Curran, Morris B. Schnapper, Louis J. Walinsky, Rita Pfeifer, Daniel Smith, Karen Berger, and Barbara Solomon for their help.

Lewis Bateman and the editorial staff of the University of North Carolina Press gave valuable guidance in publishing this work, and the staffs of the University of North Carolina Press and Iona College's Information Technology Resource Center formatted, printed, and duplicated numerous versions of the manuscript as it was being prepared.

This work, which began as a doctoral dissertation, could never have been written if I had not been given the time needed to pursue graduate studies. Brother A. Joseph Lips was a source of great encouragement and support when I began considering graduate work, and Brothers H. Michael Delaney and Paul K. Hennessy allowed me to take the time needed to complete it. I would also like to thank the Christian Brothers of the Bishop Hendricken and Iona College communities as well as the Jesuits of the St. Aloysius Gonzaga community for their help, hospitality, and companionship during the years this book was being written.

Several people have read different versions of this manuscript. When it was initially written as a dissertation, my mentor, Nancy Bernkopf Tucker, made many perceptive and challenging comments about the text while offering needed encouragement in completing the work. Dorothy Brown also read several drafts of the dissertation and made a number of helpful suggestions. George Herring, whose own interest in the American Friends of Vietnam played a role in encouraging me to choose this topic, generously set aside time to read the thesis in the final stages of its composition. William Brownell and James T. Fisher also read all or part of the dissertation and made helpful suggestions. Readers for the University of North Carolina Press, particularly Professor Gary Hess, made comments that helped me sharpen the focus of the work.

Finally, my father, James Morgan, read the dissertation and spotted a number of writing errors that I and others had overlooked. It is to him and to my mother, Joan Morgan, that this book is dedicated.

abbreviations

AFV	American Friends of Vietnam
AID	Agency for International Development
ARVN	Army of the Republic of Vietnam
CIA	Central Intelligence Agency
CIP	Commercial Import Program
CRS	Catholic Relief Services
DRV	Democratic Republic of Vietnam
GVN	Government of Vietnam
HERO	Historical Evaluation and Research Organization
ICA	International Cooperation Administration
IRC	International Rescue Committee
IRS	Internal Revenue Service
MAAG	Military Assistance and Advisory Group
MSU	Michigan State University
NAACP	National Association for the Advancement of Colored People
NLF	National Liberation Front
NSA	National Student Association
NSC	National Security Council
OSS	Office of Strategic Services
PIO	Public Information Office
RIA	Research Institute of America

RLG	Royal Lao Government
RVN	Republic of Vietnam
SEATO	Southeast Asia Treaty Organization
SVN	State of Vietnam
UN	United Nations
USIA	United States Information Agency
USIS	United States Information Service
USOM	United States Operations Mission
VNA	Vietnamese National Army

The Vietnam Lobby

chapter 1
Ngo Dinh Diem's Early American Supporters, 1950–1954

In the summer of 1950, Ngo Dinh Diem, a fervent nationalist, left Vietnam with his brother, Bishop Ngo Dinh Thuc, on a journey to Rome by way of Japan and the United States. He would not return to his country for nearly four years, coming back only after being appointed to serve as the premier of the State of Vietnam in June 1954. During this time abroad, Diem met and corresponded with French, American, and Vietnamese officials and citizens in efforts to win backing for his views on the direction an independent Vietnam should take and his future role as the nation's leader. He was particularly successful in attracting followers in the United States, where a number of politically active Americans became convinced that Diem could guide Vietnam to independence from French or communist rule. Once Diem gained power in Vietnam, these people provided him with valuable public support.

Born in 1901, Diem was raised in the central Vietnamese city of Hue, where his father, Ngo Dinh Kha, was an official in the imperial court. As a young man, Diem had a shy, retiring disposition, but this temperament was nevertheless marked by a strain of stubborn determination. A devout Catholic, Diem considered entering the priesthood but finally decided against it because, as a journalist later wrote, he regarded the Catholic Church as being "too pliant for his own unbending will."[1] He instead entered the Vietnamese civil service after graduating at the head of his class from the University of Hanoi in 1921. Diem rose rapidly as an official and attracted the favorable attention of his superiors and the French colonial authorities who effectively controlled the Vietnamese government. Emperor Bao Dai appointed him to serve as minister of the interior in 1933, but Diem soon resigned from the post because of French refusal to grant the Vietnamese any meaningful power in directing their own affairs.[2]

After quitting government service, Diem spent the next two decades in the political wilderness despite various attempts to regain power. When the Japanese overthrew the French colonial administration during the Second World War, Diem showed an interest in serving as premier of a Vietnamese government sponsored by Japan, but Japanese authorities, apparently aware of Diem's fiercely independent behavior, blocked the appointment. Another opportunity to reenter political life arose when the Viet Minh, a nationalist organization led by the veteran communist revolutionary Ho Chi Minh, staged a revolution after Japan's surrender in 1945. The Viet Minh abducted Diem and brought him before Ho, who asked Diem to take a position in his government. Diem, distrustful of the Viet Minh's communist leadership and angry about the role Ho's agents had played in the assassination of an older brother, a provincial governor named Ngo Dinh Khoi, turned down the offer and was eventually released by Ho. After war broke out between the Viet Minh and French forces in 1946, Diem took part in negotiations aimed at creating a Vietnamese administration headed by Bao Dai that would try to counteract the appeal of the Viet Minh. Diem nevertheless did not serve this regime, correctly believing that France had granted no meaningful degree of independence to Bao Dai. Although Diem held no political office, the Viet Minh, as Stanley Karnow wrote, "deemed him enough of a nuisance to be condemned to death" and ordered his assassination, a threat that played an important role in his decision to leave Vietnam in 1950.[3]

Diem and Thuc left Vietnam at a time when America's role in Vietnamese affairs had dramatically increased. Officials in Washington initially questioned the wisdom of France's attempt to reassert its authority in Indochina, but the need for Paris's support in the Cold War against the Soviet Union overrode these doubts. Moreover, the Americans worried that a Viet Minh victory would extend communist influence throughout Asia, a fear that was sharpened by the 1949 victory of the Chinese Communist Party and by the outbreak of war in Korea a year later. This alarm about the growth of communist power in Asia led to an American decision to support France's war against the Viet Minh. In 1950, President Harry Truman's administration endorsed French sponsorship of the "Bao Dai Solution" by extending diplomatic recognition to Bao Dai's regime and by inaugurating economic and military assistance programs to help ensure its survival.[4]

Diem and Thuc began their travels abroad a few months after this intervention, and American diplomats, aware of the need to enlist Vietnamese nationalists in the struggle against the Viet Minh, advised their superiors to give the two brothers a friendly reception when they arrived in the United

States. Foreign Service officers in Saigon called Diem and Thuc leading figures in Vietnam's Catholic community, "one of the principle 'fence sitting' elements now in [the] country," and they believed that meetings with the two men in the United States might open Catholic eyes to "the Communist danger to Viet-Nam."[5] Officials who saw Diem and Thuc during their brief stop in Japan reinforced these recommendations by drawing a favorable portrait of Diem. One dispatch referred to him as "an extremely keen person" who "sees political problems clearly," while another cable described Diem as being "anti-French, anti-Communist, progressive, liberal, [and] a good possibility as an American tool in Indo-China."[6]

Washington heeded the advice it received from Saigon and Tokyo, and Dean Rusk, assistant secretary of state for Far Eastern affairs, made arrangements for a small reception for Diem and Thuc in the capital. The State Department also organized tours of American factories so the two brothers would "obtain the impression of our American industrial capacity."[7] Finally, its representatives held discussions with Diem and Thuc. In these talks, the Vietnamese criticized the weakness of the Bao Dai regime, stressed the need for greater Vietnamese autonomy, and mentioned the possibility of creating a Vietnamese army with American supplies. The records of these conversations indicate that Diem did not impress the Americans in Washington as favorably as he had their colleagues in Saigon and Tokyo. Thuc, who spoke as often as, if not more frequently than, did his brother, struck some officers as being a far more significant figure in Vietnam. One official saw Thuc as a possibly "important factor in present IC [Indochina] complex" but regarded Diem as a politician "steeped in oriental intrigue and concerned equally, if not more . . . with furthering his own personal ambitions."[8]

After spending nearly a month in the United States, Diem and Thuc left for Europe in the autumn of 1950. The two brothers first traveled to Rome, and Diem then went to France while Thuc returned to Vietnam. In France, Diem approached Bao Dai on the possibility of serving as the emperor's premier, but he soon concluded that the powers he would receive from Bao Dai would be too limited. Diem then returned to the United States at the end of 1950 and lived there for the next two and a half years, residing at the Maryknoll Mission Society's seminaries in Ossining, New York, and Lakewood, New Jersey.[9]

Diem resumed his contacts with State Department officials after returning to the United States. At these meetings, he displayed less hostility toward the French than on previous occasions, but he nevertheless urged the Americans to press France into granting the Bao Dai regime more autonomy. Encouraged by these reports of Diem's attitude, the State Department told the legation at Saigon that Diem "spoke with much more balance than heretofore."[10] Some Foreign Service officers, however, voiced less enthusiasm for Diem. "He gives the impression," wrote one official, "of being somewhat out of touch with recent developments in his own country."[11]

Besides State Department representatives, Diem met many other Americans during his stay in the United States, including political activists, clergymen, journalists, academics, and politicians. He apparently first dealt with individuals active in Catholic and right-wing circles, but his contacts widened after an introduction to Peter White, a Catholic layman who had ties to both liberals and conservatives. The two men initially saw one another at the New York office of Senator William Benton, a Connecticut Democrat who had allowed White to use the office "in a Great Books merchandising operation." Diem, who was accompanied by a Belgian priest named Emmanuel Jacques, had been referred to White by the staff of *Integrity*, a magazine dealing with questions on how Catholics could practice their faith in American society. White later recalled:

> The two men blew my mind with jolts and blasts of urgent and slanted language regarding their cause, and [in] staff-officer fashion I reduced it all to a single typewritten page and gave it to them as a memo they could use to clue in others on their perplexing and wholly unfamiliar business, which added up to Diem's expectation of being president of South Vietnam. My efficiency, good French, and the size and appointments of Benton's office must have impressed Diem, as he announced to me with great magisterial authority, "J'ai besoin de vous [I need you]."[12]

White soon referred Diem to Christopher Emmet, a relative who had been passionately opposed to both fascist and communist movements for nearly two decades. Related to Robert Emmet, a nineteenth-century Irish nationalist hero, Emmet attended Harvard and went on to study at universities in Germany in the early 1930s, an experience that allowed him to witness Adolf Hitler's rise to power. Revolted by the Nazis, he returned to the United States, where he joined or formed such anti-Nazi organizations as the Christian Committee to Boycott Nazi Germany and the Committee to Defend America by Aiding the Allies. Emmet also detested communism and took an active role in anticommunist associations after World War II. He acted as the secretary of the American Friends of Captive Nations and was a member of such groups as the Committee to Aid Refugee Chinese

Intellectuals and the Committee of One Million Against the Admission of Communist China to the United Nations.[13]

After seeing Diem, Emmet introduced him to other Americans, including congressional representatives. In a letter to Christian Herter, a Massachusetts Republican on the House Foreign Affairs Committee, Emmet described Diem as "a man who is generally recognized as one of the greatest of the Indo-Chinese anti-Communist leaders" and as "a fervent, but not a fanatical nationalist." Emmet outlined Diem's proposals for obtaining greater Vietnamese autonomy and defeating the Viet Minh, and he asked Herter to introduce Diem to other lawmakers, such as Walter Judd and Mike Mansfield.[14] Diem also received Emmet's assistance in drafting a memorandum sent to Edna Kelly, a congresswoman from Brooklyn with a strong anti-communist record. Diem evidently influenced Kelly's views on Vietnam, because a State Department officer who had a tense exchange with Kelly over the issue of aid to French forces in Indochina reported that "Mrs. Kelly has been talking to and impressed by Ngo Dinh Diem."[15]

Diem also met several Catholic clergymen during his stay in the United States. He was introduced to Francis Cardinal Spellman, the powerful archbishop of New York, apparently by his brother Thuc, who told an American diplomat that he had first met Spellman in Vietnam.[16] Several accounts have made much of Diem's relationship with Spellman, claiming that the cardinal played a key role in introducing Diem to a number of influential Americans.[17] It is nevertheless difficult to determine the importance of Spellman's contacts with Diem. He apparently made arrangements for Diem's stay at the Maryknoll seminaries, but the correspondence of Diem's American supporters in the early 1950s contains no references to Spellman, and access to Spellman's personal papers is restricted. Reports of Spellman's meetings with Diem after Diem took office indicate that the two men had a high regard for one another, but the nature of Spellman's relationship with Diem in the early 1950s remains obscure.[18]

Diem also had contacts with other members of the Catholic clergy. A Maryknoll priest, Thomas O'Melia, interpreted for Diem at some of his meetings with American officials, including an abortive attempt to see John Foster Dulles a few days before Dulles became secretary of state in 1953.[19] O'Melia approached James H. Duff, a Republican senator from Pennsylvania, telling Duff that a meeting of Diem and Dulles "would be greatly to . . . [Dulles's] advantage."[20] John W. Hanes, Dulles's personal assistant, called Philip W. Bonsal, the State Department's director of Philippine and Southeast Asian affairs, about the request and received word that the Department had no objection to a talk with Diem. Dulles, however, eventually decided that he would not see Diem. When O'Melia and Diem appeared at Dulles's office, they were received by a member of Dulles's staff instead.[21]

Diem also received help from Raymond de Jaegher, a Belgian missionary who had worked in China for nearly twenty years. Living in a northern Chinese province controlled by communist forces during the Second World War, de Jaegher became a bitter foe of communism, calling it "an evil thing that grows on itself, doubling and redoubling in geometric progression." He also developed a great admiration for the Nationalist leader Chiang Kai-shek, an individual who had, in de Jaegher's eyes, "revealed a profound understanding of the needs of China and her people."[22] After fleeing from China in 1949, de Jaegher moved to America and Europe and was acting as regent of Seton Hall University's Far East Institute at the time Diem resided in the United States. De Jaegher introduced Diem to General William J. Donovan, the former head of the Office of Strategic Services (OSS), in the spring of 1951 and later sent Donovan memoranda outlining Diem's background and his ideas on the struggle against communism in Vietnam.[23]

Diem's stay in the United States gave him the opportunity to meet journalists who sympathized with his calls for an independent Vietnam. Diem won the backing of *The Reporter*, a magazine whose articles reflected liberal concerns about communism, civil rights, and social reform, after Peter White introduced him to Gouverneur Paulding, one of the journal's senior writers. Paulding, like Diem, was a devout Catholic who took an interest in the theories of Personalism, a social and political philosophy formulated by French Catholics who sought an alternative to Marxism and capitalism, and which eventually became the Diem regime's official ideology. The two men apparently struck up a warm friendship; White remembered that Diem liked Paulding "on first sight as a fellow-mandarin of the highest class."[24] *The Reporter* eventually reciprocated Diem's friendliness after he took office in 1954 by calling him "an honest man" who spoke to its staff "with earnestness and charm" in the early 1950s.[25] Diem met another associate of White, an Irish Catholic journalist named Gary MacEoin interested in the social and economic progress of developing countries. MacEoin and Diem acted as godfathers for one of White's children, and MacEoin, favorably impressed by Diem, later wrote that he regarded Diem as "a selfless, ascetic person."[26]

Diem also struck up a friendship with Sol Sanders, a reporter who had worked in Asia for several years and had been active in the anticommunist Left as a student organizer for the American Socialist Party at the University of Missouri. After receiving a bachelor's degree in journalism in 1946,

Sanders traveled to Asia as a freelance writer. He spent much of his time in Bangkok and Hanoi, where he interviewed many of the principal figures in the Indochina conflict, including Ho Chi Minh. Sanders heard of Diem during his stay in Vietnam and was told that Diem was "the only person who has the stature and the authority and the genius" to compete with Ho Chi Minh. Impressed by these claims, Sanders, who was convinced that a nationalist alternative to colonial or communist rule could be found, contacted Diem after returning to the United States in the summer of 1951. Over tea in Greenwich Village, Sanders discussed the Indochinese war with Diem, and the two men gloomily concluded that a communist victory was likely. This pessimism, however, did not prevent Sanders from regarding Diem as an impressive "nationalist figure who had no taint of corruption or opportunism connected with him." Sanders became one of Diem's most faithful supporters in the years ahead.[27]

Besides seeing clergymen, journalists, and political activists, Diem established ties with members of the American academic community, especially scholars specializing in Asian affairs. He apparently attracted the favorable notice of I. Milton Sacks, a political scientist at Brandeis University who had previously served in the State Department, but he forged far closer and more significant ties with Wesley R. Fishel, a scholar whom Diem had met in Japan in 1950.[28] Born in 1919, Fishel attended Northwestern University as an undergraduate and went on to serve as an Army military language specialist in the Pacific during the Second World War. After his wartime service, he undertook graduate studies at the University of Chicago and received a Ph.D. from the university in 1948. One critic characterized Fishel as "a run-of-the-mill academician . . . who had written a non-descript thesis on Chinese extra-territoriality," but Quincy Wright, a renowned international legal scholar who was Fishel's dissertation adviser, regarded him as "one of my best students at Chicago."[29] Fishel struck those who knew him as being a pleasant but ambitious man. After a few meetings with Fishel in 1954, Joseph Buttinger wrote that Fishel "likes to demonstrate he is important, but not offensively."[30] Chester L. Cooper, a National Security Council (NSC) official who dealt with Fishel in the mid-1960s, remembered Fishel as presenting "an image of a sort of meekness and humility . . . but he was a very smart operator, I think."[31]

Given the critical role that Fishel played in Diem's relations with the United States, analysts have assumed that it was Fishel who originally persuaded Diem to travel to America. In fact, American diplomatic reports indicate that Diem intended to go to the United States before he met Fishel.

Moreover, Fishel had not yet joined the faculty of Michigan State College, where he would have the resources to hire Diem as a consultant to the school's Governmental Research Bureau.[32] Diem received this appointment after Fishel joined Michigan State's faculty in 1951. One of Fishel's colleagues remembers only one occasion when Diem gave a presentation.[33] Although not very active at Michigan State, Diem kept in touch with Fishel, maintaining a close relationship that set the stage for the assistance program Michigan State provided for the Diem regime after its establishment in 1954.

During his last months in the United States, Diem made contact with some of his best-known supporters. Supreme Court Justice William O. Douglas had heard of Diem while traveling through Asia in the summer of 1952. After returning to the United States in the fall, Douglas wrote to Diem and asked to see him. Diem agreed to the request and went to a luncheon arranged by Douglas at New York's Yale Club.[34] The meeting between the two men went well, and in a letter to Gene Gregory, a U.S. Information Service (USIS) officer who had told Douglas about Diem, Douglas said that he had been "greatly impressed" with Diem.[35] Douglas continued to correspond and meet with Diem and asked him to proofread sections about Vietnam in *North From Malaya*, Douglas's account of his travels in Asia. When the book was published in 1953, Douglas told his readers that "Ngo Dinh Diem . . . is a hero . . . [who] is revered by the Vietnamese because he is honest and independent and stood firm against French influence."[36]

Douglas introduced Diem to Senators Mike Mansfield and John F. Kennedy on May 8, 1953. He thought that Kennedy would be particularly interested in seeing Diem because, as Douglas later recalled, Kennedy "was one of the Senators who was traveling and observing, and who was critical of American foreign policy."[37] At this meeting, also attended by representatives from the State Department, Diem repeated his earlier criticisms of the Bao Dai regime and of France's failure to give greater independence to the Vietnamese. Mansfield later recalled that Diem "possessed a deep conviction and almost buoyant confidence that he would some day steer his country between colonialism and communism toward freedom," but the senator thought that "there seemed little likelihood that this man—outlawed by both sides in the Indochina conflict—would ever have an opportunity to put his nationalist idealism into practice."[38] At the end of the discussion, Diem informed his listeners of his intention to leave the United States in order to meet with sympathizers in France. However, it was already becoming apparent that his Washington audience was becoming more useful to Diem than any group he would see in Europe.[39]

As Diem sought support in the United States and Europe, events in Vietnam dramatically improved his chances of winning power. Although aided by a growing volume of American supplies, France won few victories in its war against the Viet Minh, and French leaders decided to settle the conflict at an international conference in Geneva, Switzerland. By the time negotiations concerning Indochina began on May 8, 1954, France had suffered a decisive setback on the battlefield when Viet Minh troops overran a large French garrison at Dien Bien Phu, a remote, mountain village in northern Vietnam. The French desperately tried to avert this defeat by asking for American air strikes against Viet Minh positions surrounding Dien Bien Phu, but President Dwight D. Eisenhower turned down this request after strong objections by his senior advisers, congressional representatives, and the British government. With no relief in sight, Dien Bien Phu's defenders capitulated on May 7. Their surrender marked the complete collapse of France's willingness to continue the war in Indochina.[40]

The rapid decline of French fortunes set the stage for Diem's rise to power as France's Vietnamese protégés took steps to ensure their survival against the victorious Viet Minh. On June 4, Bao Dai signed an accord that gave his State of Vietnam (SVN) virtual independence from French control. The emperor also sought closer ties with the Americans, realizing he could no longer rely on France in the wake of the Dien Bien Phu disaster. He instructed his representatives in Europe to contact American diplomats, and he decided to appoint Diem as the SVN's prime minister since "Washington would not spare him its support." The emperor asked Diem to take office as premier on June 16. Diem acceded to the request three days later after he received full civil and military powers from Bao Dai. Diem then left for Saigon on June 24, after spending nearly four years abroad.[41]

Although the hope of winning a strong American commitment to his regime was a significant factor in Bao Dai's selection of Diem, it is difficult to determine the role that the Americans played in this process. The State Department showed a continuing interest in Diem's attitudes and activities after his departure from the United States in the spring of 1953, but its records make no mention of direct American involvement in Diem's selection until May 1954.[42] At that time, Ngo Dinh Luyen, a brother of Diem who claimed he was acting on behalf of Bao Dai, told American diplomats in Geneva of the emperor's intention to appoint Diem as premier if the United States supported Bao Dai's decision. The delegates made noncommittal replies to Luyen, but in a cable to Washington they recommended that the American embassy in Paris contact Diem.[43] Douglas Dillon, the United

States ambassador to France, met with Diem in the following weeks and told Washington that Diem's "apparent sincerity, patriotic fervor and honesty are refreshing." He nevertheless expressed doubts about Diem's abilities, calling Diem a "Yogi-like mystic" who "may have little to offer other than to reiterate that the solution to the Vietnamese problem depends on the assumption of increased responsibilities by [the] US."[44]

Members of the Eisenhower administration nonetheless favored Diem's candidacy. A military cable in early June reported that "Diem has received support and encouragement from American official quarters and this may be a reason why Bao Dai is considering him for the post."[45] It is not clear exactly who pushed for Diem's appointment, but some accounts strongly suggest that John Foster Dulles may have been one of Diem's strongest advocates. John W. Hanes, one of Dulles's assistants, later claimed that the secretary of state's support for Diem was "rammed through single-handedly, through our intelligence and military communities."[46] In his memoirs, Bao Dai mentioned a conversation he had with Dulles before asking Diem to act as premier, and in *The Lost Crusade*, Chester Cooper writes of a meeting between Dulles and Bao Dai that dealt with the role Diem would play in preventing a Viet Minh takeover of Vietnam.[47]

There has also been speculation on the role the Central Intelligence Agency may have played in securing Diem's appointment. Robert Amory, who served as the CIA's deputy director of intelligence in the 1950s, asserted that Justice Douglas had initially sparked the agency's interest in Diem. Another senior CIA officer, Richard Bissell, later recalled that the CIA was "deeply involved" in winning support for Diem.[48] A few accounts have noted that Ambassador William J. Donovan, the founder of the OSS, and Lieutenant Colonel Edward G. Lansdale, a CIA operative, appeared in Saigon shortly after Ngo Dinh Nhu, another of Diem's brothers, organized the Front for National Salvation, a group that promoted Diem's candidacy.[49]

The Americans whom Diem met while in the United States may also have played a part in securing his appointment, but their role is even more obscure than that of government officials. Some early discussions of Diem's accession to power, especially the accounts of French writers, claimed that Cardinal Spellman and American Catholics promoted Diem's cause. There is, however, no available documentary evidence to support these assertions.[50] Justice William O. Douglas believed that his activities did much to put Diem in power. "I think perhaps," he wrote in 1968, "if there is any one individual who is more responsible than any other, it was myself, and that was by way of introduction of him to Washington, D.C. and the book which I wrote."[51]

Although Amory's recollection of Douglas's role in drawing the CIA's attention to Diem lends credibility to this statement, Douglas nevertheless overestimated his importance in introducing Diem to official American circles. As made clear above, State Department records and the personal papers of individuals such as Christopher Emmet show that Diem had numerous contacts with American officials and politicians long before he met Douglas.

Wesley Fishel may also have been involved in the decision to appoint Diem. At least one account states that Fishel "worked for or with the CIA" at the time he first encountered Diem in Japan. It is not clear if this is true, although embassy reports from Tokyo stated that Diem and Thuc spoke to an "American source" during their stay in Japan.[52] Fishel nevertheless acted as an intermediary between Diem and the State Department after Diem took up residence in the United States, and one Foreign Service officer thought that Fishel served as "a sort of press agent and advisor" for Diem.[53] The nature of Fishel's activities nonetheless remains obscure because his name does not appear in State Department archives until the month after Diem became premier, and Fishel's personal papers contain little material from the early 1950s.

While the American role in Bao Dai's decision to give Diem power is unclear, there can be no doubt about Diem's success in attracting supporters during the years he stayed in America—people ready to back him publicly once he gained power. Diem won this following for a number of reasons, one of them being the favorable personal impression he made. He did not have a charismatic personality that could easily attract a large circle of admirers, but he did strike Americans who knew him as a "highly intelligent man" who "inspired confidence [and] remembered everything."[54] In the eyes of his backers, Diem's fervent patriotism and his refusal to compromise with either the French or the communists, the two groups whom the Americans saw as deadly threats to Vietnam's genuine independence, more than compensated for his lack of charisma. An individual with Diem's "all or nothing integrity," they believed, would not betray Vietnam's freedom.[55]

Diem also attracted backers with the political guidance he received from individuals such as Peter White and Christopher Emmet. "Perhaps the most useful thing I did for him," White wrote years later, "was to get him in the way of winning supporters who weren't professional Catholics or lunatic fringe anti-communists, which is what he started out with."[56] Emmet aided Diem in widening the range of his political contacts as well. In a letter to Christian Herter, Emmet stated that he had "warned him [Diem] against tying himself in within an extreme position or with extreme groups in this country." Emmet also cautioned Diem about making any outspoken condemnation of France's Vietnam policy, since that could have contributed to congressional reluctance to approve the aid requests needed to sustain the French forces fighting the Viet Minh. That advice likely contributed to the more moderate tone Diem adopted in his conversations with State Department officials.[57]

Diem did not always accept such counsel. White recalled one occasion when Diem reacted angrily to an article in *The Reporter* attacking the China Lobby, a vocal group of American citizens that often worked closely with Chinese diplomats in generating support for the anticommunist regime of Chiang Kai-shek. White had given Diem the essay in an attempt to warn him against any effort to manipulate his American backers, but Diem replied that "he was deeply offended at the US betrayal 'of your faithful ally.'"[58] Despite such disagreements, Diem usually made use of the assistance that others offered. On one occasion, he told Emmet that he had "paid the greatest attention to your excellent advice."[59]

Diem did not win a following simply by favorably impressing admirers or by accepting political guidance. He also appealed to convictions held by many American citizens. Diem forged ties with his backers at a time when international tensions and fears of internal subversion had created a virulent anticommunist sentiment that touched virtually every shade of the political spectrum in the United States. Right-wing politicians such as Senator Joseph McCarthy emerged as the most vocal exponents of this attitude, but liberals and leftists who regarded the Soviet Union's party dictatorship as a profound betrayal of socialist principles condemned communism as well. In this atmosphere of bitter anticommunism, Diem had little trouble in winning a friendly hearing when he voiced his hostility toward the communist-led Viet Minh. Christopher Emmet called Diem "one of the greatest of the Indo-Chinese anti-communist leaders" in a letter sent to Representative Christian Herter, while Justice Douglas tried to attract a magazine's interest in Diem's views by assuring an editor that Diem "is no Communist."[60]

Diem's requests for U.S. assistance in promoting Vietnam's independence also drew favorable attention to his candidacy because his pleas appealed to a long-held conviction that the United States could do much to shape Asia's future. Ever since the departure of their first missionaries to China in the nineteenth century, Americans thought that their nation had the ability and the obligation to guide the peoples of Asia into the modern world. As they became ever more deeply involved in Asian affairs, Americans began to develop "a parental self-image in their dealings with East Asians" and the belief that they had done much to modernize China, Japan, and the Philippines.[61] This notion retained its hold over American thinking well into the twentieth century; it became strikingly evident in the case of Vietnam when Diem's backers claimed that the United States could play a major role in fostering the freedom and prosperity of Vietnam, a country they often called a "young" or "new" nation.[62]

Paternalistic assumptions that America had a duty and a right to direct Asia's destiny were reinforced by the emergence of development and modernization theories in the postwar years. Formulated as a means of helping Americans, especially government policymakers, understand and cope with rapid changes in non-Western societies, these theories attempted to predict and even control the evolution of colonies and newly independent nations. They emphasized the establishment of Westernized political systems featuring written constitutions, strong national governments, and public participation. The stability of such states would be guaranteed by economic prosperity stimulated by trade with the industrialized West and by government sponsorship of moderate social reform programs. Modernization theorists distrusted revolutionary creeds such as Marxism because "radical politics . . . are unnecessary for economic and political development and therefore are always bad."[63] In a country such as Vietnam that was undergoing a complicated and difficult struggle for independence, they looked to figures who represented a "Third Force" that rejected both colonialism and communism as future national leaders. The United States, they believed, could encourage such individuals through judicious interventions in Asian affairs that would, as Arthur M. Schlesinger Jr. confidently put it, "counter the appeal of the Russian Revolutionary spirit in underdeveloped areas."[64]

Diem seemed to be a particularly promising nationalist leader because a number of his views apparently dovetailed with the salient features of development theory. In conversations with American officials and citizens, Diem called for the "establishment of representative government" and promised that he would "seek the widest possible support" and grant "customary civil liberties to the people."[65] He also expressed an interest in all forms of U.S. aid to help anticommunist Vietnamese and said he favored "wide social reforms."[66] Moreover, Diem used "Third Force" rhetoric when referring to himself and fellow Catholics in Vietnam. He told an American diplomat of his desire to work with Jawaharlal Nehru, India's prime minister, as "a 'third force' man" in Southeast Asia, and he identified Catholic districts in North

Vietnam's Red River Delta as an "organized and functioning... Third Force" in Vietnam. American assistance to these people, Diem asserted, would "promote the growth of democratic institutions in still one more area of Asia."[67]

All of these statements seemed to establish Diem as a figure who would work closely with the United States in fulfilling American aspirations in Asia. By the time it became evident that he was pursuing a very different course of action, America had already committed itself deeply to the survival of his regime.

chapter 2
The Founding of the AFV, 1954–1955

After France's defeat at Dien Bien Phu, the Eisenhower administration tried to stem the Viet Minh's growing power by encouraging the establishment of an anticommunist state in South Vietnam. The administration hoped that Ngo Dinh Diem, the State of Vietnam's new premier, would meet this challenge, but it began to have serious doubts about Diem's abilities after American diplomats in Saigon transmitted a series of discouraging reports about the Vietnamese leader's troubles with his French and Vietnamese opponents. Eisenhower and his colleagues eventually placed their complete confidence in Diem, but only after they conducted a lengthy policy debate that almost ended in a decision to depose him.

Aware of their government's ambiguous attitude toward Diem, American private citizens and politicians who had met Diem and been impressed by his zealous patriotism launched a campaign to shore up American support for the embattled premier. Meetings with journalists and editors resulted in laudatory articles about Diem in the American press. They also tried to convince administration officials and congressional representatives that Diem deserved America's support. Some of Diem's admirers decided that their work should be carried out on a more formal basis and, in the autumn of 1955, they set up the American Friends of Vietnam.

American efforts to strengthen Diem began as Diem's government struggled for survival. The signing of a cease-fire at Geneva on July 21, 1954, averted the threat of a Viet Minh military victory but placed the northern, and most populous, half of Vietnam under communist control. Moreover, most of the countries participating in the Geneva Conference on Indochina endorsed an oral declaration that called for an election by July 1956 to determine the future of a united Vietnam, a contest likely to place power in the hands of the Viet Minh leaders who led the independence struggle against France. A more immediate challenge to Diem's power emerged in the southern zone left to his administration. Here, three political-religious sects that had enjoyed considerable rights of autonomy under French rule—the Cao Dai, Hoa Hao, and Binh Xuyen—resisted Diem's attempts to assert his authority and received the support of French officials who had serious doubts about Diem's abilities. Finally, Diem had to deal with a flood of refugees from North Vietnam after the armistice.[1]

The exodus from the North attracted considerable, and sympathetic, American attention. More than 800,000 Vietnamese, mostly Catholics who had apprehensions about living under a communist government, moved south. Their anxieties were sharpened by a well-organized propaganda campaign launched by the Diem regime and the French and American intelligence services that encouraged Vietnamese to leave their northern homes for a freer life in South Vietnam.[2] In America, film footage and news stories graphically depicted the refugees' sufferings. A particularly influential account was Thomas A. Dooley's *Deliver Us from Evil*. Dooley, a navy doctor who had worked with the refugees in Haiphong, portrayed the Vietnamese as a brave people "determined to worship their God, determined to be free, determined to escape to do so" despite the relentless persecution of a ruthless communist dictatorship.[3] Dooley's book, which became a best-seller, and similar accounts dramatized the plight of a people whose hardships, as a Defense Department study of the Vietnam conflict noted, "engaged the sympathies of the American people as few developments in Vietnam have before or since, and solidly underwrote the U.S. decision for unstinting support for Diem."[4]

Although he encouraged the flight from the North, Diem had trouble coping with the swelling tide of people flooding into the South. He turned to the American government and charitable organizations for help. Washington provided assistance by sending ships to transport the refugees. The first private group to respond was Catholic Relief Services (CRS), an agency created by the National Catholic Welfare Conference during the Second World War to assist war victims and Catholic churches in war-torn countries. CRS activities in Vietnam were coordinated by Monsignor Joseph Harnett, a priest who had worked for CRS in France and Trieste before being sent to Saigon.[5] A second, nondenominational, relief organization also stepped in. This was the International Rescue Committee (IRC), originally founded to aid people fleeing from Nazi-occupied Europe. The IRC gave particular emphasis to helping artists, intellectuals, students, political figures, and labor leaders who opposed the European dictators of the 1930s. It continued this work after the Second World War, but shifted its attention to people escaping from the communist states of Eastern Europe.[6]

The IRC's assistance to the Vietnamese refugees was initiated at the recommendation of Leo Cherne, chairman of the IRC's board since 1951. A New Yorker born in 1912, Cherne had led a busy public life by the time he made his first trip to Vietnam. Besides serving as an officer of the IRC, Cherne headed the Research Institute of America, a firm that had provided political and economic information and analyses to business, labor, and public opinion leaders since the mid-1930s. He also advised the government on such matters as national mobilization during the Second World War and the economic future of occupied Japan. Cherne, whose interests in the fine arts, as well as in politics and economics, made him "a bit of a renaissance man," was a liberal who shared the anticommunist sentiments of Diem's first supporters.[7] He condemned the extremism of right-wing politicians like McCarthy, but had strong anticommunist views of his own. His work for the IRC reinforced these opinions by putting him in contact with numerous foreign leaders who opposed communism.[8]

Cherne decided to go to Saigon after hearing of the conclusion of the Geneva Conference. Flying from Berlin, where he had been inspecting IRC programs, Cherne arrived in Saigon and spent a few weeks in August and September examining the possibility of initiating IRC projects in Vietnam. He concluded that the IRC should undertake work in Vietnam by giving direct relief to the refugees and by providing assistance to students and intellectuals.[9] Cherne also formed some opinions about the political situation in Saigon. Like many of Diem's early admirers, Cherne was favorably impressed by the premier and regarded him as a man who could establish a nationalist but anticommunist state in Vietnam. He later remembered Diem as "a shy, determined, frank, devout individual," and in a memorandum sent to William Donovan, the IRC's honorary chairman, Cherne called Diem "a man of extraordinary stature and intellect whose incorruptibility is conceded even by his most violent opponents."[10]

Although a supporter of Diem, Cherne knew that the regime faced serious problems. He saw "with great pain" the development of a campaign by Diem's French and Vietnamese opponents to resist the premier's authority. Moreover, he was alarmed by the willingness of American diplomats to listen to and to work with these critics, particularly the French. "From my point of view," he later recalled, "any identification with the French by the U.S. government was contrary to the whole thrust of what it is that Ngo

Dinh Diem was trying to do," which was to create "an independent Vietnam."[11] Another challenge confronting Diem was the likelihood of a Viet Minh victory in the elections scheduled for 1956. The military success of the Viet Minh had given it tremendous prestige and had, Cherne wrote, "devitalized many of the anti-communists in Vietnam."[12] Cherne nevertheless saw reason for hope. "Future depends," he telegraphed his colleagues at the Research Institute, "on organizing all resources to resettle refugees, sustain near bankrupt government, give people something to fight for and unite them to resist communism."[13]

Cherne returned to the United States in September and recommended that the IRC inaugurate refugee assistance programs in Vietnam. The IRC's board of directors, which also had received a request for help in Vietnam from Harold Stassen, the head of the Foreign Operations Administration, a government agency that coordinated foreign assistance programs, accepted Cherne's advice and selected Joseph Buttinger, a member of the organization since the Second World War, to begin the IRC's work in Vietnam.[14] Born in Austria in 1906, Buttinger had grown up in circumstances of grinding poverty. He became an enthusiastic convert to socialism in 1921 and joined Austria's Social Democratic Party. When Chancellor Engelbert Dollfuss suppressed the Social Democrats in 1934, Buttinger helped organize an underground movement, the Revolutionary Socialists, and became one of its leaders. He fled from Austria after the German annexation of 1938 and eventually went to the United States after marrying Muriel Gardiner, a wealthy American who had helped the Revolutionary Socialists.[15]

Although committed to socialist principles, Buttinger eventually broke with his party comrades, in large part because he could not agree with their optimism about the Left's future success in Europe. He also expressed a strong hostility toward the communists, who had bitterly struggled with the Revolutionary Socialists for control of the Austrian Left. Angrily recalling communist subservience to Moscow, Buttinger called the political and intellectual world of Russian communism "the ugliest distortion of . . . Socialist ideals."[16] Buttinger's political experience made him a particularly suitable candidate for the job in Saigon. Cherne believed that working in Vietnam's complicated political environment would be "right down Joe Buttinger's alley."[17] Accepting the assignment, Buttinger left for Vietnam in late October.

Buttinger departed for Saigon as the Eisenhower administration took steps to safeguard and strengthen the Diem regime. To deter any possible Viet Minh attacks against South Vietnam, the Americans promoted the formation of an eight-nation alliance, the Southeast Asia Treaty Organization (SEATO), in September 1954. This coalition, composed of the United States, France, Britain, Australia, New Zealand, Thailand, Pakistan, and the Philippines, promised a firm response to any "communist aggression" in Southeast Asia and placed Laos, Cambodia, and South Vietnam under its protection. Washington also stepped up the flow of economic and military assistance to Saigon. Eisenhower hoped that this aid would, as he stated in a letter to Diem in late October, help "the Government of Vietnam in developing and maintaining a strong, viable state, capable of resisting attempted subversion or aggression through military means."[18] The president and his advisers decided to give this effort a greater degree of coordination by appointing General J. Lawton Collins, an officer with an impressive record of service in the Second World War and as a member of the Joint Chiefs of Staff, as a special ambassador to oversee its implementation. They sent the general to Vietnam in early November.[19]

Buttinger arrived in Vietnam a few weeks before Collins and spent more than two months organizing the IRC's assistance programs to refugee camps and to scholars and students who had fled south. He also followed the political developments in Saigon, making contact with Vietnamese from various political factions. These conversations had a tremendous impact on Buttinger, who had gone to Vietnam "firmly convinced that the South could not survive," but who now experienced a change of mind that "had something of the quality of a conversion."[20] Most of the Vietnamese to whom Buttinger spoke declared that they supported Diem because they saw him as providing the best hope for creating an independent Vietnam. Some people, especially members of the Dai Viet, a bitterly divided nationalist party that had ties with the Japanese in the Second World War, attacked Diem's dependence on his family and his autocratic behavior, but most of the Vietnamese with whom Buttinger spoke backed the premier.[21] Admitting that Diem had flaws, Buttinger concluded that "Diem is the man on whom the best people in the South and Center have pinned their political hopes." Buttinger's informants told him of French efforts in Saigon to undermine Diem by sabotaging any attempts he made to control his own army. Some of them, he informed Cherne, favored "stronger American intervention" in Vietnam's affairs, and Buttinger himself wondered whether the Americans, "like the French, [are] going to deny him [Diem] the support he needs to clean his house."[22]

Seeing Diem as "a man of exceptional political talent," Buttinger was disturbed by American press reports portraying Diem as an incompetent leader.[23] After reading a *Time* magazine article stating that the SVN was "impotently governed by its honest but ineffective Premier," Buttinger noted in his diary, "Pure nonsense what they write about Diem."[24] Other periodicals criticized the Vietnamese leader as well. "Diem has ideas—and a program," *U.S. News & World Report* reported, "but little happens to get them carried out."[25] The *New York Times Magazine* published a pessimistic article written by Peg Durdin, a journalist who, with her husband Tillman, had considerable experience in Asia. Durdin characterized Diem as "an honest but inept Prime Minister" and doubted that the eventual victory of the Viet Minh could be averted.[26] "The tragedy of Saigon," she wrote, "is that it will probably have insufficient time to shake off its heavy colonial heritage and grow into something strong—and Vietnamese—enough to withstand the Communists."[27]

Buttinger found a series of articles written by columnist Joseph Alsop to be particularly troubling. Although a fervent anticommunist, Alsop had little confidence in Diem's ability to counter the strength and appeal of the Viet Minh. He drew a grim picture of the Vietnamese political situation, calling it "an obscene basket of eels" over which "Ngo Dinh Diem, honest and virtuous but wholly out of contact with reality, presides with obstinate certainty that all will yet be well."[28] Alsop lamented Diem's disputes with Vietnamese army officers and the sects, claiming that this squabbling left "an almost total power vacuum in huge areas" that the Viet Minh exploited.[29] He criticized Diem's selection of mediocre officials and his reliance on family members such as Ngo Dinh Nhu and his "tigerish" wife in running the government.[30] Visiting a zone controlled by the Viet Minh, Alsop had hoped to find the movement weak and unpopular. "But the record of its achievements in nine years," he grudgingly admitted, "all too clearly confirms my own short observations of the efficiency, power and popular support of this Communist-built and Communist-guided machine of guerrilla government."[31] Upset by these columns, Buttinger began to draft rebuttals that he planned to publish when he returned to the United States.[32]

Buttinger also heard that people in the American embassy, especially General Collins, had lost confidence in Diem. He learned this from Wesley Fishel, who came to Saigon in August. Fishel maintained his contacts with Diem after the latter had left the United States in 1953 and was one of the first Americans to receive news of Diem's appointment.[33] Diem asked Fishel to come to Saigon a few weeks after he had been chosen premier so he could receive Fishel's advice "in [the] task of governmental reconstruction." Fishel arrived in Saigon after being assigned to the American embassy's aid bureau, the United States Operations Mission.[34]

As Diem's adviser, Fishel acted as the intermediary between the premier and American officials. Paul Kattenburg, who served as the State Department's desk officer for Vietnam at the time, regarded Fishel as "a very important" source of information concerning Diem's personality and views.[35] Ambassador Collins and his predecessor, Donald Heath, praised Fishel as well. Fishel, Heath declared, played an "important role in attempting, as personal friend, to make Diem realize [the] weakness of his position and necessity [to] show firmness and leadership and develop [a] positive program."[36] Fishel left Saigon in the autumn of 1954, but Collins soon recalled him because he thought Fishel "can be extremely useful to me as well as President Diem" because of the trust that Diem placed in Fishel.[37]

As he was working in Saigon, Fishel met Buttinger and discussed Vietnam's political situation with the IRC's representative. In one of these conversations, Fishel told Buttinger that "Collins is fed up with Diem," a remark that accurately reflected Collins's frustration with the Vietnamese leader.[38] Although he publicly supported Diem, Collins privately had serious doubts about Diem's abilities and voiced these misgivings in telegrams to Washington. Diem, Collins asserted, had demonstrated no "capacity to unite divided factions in Vietnam" and had simply relied on members of his own family in running the government.[39] Despite these criticisms, Collins's superiors continued their policy of backing Diem because, as Secretary of State Dulles told Collins, "There is no other suitable leader known to us."[40]

Buttinger did not know of Washington's decision to continue its support of Diem. Upon returning to the United States at the end of 1954, he sought help in an effort to counteract the negative reports about the Diem regime. He turned to Harold L. Oram, a fund-raiser who had worked with the IRC, for assistance in contacting prominent individuals in media and government circles. Oram had promoted liberal causes and organizations since 1937, when he generated financial support for the Spanish Republic. His firm served such groups as the National Association for the Advancement of Colored People and the American Civil Liberties Union, and it aided Adlai Stevenson's campaign for the presidency in 1952. Oram's choice of clients also reflected the powerful anticommunist sentiment then prevailing in liberal circles; he helped such associations as the Committee to Aid Refugee Chinese Intellectuals and the Committee of One Million.[41]

Oram put Buttinger in touch with Cardinal Spellman and Representative Walter Judd in the hope that Spellman and Judd would rally Catholic and Protestant politicians to Diem's support. Impressed by Buttinger, Judd "highly recommended" that State Department officials meet with Buttinger. The State Department followed Judd's advice, and Kenneth Young, an officer from the Bureau of Philippine and Southeast Asian Affairs, saw Buttinger on January 6, 1955, and received a memorandum outlining Buttinger's views on Vietnam. Oram also introduced Buttinger to the editors of such publications as the *New York Times*, the *New York Herald-Tribune*, *Life*, and *The Reporter* as a means of persuading them to publish articles or editorials reflecting Buttinger's opinions.[42]

In his writings, Buttinger called for a clear American commitment to Diem's beleaguered regime. Buttinger saw Diem as "a man of extraordinary strength, courage, integrity, and political ability" who was "nobody's pawn."[43] He portrayed Diem as a man striving to save his country from chaos in the face of determined opposition from Vietnamese sects and French officials who would not surrender their "virtually unbroken . . . position of interference" in Vietnamese affairs.[44] Buttinger claimed that American intervention on Diem's behalf would be welcomed by many Vietnamese. "United States interference," he declared, "is desired by the vast majority of politically conscious people in Vietnam."[45] Buttinger acknowledged that this course of action would strain Franco-American relations, but he asserted that "US support for South Vietnam will never become effective if we are afraid to oppose the Colonial policy of the French. We must choose between Paris and Saigon."[46]

Leo Cherne also advocated an unambiguous American commitment to Diem. After returning from Vietnam in September 1954, he met officials in Washington in an effort to convince them that Diem was a strong leader. "I rather presumptuously insisted," he recalled, "this man would last. This man is an almost unbreakable patriot."[47] Cherne, like Buttinger, tried to counter unfavorable reports of the Diem regime. In a letter to the *New York Times Magazine*, he said Peg Durdin's article about Saigon presented a "striking . . . portrait" of conditions in the city but had overlooked a number of significant points, especially the fact that "a new nation is being born in Vietnam — a nation which rejects equally and simultaneously the moribund Western colonialism from which it is emerging and the alien Communist creed by which it is threatened."[48] Cherne also wrote a memorandum in the spring of 1955 charging that some American journalists had "seriously misrepresented" Diem's problems by minimizing the trouble caused by "the French colonialists" and the sects. Diem needed to overcome this opposition, he argued, if "Free Vietnam is to cross the bridge to the Twentieth Century and establish itself as a free and democratic society."[49]

As Buttinger and Cherne campaigned on Diem's behalf in America, Ambassador Collins continued his criticisms of the Vietnamese premier in cables to Washington. Collins briefly expressed optimism about Diem's prospects during a period of relative calm in early 1955, but he voiced renewed doubts about Diem when a new political crisis erupted. On March 4, the leaders of the political-religious sects banded together and called for the reorganization of Diem's government, a demand that received the backing of Vietnamese nationalist leaders, including Bao Dai, who opposed Diem's attempt to centralize power. Diem at first temporized by making vague promises. He then decided to force the issue in late March by ordering the seizure of police barracks held by the Binh Xuyen, a criminal organization that controlled Saigon's police force. This action led to the outbreak of fighting between Diem's Vietnamese National Army (VNA) and the Binh Xuyen that was stopped only by the intervention of French forces. The battle in Saigon was followed by resignations from Diem's cabinet and French calls for Diem's removal from office. It also convinced Collins that Diem had "almost entirely isolated himself" politically and that the United States should no longer back a man who could not effectively govern Vietnam.[50]

Collins recommended that Washington consider plans to replace Diem, but his superiors demurred. Eisenhower expressed a reluctance to oust Diem "because we have bet on him heavily," while Dulles told Collins that no suitable successor to Diem could be found.[51] Moreover, Dulles warned Collins that Diem's dismissal would jeopardize congressional approval of the funds needed to carry out American programs in Vietnam. This concern about congressional opinion centered on Senator Mike Mansfield's reaction to a potential withdrawal of American support from Diem. Mansfield, who had been a partisan of Diem since his 1953 meeting with the Vietnamese leader, had been pushing for a firm commitment to the Diem regime since Diem's appointment as premier. In a report published after a trip to Indochina in the fall of 1954, Mansfield declared that Diem's overthrow "would raise . . . serious doubts about the salvageability of any of our present policy with respect to Vietnam."[52] His support did not waver when the State Department showed him the cables Collins had written about Diem's flaws in December 1954, or when Collins raised the possibility of replacing Diem in the spring of 1955. When Dulles called Mansfield to the State Department on April 1 and showed the senator the telegrams in which Collins recommended Diem's removal, Mansfield objected and predicted that if "Diem quit or was overthrown, there would very likely be civil war; and that as a result . . . Ho Chi Minh could walk in and take the country without difficulty."[53]

Despite opposition from Washington, Collins continued pushing for a change in government. Summoned to Washington in late April, Collins repeated his criticisms of Diem in meetings with administration officials. These arguments finally had their effect, and Eisenhower and his advisers made plans for Diem's replacement. The plans were canceled only by reports of renewed fighting between Diem's troops and the Binh Xuyen. The news of the street battles in Saigon led to fervent declarations of support from Diem's congressional backers. Senator Mansfield called for the suspension of aid programs to Vietnam in the event of Diem's overthrow, and Representative Edna Kelly told Kenneth Young that the House Foreign Affairs Committee opposed any decision to abandon Diem.[54] The administration decided to wait upon the outcome of the conflict in Saigon, even though Collins continued to insist that "Diem's number was up."[55] The outcome of the battle became apparent by May 1, when soldiers of the VNA began to drive the Binh Xuyen out of Saigon. The Binh Xuyen's defeat persuaded Washington to put its support behind Diem and to stop considering any cooperation with the French in discussing his removal. In the weeks following Diem's victory, the Americans fended off French attempts to reconsider Diem's suitability and publicly committed themselves to the Diem regime.[56]

Joseph Buttinger made the decision to form a private organization supporting the Diem regime, the American Friends of Vietnam, during the weeks the Eisenhower administration was reconsidering its support of Diem. Documentary evidence concerning the formation of the AFV is scarce, but the idea for its creation may have been suggested during Buttinger's stay in Saigon in 1954. Buttinger's diary records a discussion with a Vietnamese about Diem's political troubles in which the Vietnamese spoke of an American officer's suggestion that "a Committee of Friends of Vietnam" be established to rally American public opinion to Diem's side.[57] Buttinger, however, did nothing about the matter until the spring of 1955, when rumors about the withdrawal of American support from Diem and the appearance of a new series of Alsop columns announcing that the "Diem experiment has failed" apparently prompted him to act.[58]

Whatever the immediate circumstances leading to the AFV's creation may have been, the decision to form the group was made in April, and Buttinger informed Oram of this step in a letter dated April 22. In authorizing Oram to establish the AFV, Buttinger wrote: "It is my intention to do everything possible to aid the government of Viet Nam (South), now headed by Premier Ngo Dinh Diem, to maintain its integrity against the attempts of the Communist Viet Minh to overthrow that government. I believe this to be in the interests of American policy and of the Free World."[59]

For help organizing the AFV, Buttinger and Oram turned to three groups.

They asked several colleagues from the International Rescue Committee to join the AFV and received a favorable response. Leo Cherne became an AFV officer, as did Christopher Emmet and Richard Salzmann, the IRC's executive director. Admiral Richard E. Byrd, the renowned polar explorer who held an honorary chairmanship in the IRC, was elected to the AFV's executive committee, while General William J. Donovan, who also had been associated with the work of the IRC, was chosen as honorary chairman.[60] The IRC's president, Angier Biddle Duke, also assumed a leadership position in the AFV. A member of the family that had made its fortune from tobacco, Duke had worked in the diplomatic service of the Truman administration before joining the IRC in 1955. He initially became acquainted with Vietnamese affairs while inspecting IRC projects in Vietnam. Like his colleagues, Duke had been impressed by Diem's devout patriotism and moved by the plight of "hundreds of thousands of refugees fleeing from a totalitarian society." Duke's visit to Vietnam convinced him that the United States could play a constructive role in that country by aiding "democratic elements . . . struggling to achieve an independent, pluralistic, and socially equitable nation."[61]

Besides drawing on the IRC's membership, Buttinger and Oram sought the help of friends and acquaintances in forming the AFV. Buttinger seems to have played a particularly active role in this effort by using his ties with the American Left to recruit for the AFV. The journalist Sol Sanders, who had been active in socialist politics in the 1940s, remembered that Buttinger had asked him to join.[62] A far more prominent figure who joined the AFV was Norman Thomas, the leader of the American Socialist Party. According to Thomas, Buttinger had worked with Sanders in drawing Thomas's attention to Vietnam's problems in the spring of 1955. Buttinger then approached Thomas and urged him to become an AFV member because, as Thomas later wrote, "It was desirable to include socialists so that it [the AFV] would not seem to be a partisan group."[63] Thomas also had received a letter from Duke encouraging him to enter the AFV, which Thomas agreed to do with the proviso that "my interest in Viet-Nam does not extend to automatic endorsement of American participation in war to that end."[64]

Finally, the AFV's organizers mailed letters of invitation to American citizens concerned with Asian affairs. These notes, which had been drafted by Oram and signed by Duke, were sent to academics, journalists, clergymen, and political activists. Congressional representatives and government officials also received invitations, and by the time the AFV's officers first met in December 1955, Harold Oram reported that "a large proportion" of the AFV's eighty founding members came from Capitol Hill.[65] Attempts to bring in figures from the executive branch, however, met with little success. After Vice President Richard Nixon and Sherman Adams, the White House chief of staff, received letters from Duke, the State Department called the AFV "one of the worthy organizations conducting humanitarian activities overseas" but recommended that the two men refrain from joining "since it is considered inadvisable" to give a private group "special consideration by the White House."[66] Despite this rebuff, Oram would boast that the AFV had become "one of the most distinguished groups ever to promote relations between the U.S. and another friendly country."[67]

Membership in the AFV included no Vietnamese, but the association nevertheless worked closely with the Vietnamese government, especially after Oram was designated as the Diem regime's public relations representative in the United States. At the same time he was organizing the AFV, Oram negotiated a contract with Saigon. The initial suggestion that Diem should make use of Oram's services apparently came from Cherne during his visit to Vietnam in 1954. Diem, however, did not act on this advice until March 1955, when he heard news of the help that Oram had given to Buttinger. Contract negotiations lasted until the summer of 1955, when Diem finally decided to hire Oram as his agent in the United States.[68]

Oram outlined the objectives of his public relations program in a September memorandum to Ambassador Tran Van Chuong, Ngo Dinh Nhu's father-in-law and Diem's representative to the United States. The primary purpose of the program was to keep influential figures in government, politics, and the media informed of the "true situation in Vietnam."[69] This information would be presented to key individuals "in such a manner as suits their respective needs and that responsible assistance is offered them in making their favorable points of view effective."[70] Oram also told Chuong of his intention to assist groups of American citizens who were "conscious of the importance of the issue," and, in this connection, he emphasized the need to work closely with the AFV.

> They will have the great advantage in their work of being well informed on the issues since many of them have visited in Viet Nam recently, and have kept abreast of developments. . . . I am informed that they intend to augment their group by the inclusion of a number of leading personalities drawn from throughout the country. They can be a rallying point around which American public opinion may gather in the true interests of the United States. One of our principal duties is to see that this group

is kept well informed with respect to the actual situation in Viet Nam so that they may be effective in their work.[71]

Diem took a number of steps to consolidate his political power during the months of the AFV's formation. The VNA drove the Binh Xuyen out of Saigon in early May, and, in the following month, it dispersed most of the Hoa Hao units that had not submitted to Diem. The Cao Dai retained a degree of independence until October, but Diem then sent troops to Tay Ninh—the spiritual and political center of the Cao Dai religion—and the Cao Dai leader, Pope Pham Cong Tac, fled to Cambodia. Besides crushing the sects, Diem won greater independence as French troops withdrew from the Saigon area and the French relinquished their remaining control over the VNA. Finally, Diem took steps to win full power for himself by staging a referendum for Vietnamese voters to choose between him and Bao Dai, his nominal superior, as chief of state. Diem waged what the American embassy called "a one-sided pre-election campaign" against the emperor, using a combination of intimidation and propaganda in calling for Bao Dai's deposition.[72] Held on October 23, the referendum gave Diem a lopsided 98.2 percent of the vote. Diem, however, showed no embarrassment about this result and was proclaimed president of the Republic of Vietnam on October 26, 1955.[73]

Diem's success in retaining and strengthening his power in 1955, especially his victory over the sects, has raised questions about the role his American supporters played in securing the Eisenhower administration's complete backing of Diem. An article in *Ramparts* magazine asserted that Diem's backers, especially Lansdale, Buttinger, and Spellman, took "the steps that had to be taken to swing the wavering Eisenhower Administration solidly behind the young regime of Ngo Dinh Diem."[74] Buttinger and his friends did not make such claims about their influence, but they did believe that they had affected the tone of American press coverage of the Diem regime. "Joe Buttinger," declared one of Buttinger's friends, "had almost singlehanded[ly] (but with the assistance of H. L. Oram) changed the climate of American public opinion in the course of one month."[75] Cherne told Wesley Fishel that a letter he had sent to Henry Luce "has had its effect in that shop."[76]

Doubts nevertheless can be raised about the impact Cherne, Buttinger, and Oram had on press coverage of Vietnam. Their views were printed in a number of American publications and are sometimes quite evident, as in a *New York Times* editorial calling Diem "nobody's puppet," an echo of Buttinger's "nobody's pawn."[77] Nevertheless, the campaign of Buttinger and Oram took place at a time when members of the American mission in Vietnam, including Collins, expressed optimism about the future of the Diem regime. The *New York Times* editorial that had used a variation of Buttinger's "nobody's pawn" also referred to a "moderately promising" report made by Collins.[78] The change in the American press coverage of Vietnam may have been due as much, if not more, to the optimistic statements coming from government sources as to the efforts of people like Cherne and Buttinger.

It also can be argued that Diem's congressional supporters did much to secure the Eisenhower administration's commitment to Diem, since government officials worried about congressional reaction to withdrawing U.S. support. Anxieties about congressional opposition to Diem's removal are reflected in a memorandum predicting "real difficulties on the Hill if Diem is forced out by what appears to be French–Bao Dai action."[79] Yet concern about congressional opinion did not prevent the administration from deciding to discuss Diem's replacement with the French, a step it refrained from taking only after Diem took decisive action against the Binh Xuyen. Paul Kattenburg, who took part in the deliberations concerning Diem at the time, recalled that although the efforts of Diem's backers "*did* have a cumulative impact in maintaining support for Diem," they did not have "a decisive one at the key moment" of Diem's confrontation with the sects in the spring of 1955.[80]

There is nevertheless a possibility that Diem's American supporters may have made a significant contribution to the American decision to back Diem, albeit indirectly. There are a few sources that indicate that some of Diem's American backers may have encouraged him to confront the sects, an action which, when it ended with the Binh Xuyen's defeat, secured the Eisenhower administration's full support for the Diem regime. In an interview given years later, Mike Mansfield said, "It was . . . the impetus given by some of us . . . in behalf of Diem that gave the President (that is Ngo Dinh Diem) the initiative to wipe out the Binh Xuyen, and to put down the Cao Dai and the Hoa Hao."[81] Diem may have received this advice not only from Mansfield but from Wesley Fishel. State Department records state that Fishel was "in frequent contact with Diem" at this time.[82] Colonel Lansdale, who had worked closely with Diem in undermining the sects, may also have influenced the premier, but his role remains obscure because much of the documentary evidence concerning his activities remains classified.[83] Nevertheless, if figures such as Mansfield, Fishel, and Lansdale recommended that Diem seek a showdown with the sects, they may have very well helped convince the Eisenhower administration that the Vietnamese leader deserved America's complete support.

Although the influence exercised by Diem's backers is debatable, there can be no doubt about their commitment to Diem and their confidence that a new society could be built in Vietnam with America's help. "I was totally impressed," Leo Cherne said years later, "with the patriotism, in the purer sense of the word, of the Ngo Dinh Diem that I met."[84] Moreover, they felt great sympathy for Diem as he tried to establish his authority over a divided and demoralized society. Speaking of Diem years later, Lansdale summed up this attitude by saying, "To me he was a man with a terrible burden to carry and in need of friends, and I tried to be an honest friend of his."[85]

Diem's backers, however, were not uncritical. Even Cherne and Buttinger, who at times praised Diem in extravagant terms, saw him as suffering from a small political base, dependence on family support, and a rigid character. An American diplomat recalled Buttinger saying that he "had been immediately struck by what he termed as the narrow and unhealthy atmosphere surrounding the President, who appeared intensely suspicious of everyone except his immediate coterie and unwilling to take his collaborators into confidence."[86] Although troubled by this behavior, Buttinger and others set aside their misgivings in the hope that Diem would run a more open administration once he overcame the opposition of the sects and France.

The notion that Diem would be able to establish a viable anticommunist state apparently was confirmed by the flight of refugees from the North in the months after the Geneva Conference. Critics later condemned Diem's supporters for promoting a "refugee myth" that portrayed the Viet Minh as ruthless oppressors and Diem's regime as "the sanctuary of freedom."[87] However, some of Diem's supporters did believe that the movement of refugees signified a widespread rejection of communism. They realized that most of those who fled the North were members of Vietnam's Catholic minority and were aware that the United States "had helped and encouraged the flight of refugees from Communism."[88] They nevertheless saw this exodus as a significant repudiation of the Viet Minh regime that "came to be described as 'voting with their feet,'" as Cherne remarked, "and was one of the largest votes of the kind which ever took place."[89] Moreover, America's role in encouraging the departure from the North had given it "an inescapable moral obligation to see that the South remains free."[90]

The Americans who backed Diem realized that the Viet Minh's ability to win a popular following was a formidable challenge, but they ascribed the Viet Minh's success to the obstructive colonial policies of the French and thought that the establishment of a genuinely independent state in Vietnam would undercut the Viet Minh's popularity. As did Diem's earliest supporters, they believed that the United States could play a vital role by helping Vietnamese nationalists break away from French control and set up a popular government. It could achieve this goal by providing financial and, even more important, political help to Vietnamese leaders like Diem, thus enabling Vietnam "to stand as a free and viable society."[91] Cherne thought the successful outcome of such a policy would affect not only Vietnam but the rest of Asia: "Free Vietnam can be rapidly helped to become the single economic and political paradise of Asia. . . . Having weathered the struggles of the most difficult six months, Vietnam can become, on the mainland of Asia, the moral, physical and economic spear in the side of Asian Communism. It can be a laboratory of freedom, capable of exercising an influence over India such as no American behavior or generosity of example could produce."[92]

It was with this hope of building a new nation, as well with confidence in Diem and a belief in the anticommunist sentiments of the Vietnamese people, that the American Friends of Vietnam began its public activities.

chapter 3
The Early Activities of the AFV, 1955–1956

In its first months, the American Friends of Vietnam faced the task of organizing a sustained campaign on behalf of the Diem regime. The association established an executive committee to set its policies and direct its activities. It focused most of its initial work on an effort to convince the American public and the Eisenhower administration that the future of Diem's government should not be jeopardized by an agreement to hold the all-Vietnam elections for which the Geneva accords had called. By the late spring of 1956, the AFV had sponsored a major conference in Washington that attracted dozens of guests, including Senator John F. Kennedy and the State Department's assistant secretary for Far Eastern affairs. Moreover, reports from Vietnam indicated that no plebiscite would take place. Despite this impressive opening performance, the AFV's role in averting the elections proved to be marginal, since Eisenhower and his colleagues already had decided to prevent a vote.

The American Friends of Vietnam publicly announced its formation on December 1, 1955. Short accounts appearing in the *New York Times*, *Washington Post*, and *New York Herald-Tribune* reported that General William J. Donovan would serve as the honorary chairman and that Angier Biddle Duke would act as the chairman of the AFV's executive committee.[1] In addition to providing information about its membership, the AFV released a copy of a telegram congratulating Ngo Dinh Diem on the creation of the Republic of Vietnam. Expressing confidence in Diem's leadership, the message declared, "Like our pioneer fathers who experienced the gravest difficulties in both internal and foreign affairs, and carried on to victory, we count on you to lead the great Vietnamese people through manifold vicissitudes to a future of peace, democracy, and prosperity." The dispatch then proceeded to make a pledge that foreshadowed trouble between Diem and the AFV. "As long as you continue to remain firm in the service of our common heritage of liberty," it promised the Vietnamese president, "we assure you of our enthusiastic support and that of the overwhelming majority of the American people."[2]

The AFV also issued a statement of purpose explaining that it had to "enlighten American public opinion" on three issues: the character of the communist government in the North, with an emphasis on its violations of the Geneva accords; "the nature of the Diem regime" in the South; and the "vital strategic, political, and moral interests of the United States in the survival of South Viet Nam as a bulwark of freedom in Southeast Asia." The document then asserted that "the freedom of South Viet Nam is a matter of the utmost concern, not only to the Vietnamese people, but to free peoples throughout the world" and that a communist victory in the South "would constitute one of the greatest defeats of freedom in the modern world." Citing Diem's successes in resettling refugees, suppressing the sects, and creating a new political order in the South, the statement urged the U.S. government to support Vietnamese efforts to remain free, develop democratic institutions, and win the acceptance of the international community.[3]

Responding with gratitude to the creation of the AFV and its congratulatory telegram, Diem wrote, "Please be assured that the Vietnamese people under my leadership will not betray the confidence that their friends of the great American democracy have placed in them."[4] Diem's appreciation could also be seen in Vietnam. G. Frederick Reinhardt, the United States ambassador to the RVN, informed the State Department that the authorities in Saigon saw the AFV as a sign of significant American help. "It is clear," he wrote, "that the activities of the organization are regarded by the Vietnamese Government as encouraging evidence of increased interest in Vietnam." He cited statements by the RVN's press organs about the importance of the AFV. Vietnam Presse, the RVN's news agency, implied that the American Friends would be an "an active and powerful pressure group to promote increased interest in and support for the present government of Vietnam." The French-language newspaper of the Diem regime, *La Gazette*, saw the AFV's congratulatory telegram to Diem as an expression of unconditional American support for the RVN. "America, by the voice of the Association of 'American Friends of Vietnam,'" the journal asserted, "is determined to support Vietnam, whatever trials await us."[5]

The formation of the AFV also attracted the attention of the communist government of the Democratic Republic of Vietnam (DRV). In a dispatch entitled "Americans Form Aid Group," the Vietnam News Agency charged that the AFV had no real intention of fostering friendship between the American and Vietnamese peoples. "It is," the report claimed, "but an organization set up by the American imperialists to further American intervention in all fields in South Vietnam to speed up the sabotage of the Geneva Agreements, to partition Vietnam forever, and to transform South Vietnam into an American base."[6]

Having announced its formation, the AFV faced a great deal of work in creating an effectively functioning organization. The executive committee usually had sixteen people who met five to seven times a year to make decisions concerning AFV programs, finances, and membership. Its members also sat on a board of directors that met annually to elect new officers and approve an annual budget. Many of these people, including Joseph Buttinger, Leo Cherne, Christopher Emmet, Angier Biddle Duke, Harold Oram, Richard R. Salzmann, and Admiral Byrd, had been associated with the International Rescue Committee. Another officer, William vanden Heuvel, had been active in IRC projects and had worked closely with General Donovan during the latter's service as ambassador to Thailand and as a lawyer in New York. Another member, Elliot Newcomb, was one of Oram's colleagues. Others who served on the AFV's board included such early acquaintances of Diem as Professor I. Milton Sacks and the journalist Sol Sanders. Dr. M. L. Anson, a nutritionist, acted as the AFV's treasurer for the first year. Finally, another early AFV officer was Norbert Muhlen, a German émigré who frequently contributed articles to *The New Leader*, a journal whose editorial policy of "militant anti-communism, plus sympathy for government-inspired social reform, best summarizes the philosophy of most of the executive committee members."[7]

Individuals who joined the AFV but held no office were designated as national committee members. For nearly a decade, AFV letterheads listed the names of more than ninety members of the national committee. Those members received periodic reports by mail and fund-raising appeals two or three times a year. They were not expected to play active roles in the organization, although AFV leaders occasionally asked them to serve on special committees or to perform a service on behalf of the AFV. On one occasion, Justice William O. Douglas agreed to lead a drive to secure aid for a newly established university at Hue. When the first shipment of books for the school arrived in Vietnam, national committee members residing in Saigon were asked to make a formal presentation of the gift. The AFV's leaders also created a category of associate membership in an effort to affiliate even more people, but AFV records list fewer than a dozen associate members and there is no available evidence indicating what role, if any, they played.[8]

New members were recruited into the national committee by AFV officers who nominated candidates for executive committee approval. The group's leaders chose individuals who had been early backers of Diem, who had a record of interest in foreign policy, or who had worked in Vietnam. They also picked people in an effort to make the AFV's membership base "as wide as possible" in order to "add credibility" to its claim that it was a "non-partisan group organized in support of a free and democratic Republic of Vietnam."[9] This effort met with considerable success in the 1950s as the AFV drew people from diverse political and professional backgrounds into its ranks. Early supporters of Diem such as Justice Douglas and Father Raymond de Jaegher joined the AFV, as did academics such as William Henderson and Frank Trager who specialized in foreign affairs. The names of publishing moguls Henry Luce and William Randolph Hearst Jr. appeared on the AFV's letterhead, as did that of Tom Dooley, the navy doctor who had dramatized the sufferings of the North Vietnamese refugees in *Deliver Us from Evil*. Even Hollywood was represented in the AFV. The executive committee invited the film producer Joseph Mankiewicz, who produced a film version of Graham Greene's novel *The Quiet American*, and the war hero and actor Audie Murphy, who played the title role in the movie, to join the group.[10]

The AFV's board also tried to draw attention by asking prominent figures to serve as its leaders. General Donovan held the title of the AFV's honorary chairman, but the AFV's officers wanted another well-known individual to actively promote the group's programs. They soon chose Lieutenant General John W. O'Daniel, a recently retired army officer, as the AFV's chairman. Awarded the sobriquet of "Iron Mike" while in the service, O'Daniel had been a soldier since 1916, when he enlisted as a private at the age of twenty-two. He saw extensive combat in both world wars and finished World War II as commander of the Third Infantry Division, a unit that fought from the Anzio beachhead to Hitler's mountain retreat at Berchtesgaden. In the postwar years, O'Daniel served as a military attaché in Moscow, leader of a corps in the Korean War, and commander of all army forces in the Pacific.[11]

O'Daniel spent his last years of military service as the head of the American Military Assistance and Advisory Group (MAAG) in Vietnam. Assuming the post in the spring of 1954, he supervised the transition of the VNA's training and support from French to American hands. During this time, he displayed two traits that later marked his performance as chairman of the AFV: a stubborn adherence to his own views and a strong devotion to Ngo Dinh Diem. Donald Heath, the first ambassador with whom O'Daniel worked, complained about the general's stubbornness in dispatches to Washington. While praising O'Daniel for his "friendly and respectful cooperation" and as "an effective spokesman for our policy and needs in Indochina," Heath complained that the general had "a tendency to believe that all matters can be portrayed in sharp black and white" and that O'Daniel "rarely listens to criticisms and countersuggestions because he is already thinking up new arguments for his statements."[12]

O'Daniel's devotion to Diem also became evident during his tour of duty in Saigon. When Diem confronted the sects in the spring of 1955, O'Daniel objected to suggestions that Washington replace Diem by declaring, "Any change [of] leadership at this time would result in chaos."[13] Edward Lansdale recounted an even more open expression of O'Daniel's support for Diem during the battle against the Binh Xuyen. Driving past a battalion of Diem's troops that was marching toward the fighting, O'Daniel "leaned out of the car and impulsively shouted, 'Give 'em hell, boys, give 'em hell!'"[14] When Diem defeated the sects and consolidated his control over the South, O'Daniel expressed his satisfaction. "Diem has his ship of state headed in the right direction," the general wrote in a memorandum, "and with continued U.S. support it is felt that he will succeed provided the enemy does not launch an all-out attack."[15]

The suggestion that O'Daniel be invited to act as the AFV's chairman came from Harold Oram, who had read of O'Daniel's return from Vietnam. In early December, Oram asked O'Daniel to attend a reception being held in his honor by the American Friends and to accept the chairmanship of the AFV.[16] Duke also sent an invitation to O'Daniel declaring that the general's chairmanship "would serve to emphasize to the American people the strategic importance of Viet Nam in our foreign relations."[17] O'Daniel initially hesitated but received assurances from the State Department that the AFV was "sound in every respect."[18] He then agreed to attend the gathering on December 19, telling reporters covering the event that he was "pleased and honored" with the request that he join the AFV.[19] In a letter to Samuel T. Williams, the officer who succeeded him as the chief of the MAAG, O'Daniel wrote, "I am glad to be able to continue to fight for the country from here while you fight for it from there."[20]

In the letter asking O'Daniel to work with the American Friends of Vietnam, Harold Oram stressed an issue that preoccupied the organization in its infancy: the prospect of all-Vietnam elections scheduled to take place under the provisions of the Geneva accords. Some of the AFV's founding members expressed fears that, if conducted in July 1956, the plebiscite would place all of Vietnam under the control of the Viet Minh. A vote for Ho Chi Minh, Leo Cherne believed, would reflect a Vietnamese "protest against French colonialism and French capitulation at Geneva."[21] He also thought that rigid communist control of the more populous North favored the Viet Minh, a view shared by Joseph Buttinger, who stated that no regime like the DRV "held elections without producing the desired majority of favorable votes." Buttinger regarded an election held under such circumstances as an injustice to the people of the South. Most southerners, he contended, held anticommunist sentiments and should not be forced to join the North. Buttinger declared that any attempt by the Eisenhower administration to collaborate in efforts to implement the provisions concerning elections should be strongly opposed. "The spokesmen of American Public [sic] opinion," he asserted, "should make it clear immediately that the American people will not allow our government to lend a helping hand in the execution of a scheme which will enslave ten million people in the name of a democratic right."[22]

The AFV publicly expressed its opposition to the election in an analysis appended to its statement of purpose. This document argued that the declaration concerning elections was little more than a "pious wish" because it had not been ratified or accepted by the governments of the United States and the Republic of Vietnam. Moreover, Viet Minh violations of the Geneva agreements had "absolved" the parties involved "from whatever obligation" to hold a plebiscite. The paper also claimed that the accords had failed to establish adequate machinery for the supervision of the vote and that the International Control Commission, which could not perform "the far easier task of enforcing the military and refugee terms of the Armistice," could not be expected to carry out this task. It went on to stress America's need to protect Southeast Asia from further communist advances and its "inescapable moral obligation" to the northern refugees who had fled to the South. "Thus," the statement concluded, "we should resist to the utmost any attempt to use the Geneva declaration extorted from the defeated French, as blackmail to force the South Vietnamese people under Communist slavery."[23]

The AFV's anxiety about the all-Vietnam elections also stemmed from the belief that international pressure, especially from Britain and France, might force the Eisenhower administration to agree to a vote in July. In a memorandum sent to Christopher Emmet, David Martin, a political activist who occasionally worked with Oram on matters concerning Vietnam, wrote, "It is impossible to ignore the danger that the combined pressure of our two major allies might result in a serious situation." Worried that the French and British might make an accommodation with the communists in Indochina, Martin recommended that a "campaign of action" be undertaken to avert such a development, particularly in Britain, which Martin saw as being "much wiser and more flexible" than France. British opinion could be swayed, Martin asserted, by sending letters and articles to British periodicals and by corresponding with prominent Britons who took an interest in Vietnamese affairs.[24]

The communist governments of Vietnam, China, and Russia exerted what the AFV regarded as even more disturbing pressures for a Vietnamese election. When Chou En-lai, the Chinese premier and foreign minister, asked for a reconvocation of the Geneva Conference on January 25, 1956, William Donovan, in his capacity as the AFV's honorary chairman, sent a letter to the White House objecting to Chou's request, calling it an "impertinent demand." "The Friends of Vietnam (of which I am one) respectfully submit our belief that the demand of Chou [E]n-lai should be rejected," Donovan wrote. He cited the refusal of the United States and the RVN to assent to the accords, America's obligation to the refugees who had fled to the South "despite threats of punishment and death," and the need to protect the South from communist attacks. "Is it not possible," Donovan asked, "to defer the elections to a later date and in the meantime to establish the necessary safeguards under an international commission distinct from the impotent neutral armistice commission now in existence?"[25]

Eisenhower sent a quick and positive response to Donovan, who had served as ambassador to Thailand from 1953 until 1954. "As you know," the president assured Donovan, "I consider that President Diem is the most potent force we have in South Viet Nam to help halt the arrogant march of Communism." He also promised that he would "instantly" take up the matters raised by Donovan with the State Department.[26] Dulles soon sent a reply to the White House about the issues discussed in Donovan's letter. He concurred with its opinions and informed Eisenhower that Donovan's suggestion of creating a new commission to monitor the elections "is under urgent consideration in the Department." The secretary of state also told the president that the American government, after consultations with the British in late January, had decided to reject Chou En-lai's call for a reconvocation of the Geneva Conference. The administration's Vietnam policy, Dulles wrote, aimed at strengthening the RVN, preserving peace "under some new arrangement which would permit gradual termination of the old Geneva Accords," and undermining the DRV through political and psychological warfare operations.[27]

Eisenhower's reply to Donovan and Dulles's memorandum to the White House show that the president and his colleagues, like the AFV, feared the consequences of a communist electoral victory. Although a few officials believed that Ho Chi Minh had won the backing of many Vietnamese because of his success against the French, most seemed unwilling or unable to admit that Ho had actually built up a broad base of popular support. In his oft-quoted remark that "possibly 80 per cent" of Vietnam's voters would have cast their ballots for Ho, Eisenhower attributed the communist leader's popularity to the torpid leadership of Bao Dai.[28] Other officials, especially Dulles, saw the Viet Minh's tight control of the more populous North as the primary reason for the likelihood of an electoral success. Meeting with his subordinates in the autumn of 1954, the secretary of state claimed "that there was no possibility of fair elections in the North and that, when the time came, we would have ample grounds for postponing or declining to hold them in the South."[29]

Although anxious to avoid the election, the administration refrained from expressing its open opposition because of fears that such a stance would trigger renewed fighting in Vietnam. Washington instead suggested guidelines for international supervision of the plebiscite similar to proposals that the communists already had vetoed in negotiations concerning the reunification of Germany and Korea. Adopting such a position, Dulles asserted in a telegram to Saigon, "is unassailable in intent but probably unacceptable to [the] Communists," and he encouraged Diem's government to take this line in discussions it was supposed to hold with Viet Minh representatives in July 1955.[30] Diem, however, refused to negotiate with the DRV and declared that his government was not "bound in any way" by the Geneva agreements.[31] Americans worried about the consequences of Diem's rejection of talks with the Viet Minh, but they acquiesced in his decision and provided Saigon with valuable diplomatic support in fending off communist demands for elections.[32]

Unaware of the administration's determination to avoid the plebiscite and alarmed by what it regarded as public apathy toward Vietnam, the AFV prepared a plan to alert American opinion to Vietnam's "significance from the standpoint of the national interest and of the defense of the Free World."[33] Three AFV members, Christopher Emmet, David Martin, and I. Milton Sacks, drew up a program of activities scheduled to begin on March 1. In order to coordinate this project, a central office in New York would be established and given the responsibility for raising funds, distributing literature, and scheduling meetings. Suggested AFV activities included the publication of an intelligence digest concerning Vietnam, the collection of literature dealing with Vietnam, and the sponsorship of lecture tours by AFV members. The program also called on the AFV to win the cooperation of key media figures such as editors and columnists in focusing the public's attention on Vietnam. Finally, AFV members should foster ties with "the leaders of the key group of national organization[s] and develop their interest" in Vietnam.[34]

In carrying out its activities, the AFV made full use of the services of General O'Daniel and of Gilbert Jonas, a young man who was the organization's assistant treasurer and executive secretary. Raised in Brooklyn, Jonas attended Stanford University and graduated with a bachelor's degree in journalism in 1951. While at Stanford, Jonas became involved in liberal causes such as international cooperation and civil rights and joined the United World Federalists and the NAACP. He also took an interest in African and Asian affairs, especially in China. After graduating from Stanford, Jonas went to Columbia and received a graduate certificate in Chinese studies in 1953. The army drafted him shortly thereafter and eventually assigned him to its public information office. Jonas found his experience in the PIO to be extremely useful because, as he recalled years later, "It gave me a lot of ideas about what I could do for the causes I agreed with."[35] Discharged from the army in 1955, Jonas unsuccessfully sought employment for several months, finding few opportunities that suited his interests. A chance arose when Jonas met Oram at a party in the fall of 1955. Upon hearing that Jonas had a background in Asian affairs, Oram asked Jonas to assist him in running the American Friends of Vietnam. Although he initially protested that he had specialized in Chinese studies, Jonas decided to accept Oram's offer and began working for the AFV in early 1956.[36]

Aided by the availability of Jonas and O'Daniel for full-time work, the AFV began implementing its program of activities in March. The work included the release of a statement attacking Chou En-lai's call for a reconvocation of the Geneva Conference, the promotion of speaking engagements by O'Daniel and Tran Van Chuong, the RVN's ambassador, and mailings to AFV members (numbering approximately ninety at this time) encouraging them to utilize their contacts in the government and the media to express opposition to the all-Vietnam elections.[37]

The AFV devoted most of its energy, however, to holding a conference on Vietnam in the spring of 1956. Discussion about this symposium began at an executive committee meeting held on February 14, when the group asked Oram to chair a subcommittee to study the matter. The following month, the executive committee decided to go ahead with plans for organizing a conference in Washington on the grounds that such an event "would be desirable in terms of educating the American public on current Vietnamese situations." Joseph Buttinger and I. Milton Sacks agreed to set an agenda for the gathering.[38]

The AFV's intention to hold the meeting received encouragement from officials in the administration, especially those in the State Department. In a meeting with Jonas on April 25, Paul Kattenburg, the officer in charge of Vietnamese affairs, said, "The Department at this time looks quite favorably upon the holding of . . . [the] Conference." Kattenburg also told Jonas of the willingness of Walter Robertson, the assistant secretary of state for Far Eastern affairs, to come as a speaker, but he suggested that the AFV "ask for a policy speech quite apart from the panel [discussions] so that the Department spokesman would not be subjected to a question and answer session."[39] Robertson, who had left a banking career in Richmond to serve in China during the Second World War, became, as one historian has noted, "a staunch advocate of a tough line in support of Chiang Kai-shek and other nationalist foes of Asian communism" and established close ties with such China Lobby figures as Walter Judd.[40] He confirmed his intention to speak at the AFV conference in a letter to Angier Biddle Duke on May 17 in which he wrote, "I feel that this is a most worthwhile effort and an excellent opportunity to focus public attention on the excellent progress the Republic of Vietnam has been making."[41]

Nevertheless, reservations about the meeting came from the American embassy in Saigon. In a telegram to the State Department on May 6, Ambassador Reinhardt voiced concern about the announced purpose of the symposium. Referring to a letter from O'Daniel stating the AFV's intention "to focus American public attention on [the] nature of [the] current threat posed by Communist demands for holding all-Vietnamese elections," Reinhardt questioned the wisdom of stressing this matter. "Since I do not believe this issue is likely to develop into any real threat to Diem's government," he contended, "I deem it unwise and untimely to focus attention on it." He asked the department to urge the AFV to "concentrate instead on means of expanding US-Vietnamese relationships through efforts of private organizations, investors, and charities."[42]

The State Department agreed with Reinhardt's concerns and made efforts to persuade the AFV to shift the attention of the conference away from the plebiscite. It also enlisted the support of Ambassador Chuong, who promised to take a similar line in his conversations with the AFV's officers. Kenneth Young of the department's Office of Southeast Asian Affairs saw O'Daniel on May 10 and convinced the general that the meeting's focus should be changed.[43] The administration, he told O'Daniel, did not think that the plebiscite would be held in 1956, and a number of other governments, including those of France, Britain, and India, held similar views. Informed of this situation, O'Daniel suggested to Jonas that the AFV downplay the election issue. "Maybe," he wrote, "we hadn't best say too much on that at the conference other than that they, the elections, can't be held unless only free elections are guaranteed etc." He then recommended a switch in emphasis to refugee, charitable, educational, and investment activities.[44]

Although O'Daniel agreed to cooperate with the State Department, the question of the plebiscite nevertheless arose in a number of the talks given at the conference at Washington's Willard Hotel on June 1, 1956. The approximately 200 people who attended came from a wide variety of professions and organizations with interests in Vietnam. Academics, diplomats, and military officers sat beside representatives of business firms, church groups, and labor and educational associations while listening to speakers selected by the AFV.[45]

In his presentation, Joseph Buttinger claimed that the controversial agreement about a referendum *"does not exist."* He argued that no document concerning elections was signed by the Geneva Conference participants and that the United States and the RVN had made their reservations about a vote clear.[46] Senator John F. Kennedy addressed the issue of a plebiscite in a luncheon address. Calling the Republic of Vietnam "the cornerstone of the Free World in Southeast Asia, the keystone to the arch, the finger in the dike," the Massachusetts senator asserted that "neither the United States nor Free Vietnam is ever going to be a party to an election obviously stacked and subverted in advance."[47] Professor Hans J. Morgenthau sounded a dissenting note by declaring, "I shall defend the legal validity of that agreement to the last drop of my blood." He nevertheless minimized the binding character of the Geneva Accords by calling the provisions for a referendum "a device to hide the incompatibility of the Communist and western positions."[48]

Walter Robertson also mentioned the Geneva accords in his speech but, following administration policy, he did not emphasize them in his talk. He claimed that the United States and the RVN had "scrupulously respected" the cease-fire provisions of the agreement while the communists "had violated them in the most blatant fashion." In brief remarks about the proposed plebiscite, Robertson expressed American support for Diem's demands that "conditions which preclude intimidation or coercion of the electorate" be established before any balloting takes place. The thrust of Robertson's speech, however, outlined the major points of America's policy toward Vietnam. This consisted of backing the Republic of Vietnam, establishing Vietnamese forces "necessary for internal security," encouraging "support for Free Viet Nam by the non-Communist world," and providing the aid needed to repair damage resulting from the war against the French. Robertson concluded his address by assuring his listeners of "the determination of this Government that there shall be no weakening in our support for Free Vietnam."[49]

Other speakers at the conference dealt with matters besides the Geneva agreement. Leo Cherne analyzed the RVN's economy and declared that, although the South faced serious problems, "there is an opportunity to create, as has been created in West Berlin, with such remarkable effect, a window for freedom, a window into which all in Asia who hunger for dignity may look and find their lesson."[50] Frederick H. Bunting of the International Cooperation Administration, the government's foreign aid agency, discussed American assistance programs that had trained Vietnamese soldiers, resettled refugees, and financed land reform efforts.[51] Monsignor Joseph Harnett and Dr. Thomas Dooley recounted their experiences dealing with displaced Vietnamese. Calling the refugees "a great and dignified people," Harnett told of the procedures established to help them.[52] In his presentation, Dooley dwelt upon the hardships the Viet Minh had inflicted on the people who had decided to flee south, sufferings that forced him and his navy comrades to see communism "not as a distant, far away, nebulous, ethereal thing—but as an evil, driving, malicious ogre which in 38 meager years of existence has succeeded in conquering half of all mankind."[53]

Besides listening to addresses and panel discussions, conference participants heard the AFV's officers read messages sent from the Vietnamese and American governments. Diem cabled a lengthy dispatch outlining his regime's accomplishments and problems and thanking the AFV for its interest in Vietnam. "The very name of your group is warming," he wrote, "for we have learned to trust the Americans."[54] Another telegram came from Secretary of State Dulles, who voiced his "deep appreciation" of the activities of the AFV. He predicted that the RVN's development would be greatly assisted because of the "continued support of the American people through their government and through private organizations such as yours."[55]

The most impressive sign of official recognition came from the White House, which sent a congratulatory message despite objections from the State Department. Fisher Howe, director of the State Department's executive secretariat, told the White House staff that Dulles's telegram and Robertson's speech had provided "an adequate indication of the United States Government's interest in, and support of, the activities of the American Friends of Vietnam."[56] The White House nevertheless overrode Howe's demurrals, probably because of the influence of Wilton B. Persons, an old friend of Eisenhower who served as the president's deputy assistant. It dispatched a letter to O'Daniel extending Eisenhower's "warm greetings" to the conference participants. The president praised the American Friends by declaring, "They aid the American people [to] achieve a better understanding of the Republic of Vietnam, an ally of the free world, and of the problems it faces as a newly independent nation."[57] O'Daniel, who had requested a note from Eisenhower, expressed his gratitude for such a positive response. The presidential message, he told Persons, "gave the meeting the prestige that was needed," and he publicly read it twice at the gathering.[58]

The June 1 conference attracted overseas attention as well. Radio Hanoi broadcast a denunciation of the AFV on June 4, calling the organization an "association of the enemies of the Vietnamese people" and its leaders "sworn and dangerous enemies who have committed countless crimes on our territory."[59] The British Foreign Office also took an interest in the symposium. Sir Hubert Graves, the minister of the British embassy in Washington, informed London that he had received an invitation to the meeting. He listed such speakers as Robertson, Judd, and Kennedy and called them "protagonists . . . who have been fighting against the admission of Communist China to the United Nations."[60]

Graves and other British officials worried that the meeting might undermine London's efforts to persuade Diem to adopt a more flexible posture on the issue of election consultations with the DRV. The minister thought that the conference would pass a resolution opposing an all-Vietnam plebiscite, and his superior, Sir Roger Makins, expressed his concern about such a gesture in a discussion with Douglas MacArthur II, the counselor to the State Department. In this conversation, Makins worried that, although Robertson's speech had not departed from the administration's previous statements about Vietnam, "one never knew what might come out of these meetings and the twists which might be given to the proceedings at a time when we were engaged in some rather tricky negotiations in Saigon."[61]

British anxieties about the symposium's impact, however, quickly faded within a few weeks of its adjournment. In a letter written on June 4, Graves observed that the meeting "shows all the signs of the old 'China Lobby,'" and he criticized Kennedy and Morgenthau for making anticolonial remarks that were "tactless in the extreme" because they had been made in the presence of a secretary from the French embassy. He nevertheless regarded the messages sent by Eisenhower, Reinhardt, and Dulles as being "innocuous," and he wrote that Robertson's address "was not very startling."[62] Subsequent dispatches to London indicated that the AFV conference had a minimal impact on the British. The British ambassador in Saigon concluded that it had no "significant effect on Vietnamese opinion" despite the attention given to it by the Saigon press, and an officer in the Washington embassy declared that the gathering "had attracted no attention here."[63] The Foreign Office's rapid loss of interest in the AFV can be seen in a minute written by John Cable, an official in its Southeast Asia Department, who declared, "It is all over and forgotten now and I certainly see no point in pursuing the matter."[64]

The conference marked an end to an apparently promising beginning of the AFV's work. The association's activities had attracted the favorable notice of leading figures in Washington and Saigon, and officials in those cities had shown a willingness to assist the AFV. Moreover, the American and Vietnamese governments saw the AFV as a useful vehicle for promoting their own interests. The South Vietnamese press used the organization's congratulatory messages to Diem to back up claims that the RVN's president enjoyed the support of a host of prominent Americans, and the AFV's meeting provided the Eisenhower administration with a platform for Robertson to deliver a major policy statement that received extensive press coverage and would be cited by State Department officers for nearly two years.[65]

Despite these initial successes, the AFV had done little to shape American actions in Vietnam in early 1956. A primary reason was that the officials the AFV tried to influence shared many of the same assumptions held by those who belonged to the organization. As did the AFV's members, Eisenhower and his colleagues worried about the consequences of a communist victory in Vietnam and saw Ngo Dinh Diem as the most promising leader of anticommunist nationalists. They also believed that American aid and advice could do much to shape Vietnam's future and that this assistance, unlike France's attempt to transform Vietnam through imperial rule, would be gratefully accepted by Vietnamese willing to follow American guidance.

The shared premises of the AFV and the Eisenhower administration can be seen most clearly in the negative attitude both parties had toward the plebiscite scheduled to take place in 1956. An article in *Ramparts* magazine later charged that the elections "were never held because the Viet-Nam Lobby didn't want them," but such an accusation vastly overstates the AFV's influence while paying little heed to Washington's opposition.[66] Both AFV members and government officials believed that the vote would give the Viet Minh control of all of Vietnam, and they held similar views as to why such a result was likely. Although occasionally conceding that Ho Chi Minh might be a genuinely popular figure, individuals in both groups usually ascribed the likelihood of communist success to other factors, such as Bao Dai's unpopularity, the advantage the Viet Minh enjoyed from controlling the more populous North, and the probability of unfair voting conditions in the DRV. Eisenhower and his colleagues needed no pressure from the AFV to take steps to prevent a vote from taking place, and a former Foreign Service officer has characterized the AFV's campaign against the elections as a "superfluous" effort.[67] The AFV therefore acted more as a partner of the administration than as a potentially troublesome pressure group in attacking the elections.

chapter 4
Promoting the Diem Regime, 1956–1959

In the years following its opening conference, the American Friends of Vietnam organized a number of activities aimed at generating U.S. support for the South Vietnamese state headed by Ngo Dinh Diem. The association hosted meetings dealing with such topics as investment conditions in Vietnam, U.S. aid programs to the RVN, and social and economic developments in the country. It also sponsored special events such as receptions, awards ceremonies, and movie premieres, and it organized direct aid projects for Vietnam. All of this work was carried out for what Joseph Buttinger called the "essentially political reason" of saving South Vietnam from communist rule, and AFV members made this quite clear in writings and speeches praising the Diem regime.[1] The organization's efforts in the late 1950s met with considerable success as the AFV received friendly hearings from journalists, academics, politicians, and government officials who shared the AFV's confidence in Diem. Certain problems nevertheless troubled the AFV during this period and limited its effectiveness.

In March 1957, William J. Donovan resigned as the AFV's honorary chairman, and Leo Cherne and Harold Oram stepped down as executive committee members. Donovan quit because of health problems, and Cherne and Oram cited the demands of "very heavy schedules."[2] In Oram's case, however, questions about the propriety of his presence on the board while his firm acted as Saigon's public relations representative also played a role. Although the AFV's leaders were well aware of Oram's ties to the Diem regime, his position as an officer in the group left the organization open to charges that its policies were shaped by an agent of the Vietnamese government, and Oram decided that it would be best that he hold no office.[3] Finally, Angier Biddle Duke announced his resignation as head of the AFV's executive committee because the "pressures of other duties" demanded his time, but he agreed to serve as the AFV's vice chairman after Joseph Buttinger took his place in September 1958.[4]

As some AFV members took less active roles in the group, others became more involved in its work. Gilbert Jonas stepped down as executive secretary in the spring of 1957 but retained a seat on the executive committee. He also served as a vice president of Oram's company, which allowed him to act as a link between the Oram firm and the American Friends. Wesley Fishel also emerged as a more influential figure in the AFV after he completed a two-year stint as director of Michigan State University's advisory team to the Saigon government. William Henderson, a political scientist who was an officer in the Council on Foreign Relations, and Monsignor Joseph Harnett took the seats that Cherne and Oram had vacated on the executive committee.[5] Others soon followed Henderson and Harnett, including Frank Trager, a fervent anticommunist academic, Franklin Leerburger, an engineer who had worked in Vietnam in the mid-1950s, and Diana Lockard, who also worked with the Council on Foreign Relations. The position of executive secretary, the officer who administered the AFV's day-to-day business, changed hands three times within the two years following Jonas's resignation. Two women, Elinor Dubin and Joan Clark, served in this position until the AFV hired a young man named Louis Andreatta at the end of 1958.[6]

Changes in its leadership signified no diminution of the AFV's enthusiasm for Diem. For many months, the AFV devoted much of its energy to a campaign to foster an American business interest in Vietnam. This project had its beginnings in a trip General O'Daniel made to Vietnam in the summer of 1956. During his visit, O'Daniel received a memorandum from Diem outlining the RVN's need for foreign investment to develop its economy and promising cooperation with firms that operated in Vietnam. O'Daniel enthusiastically declared that the proposals were "the quickest way to get on with developing the country," and he received the backing of Harold Oram at an executive committee meeting on September 28.[7] Oram, who had spoken to O'Daniel after the general's return to the United States, submitted a memo of his own calling for "a shift in program emphasis" from political to economic matters because "the economic needs of Vietnam are equally, if not more, important for survival" and suggesting that the AFV sponsor a conference focusing on the RVN's economy.[8]

The AFV's officers accepted Oram's proposal and began immediate preparations for a meeting to be held in early 1957. On October 3, the AFV hosted a New York reception for Vietnamese officials en route to an International Monetary Fund conference. Oram called the gathering "a considerable success since about thirty corporations and banking institutions were represented."[9] Gilbert Jonas, who had been given the responsibility for organizing the conference, secured the services of Carter Goodrich, a distinguished economist from Columbia University who had headed a United Nations mission to Vietnam, in organizing the event, and Goodrich later agreed to act as the chairman for the gathering.[10] Jonas also sought and received Washington's assistance after he met three State Department representatives, Kenneth Young, Paul Kattenburg, and Hoyt Price, in the autumn of 1956. These officials reacted to the AFV's decision to emphasize economic matters with what Oram called "enthusiastic, though unofficial, support," and the State Department later promised its help to the AFV in submitting a request for the publication of a Commerce Department booklet concerning investment possibilities in Vietnam.[11]

After several months of preparation, the AFV's conference on Vietnam's economic needs took place on March 15, 1957. Approximately forty people, including academics, technical experts, journalists, and government officials, met in a closed session to discuss the RVN's economy. AFV officers including Buttinger, Duke, Emmet, O'Daniel, and Jonas took part in the proceedings, as did Oram and two national committee members who resided in Saigon: Eugene Gregory, a former USIS officer and the editor of the *Times of Vietnam*, and Wolf Ladejinsky, Diem's land reform adviser. The symposium opened with presentations covering the RVN's economic condition and energy resources and U.S. aid programs to Vietnam. In an exchange of views following these talks, the conferees addressed such matters as South Vietnam's economic potential and government policies. They also expressed concern about "the almost total absence of relevant statistics and other economic information" the RVN needed for formulating a sound development strategy, and they criticized the vagueness of Diem's declarations concerning foreign investment. As the meeting drew to a close, the participants recommended that Saigon employ the services of a private company and technical advisers in drawing up national development plans and surveying investment possibilities.[12]

The AFV's leaders concurred with the conference findings and made plans for a follow-up meeting that would provide detailed information about investment conditions in Vietnam. They scheduled the event for February 1958 and asked Leo Cherne to act as the chairman. A letter signed by O'Daniel that hailed South Vietnam as "a staunch advocate and friend of free enterprise" informed AFV members and potential investors of the gathering.[13]

As the AFV made its preparations, the Diem regime took steps to create a friendly business environment for foreign firms. It established the Industrial Development Center, which was given the task of providing loans and technical advice for private industry and government enterprises. It also signed International Cooperation Administration guarantee agreements protecting American companies from nationalization, currency incontrovertibility, and war damages. Finally, Saigon announced its approval of twelve industrial projects, including several funded by foreign businesses, in a telegram sent to the AFV on the day it held its conference.[14]

Opening at New York's Ambassador Hotel on February 28, the meeting on investments in Vietnam drew more than 130 participants from the U.S. government, the Vietnamese embassy, American corporations, and the AFV itself.[15] In introductory addresses, O'Daniel asserted that Vietnam needed America's technical knowledge and capital resources to transform itself into "a showcase for democracy in Southeast Asia," while Cherne claimed that the Diem regime's recent investment decrees and agreements had given the gathering "a climate in which it has real purpose."[16] Presentations following these remarks drew a generally positive picture of the RVN as a country with a strong agricultural base, a modest industrial capacity, and a stable economy. Tran Kim Phuong, the Vietnamese embassy's first secretary for economic affairs, assured his listeners of his government's eagerness in encouraging investments and of its intention to refrain from participating in any enterprise unless Vietnamese capitalists didn't have the funds needed to work with foreign firms. Cherne backed this claim in a closing statement asserting that Vietnam was "a unique country" whose leaders quickly responded to companies interested in exploring investment possibilities. He then thanked the conferees for showing concern for an issue "deeply involved in the vital interests of the American nation and the very survival of the Vietnamese nation."[17]

The investment meetings were followed by two other gatherings sponsored by the AFV. On April 17, 1959, it hosted a conference in Washington where speakers from government and private agencies hailed the U.S. aid program to Vietnam as an "American Success Story."[18] Six months later, the association held another, much larger, affair as more than 200 journalists, academics, and government officials met at New York's Roosevelt Hotel on October 23–24 to listen to favorable descriptions of South Vietnam's political, social, and economic development. They heard AFV members such as Wesley Fishel and Wolf Ladejinsky claim that most Vietnamese supported an administration that had made impressive strides in rebuilding the South, developing its economy, and promoting a new land reform program as "a primary social need of the country."[19] As the symposium drew to a close, General O'Daniel thanked the participants and asserted that the very interest they had shown in the RVN's progress was "a great weapon in this war we are fighting."[20]

Conferences were not the only events staged by the AFV to draw favorable attention to Diem's government. The association hosted several receptions for Vietnamese officials, politicians, and educators in an attempt to create a greater public interest in Vietnam as well as acquaint the visiting dignitaries with their American counterparts. In April 1957, it invited members to a luncheon honoring Ngo Dinh Nhu, Diem's ambitious and influential younger brother, and declared that attendance at the meal would serve as a "great demonstration of comradeship with those friends who have stood with us in defense of our common cause — the freedom of mankind."[21] The AFV's leaders regarded Nhu's reception as a "highly successful" affair and held similar gatherings for Vietnamese visitors who followed Nhu, including representatives from the RVN's National Assembly, Vietnamese students residing in the United States, and prominent figures in the Diem regime such as Vu Van Thai, Diem's director general of the budget and foreign aid, and Vu Van Mau, the RVN's foreign minister.[22]

The AFV's most impressive reception for a Vietnamese dignitary, however, was the welcome it extended to Diem himself in May 1957. Arriving in Washington on May 8, Diem was greeted personally by Eisenhower, a gesture that the president had made only once before to a head of state during his term of office. Diem spent the next four days talking to Eisenhower and his advisers about the political situation in Southeast Asia and American military and economic aid to the RVN. He also addressed a joint session of Congress and asked for continuing U.S. assistance to South Vietnam, a plea that received a warm reception. Leaving Washington after four days, Diem traveled to New York, where he was honored at various banquets and receptions and extolled as a "God-fearing" statesman "to whom freedom is the very breath of life itself."[23] While in New York, Diem visited the Maryknoll seminary where he had lived in the early 1950s, and he returned to another site of his years in exile when he flew to Michigan on May 14. There, he received an honorary degree from Michigan State University, the institution that had hosted Diem at Wesley Fishel's behest. In an acceptance speech, Diem compared his trip to MSU to a "home-coming" and assured his listeners that, although his regime was not yet "a perfect Jeffersonian democracy," it had established the "foundation of a democratic government."²⁴ Diem returned to Saigon after making stops in Tennessee, California, and Hawaii.

Diem's visit marked the height of American enthusiasm for his leadership, and the members of the AFV did a great deal to bring this about. Joseph Buttinger's Saigon journal discusses the possibility of an American trip as early as the autumn of 1954, and State Department records mention efforts by Buttinger's colleagues on the International Rescue Committee—Richard Salzmann and Angier Biddle Duke, who later became AFV officers—to invite Diem to the United States. A year later, Harold Oram told Wolf Ladejinsky that Diem had accepted a suggestion that he go to America. Diem approached the U.S. embassy about the matter in February 1957 and received American approval.²⁵ When he arrived in the United States in May, Diem received valuable help from the American Friends of Vietnam and its members. The Oram firm handled Diem's public relations during his tour, and Oram himself accompanied the presidential party as it traveled across the country. AFV members such as Joseph Buttinger and Sol Sanders composed some of the speeches Diem gave to American audiences.²⁶

The AFV's most impressive work, however, involved its collaboration with the International Rescue Committee in sponsoring a banquet to honor Diem. This dinner, held in New York's Ambassador Hotel on May 13, provided the IRC with an opportunity to present Diem with an award commemorating Richard E. Byrd, the famous polar explorer who had served as the honorary chairman of the IRC's board of directors from 1949 until his sudden death on March 11, 1957. Diem, whose government had given the IRC $100,000 to assist Hungarian refugees, received the award after the IRC's officers, including several AFV members, unanimously voted to bestow it on him.²⁷ Henry Luce presided at the meal and Cardinal Spellman gave an invocation. General O'Daniel congratulated Diem on behalf of the American Friends of Vietnam, while Leo Cherne, acting as spokesman for the IRC, said the organization felt privileged in helping "so brave a people and so great a leader in their hard but successful fight for freedom."²⁸ The guests then heard a message from the White House lauding Diem as a figure who "stands for the higher qualities of heroism and statesmanship."²⁹

After hearing these accolades, Diem received the Byrd award from Angier Biddle Duke, the IRC's president. The citation praised the Vietnamese leader for rebuilding a war-torn country and for instilling "a sense of pride and spiritual unity" in the Vietnamese people. "In accomplishing these things," it concluded, "President Ngo Dinh Diem has made Viet Nam a beacon of freedom for the whole of Asia."³⁰ In accepting the award, Diem stressed the theme of friendship and made references to his early American supporters, the members of such relief agencies as CRS and the IRC, the U.S. military advisers, and friendly journalists and publishers such as Henry Luce. He spoke of the RVN's need for continued American help and friendship, especially because of the RVN's position in the struggle against communism. "Your aid," Diem reminded his audience, "enables us to hold this crucial line, and to hold it at less expense to you, and at less danger to the world than you could have done it yourselves."[31]

The AFV played a key role in securing another award for Diem two years later. In the summer of 1958, Colonel Lansdale and General Samuel T. Williams, the commander of the U.S. military advisory team in Saigon, suggested that the AFV nominate Diem for the Freedom Award, a prize granted by the Freedoms Foundation, a conservative group promoting American political and social values. O'Daniel, who received a note from Lansdale, enthusiastically agreed that the AFV "should take the lead" in pushing Diem's candidacy.[32] He corresponded with the Freedoms Foundation's officers and kept the AFV's executive committee informed of Diem's prospects in the autumn of 1958. On May 6, 1959, the Freedoms Foundation announced its decision to honor Diem for "his resistance to communism." Impressed by this recognition, the *New York Times* editorialized that "the Freedom[s] Foundation has made an appropriate award."[33]

The AFV also used a movie premiere to put Diem's government in a favorable light. On January 22, 1958, it sponsored the Washington screening of *The Quiet American*, a film version of Graham Greene's novel. The book bitterly condemned the American intervention in Vietnam, but movie producer Joseph Mankiewicz instead offered a ringing affirmation of America's involvement by portraying the protagonist as a dedicated idealist instead of the dangerous and ignorant meddler in the novel. Ironically, Mankiewicz received assistance from Edward Lansdale, the model for the work's title character. Lansdale, according to Jonas, "actually helped in the rewriting of 'The Quiet American' script."[34] When the film opened at Washington's Playhouse Theater, AFV officers including Duke and O'Daniel joined Ambassador and Mme. Tran Van Chuong in greeting guests at the movie house and at a reception held by Perle Mesta, the celebrated Washington hostess. The event attracted notable figures such as Justice William O. Douglas, Senator Mike Mansfield, and General J. Lawton Collins, and the AFV's leaders regarded it as an "unqualified success."[35] Graham Greene took a far different view of the affair. "Far was it from my mind, when I wrote 'The Quiet American,' that the book would become the source of profit to one of the most corrupt governments in Southeast Asia."[36]

The AFV also sponsored direct aid projects, occasionally collaborating with other private groups, such as the Institute of International Education and the Asia Foundation, but forming no long-lasting partnership with any of them. The AFV's first assistance program involved a grant of $5,000 for the purchase of equipment to rehabilitate Vietnamese veterans of the First Indochina War. The AFV directed most of its other aid efforts toward educational needs. It awarded small amounts of scholarship money to Vietnamese studying in the United States and created a subcommittee on education to answer inquiries about American help for schools in Vietnam. The AFV's most ambitious project was an attempt to extend assistance to a newly established university at Hue. The American Friends procured several thousand books for the new school in a campaign endorsed by Justice Douglas, author James Michener, the president of Cornell University, and deans from Columbia, Michigan State, and Johns Hopkins Universities. This work lasted several years, with the AFV obtaining books and supplies for the institution until the mid-1960s.[37]

As the AFV tried bolstering Diem's government through special events and projects, individual members extolled the regime in various publications. Wesley Fishel called Diem's administration "one of the most stable and honest on the periphery of Asia," while General O'Daniel declared that he had been "struck by the remarkable, indeed unparalleled progress" that South Vietnam had made when he visited the country in the summer of 1958.[38] O'Daniel attributed this success to the "wise, decisive, and far-sighted leadership" of Diem, an individual characterized by Wolf Ladejinsky as an "austere and incorruptible" individual and by Fishel as the man who had "steered his little country from the edge of chaos to peace, stability, and a gradually increasing tempo of development."[39]

The AFV directed its energies toward the U.S. government as well as the general public. The executive branch, a former State Department official recalled, "didn't need much persuasion" from the AFV to back Diem after the president's 1955 victory over the sects, and it readily gave help to the association.[40] The Eisenhower administration sent representatives from federal agencies and departments to the AFV's conferences and made arrangements for the donation and shipment of books to Vietnam. Senior officials, including the president, applauded the AFV's work. In a note sent to the meeting concerning U.S. aid to Vietnam, Eisenhower praised the AFV for focusing national attention on "the substantial progress being made in Viet-Nam under the leadership of President Ngo Dinh Diem."[41] Approbation also came from J. Graham Parsons, Walter Robertson's successor as assistant secretary of state for Far Eastern affairs, who wrote to O'Daniel in the summer of 1959 and expressed his "appreciation for the fine job being done by the American Friends of Vietnam."[42]

The AFV had friendly ties with Congress as well as with the Eisenhower administration. One of the group's first letterheads shows a membership including five senators and thirty-two representatives. Among them were James P. Richards (D-S.C.), chairman of the Committee on Foreign Affairs; Emmanuel Celler (D-N.Y.), head of the House Judiciary Committee; and John J. Rooney (D-N.Y.), a ranking member of the House Appropriations Committee. Early partisans of Diem such as Edna Kelly (D-N.Y.) and John F. Kennedy (D-Mass.) also joined the AFV, and Diem's most powerful advocate on Capitol Hill, Senator Mike Mansfield (D-Mont.), joined the organization within a few years of its founding. Individuals with such widely differing views as those of conservative William Jennings Bryan Dorn (D-S.C.) and liberal Adam Clayton Powell (D-N.Y.) sat on the AFV's national committee, bound together by a belief that communism must be stopped in Vietnam and that America could help a leader like Diem accomplish this task.[43]

Legislators endorsed the AFV by praising Diem on the floors of Congress and inserting the opinions of AFV officers into the *Congressional Record*, the daily journal of activities on Capitol Hill. Addressing the House in the spring of 1956, Adam Clayton Powell congratulated Diem on the second anniversary of his accession to power and wished "President Ngo Dinh Diem and the people of Vietnam every success which they so richly deserve."[44] Mansfield hailed Diem in extravagant terms a year later, asserting that Diem "is not only the savior of his country, but in my opinion he is the savior of Southeast Asia."[45] Michael Feighan, an Ohio Democrat sitting on the AFV's national committee, placed a letter signed by O'Daniel and denouncing the Geneva accords into a 1956 issue of the the *Congressional Record*. Two years later, Patrick J. Hillings (R-Calif.) inserted into the record an "extremely interesting" rebuttal that Leo Cherne directed against Diem's opponents.[46]

Although generally successful in putting Diem's government in a favorable light, the AFV had to respond to persistent and growing criticisms of Diem's repressive policies. Diem had adopted democratic trappings such as an elected National Assembly and a constitution, but he effectively created a family dictatorship that ruthlessly suppressed all opposition. He paid close attention to the advice of his older brother, Bishop Ngo Dinh Thuc, "a genial, worldly cleric" who nevertheless tarnished the regime's image by enriching the Catholic Church through extensive real estate purchases and by dealing with Vietnam's Buddhist majority in a high-handed manner.[47] Diem gave another brother, the reclusive Ngo Dinh Can, authority to safeguard the family's interests in Central Vietnam, and he appointed his youngest sibling, Ngo Dinh Luyen, as the regime's representative in Europe. The president relied most heavily, however, on the counsel of his brother Ngo Dinh Nhu and Nhu's "attractive, compulsive, and ultimately destructive" wife.[48] The power of the Nhus rested on their daily access to Diem and their control of various political fronts and intelligence services, especially a secretive organization called the Can Lao Party, that exercised powers of surveillance and arbitrary arrest to intimidate the Vietnamese population. With the support of his ambitious family and the repressive apparatus they had forged, Diem tried to smash all opposition in relentless campaigns that led to the deaths of hundreds of Vietnamese and the arrests of thousands more by the late 1950s.[49]

Diem's opponents attacked the regime, and even sympathetic observers expressed misgivings about Diem's policies. Vietnamese critics of the administration warned of growing anti-American sentiment in Vietnam, claiming that most Vietnamese saw Diem as "an American puppet" who depended on U.S. "dollars and guns to keep himself and his family in power."[50] An American critic, a right-wing activist named Hilaire du Berrier, asserted that "the corruption and despotism of the Diem government is daily pushing" the Vietnamese people into the communist camp.[51] Other commentators were less strident but nevertheless voiced uneasiness about developments in the RVN. David Hotham, a British journalist who visited Vietnam in 1957, worried that a lavish but poorly conceived American aid program and Diem's harsh treatment of his opponents had made Vietnam "one of the least stable countries in Southeast Asia."[52] Bernard B. Fall, a French-born U.S. citizen who became one of the first American authorities on Vietnamese affairs, shared this apprehension in an article written for a 1958 issue of *The Nation*. He asserted that "growing insecurity in the countryside and an economic crisis" in the South threatened to wipe out any gains the RVN had made since independence.[53]

The AFV adopted a variety of responses to the charges leveled against the Diem regime. In a few cases, its members raised objections of their own. The most notable example occurred in the summer of 1957, when a Saigon military tribunal meted out death sentences to eight Binh Xuyen members and to Ho Huu Tuong, a former Trotskyite who had collaborated with the sects. The sentences evoked strong protests from AFV officers who had been involved in socialist politics, figures like Buttinger and Sanders, as well as national committee members Norman Thomas and I. Milton Sacks. Sanders, Buttinger, Cherne, and Duke sent telegrams to Saigon warning that "even [Diem's] best American friends" could not understand the sentences and that the executions could lead to a "dangerous reaction" in the United States.[54] These entreaties evidently had some effect since Diem spared Tuong and sent him into exile, but other factors, such as possible pressures from Washington, fears of aid cutbacks, and Tuong's relatively inconsequential political status, may also have influenced Diem's decision to commute the sentence.[55]

Although they occasionally questioned Diem's actions, AFV members usually defended the president or rationalized his behavior. When Norman Thomas sent a letter to O'Daniel expressing concern about accounts of repression in Vietnam, he received a reply from the executive committee that reaffirmed the AFV's commitment to Diem. The committee admitted that the Saigon government had its "shortcomings" but said it had generally served the Vietnamese people "with admirable devotion," and that the AFV was "profoundly convinced that Diem is moving in the right direction."[56] In an article written in 1959, Wolf Ladejinsky justified Diem's policies by arguing that Diem "believes in democracy, but he is compelled to ration it" because of threats from communist agents who would subvert the democratic process in their campaign to destroy the RVN.[57] Wesley Fishel blamed the apparently slow development of representative institutions in the RVN on Southeast Asia's political traditions, which made it difficult for its peoples to "understand, let alone embrace, the difficult articles of our democratic faith and practice."[58]

The AFV also resorted to attacking critics of the Diem regime. Joseph Buttinger told Norman Thomas that one of Diem's Vietnamese opponents "is a decent human being but politically a rather confused and weak man." He went on to say that such people had few opportunities "to express their political thinking in positive and constructive terms."[59] When a young woman identifying herself as a "Little Vietnamese Girl" denounced America's support of Diem in a letter to the *Washington Post*, Leo Cherne called the note "a masterpiece of calculated confusion" and sarcastically refuted her charges in a speech that a White House official praised as a "hard-hitting" response.[60] On another occasion, the Oram firm persuaded the editors of *American Mercury* to print an article signed by O'Daniel that contradicted a gloomy piece Hilaire du Berrier had written for an earlier issue of the magazine. The

AFV or Oram's company also persuaded other periodicals and newspapers to print rebuttals signed by AFV members.[61]

The strongest reaction to a critical appraisal of developments in Vietnam was prompted by a newspaper exposé of the shortcomings of Diem's government and the U.S. aid program. Journalist Albert M. Colegrove worked for the Scripps-Howard papers and had been sent to Saigon in the summer of 1959 to investigate U.S. foreign assistance projects. After a ten-day stay in the RVN, he returned to the United States and wrote six articles asserting that the American program had done little "to guide Vietnam to the day when she can support herself" and that Diem ran "a hard-fisted government" that ruled through "countless laws promulgated after police state practices."[62] Colegrove's articles sparked an uproar in Washington and Saigon. U.S. and Vietnamese officials angrily refuted them and congressional committees made plans to investigate their credibility.

The Colegrove articles also provoked an angry response from AFV members, who worried that the allegations posed a threat to the U.S. aid program to Saigon. Walker Stone, the managing editor of the Scripps-Howard papers, received a letter from O'Daniel that castigated the pieces as "disgraceful" examples of journalism. A memorandum appended to this note disputed the articles, questioned Colegrove's qualifications and professional conduct, and asserted that the series had been the source of "much joy in Moscow, Hanoi and Peiping . . . because what the Communists failed to achieve in five years—to cast doubt on the Free Vietnamese and the American aid program there—was accomplished in one week of headlines."[63] Father Raymond de Jaegher accused Colegrove of engaging in "unfactual muckraking," and Wesley Fishel condemned the reporter for writing "silly and irresponsible" pieces "filled with falsehoods, half-truths, and distortions."[64]

The AFV also tried to influence the congressional hearings sparked by Colegrove's articles. It sent copies of O'Daniel's letter to Stone to the Senate Foreign Relations Committee and asked if the general could appear as a witness. That request was turned down when the subcommittee conducting the inquiry decided to confine testimony to evidence given by Colegrove and senior U.S. officials from Saigon, but the AFV had better success with the House Foreign Affairs Committee.[65] No one from the AFV spoke to the representatives, but the head of the subcommittee conducting the hearing, Clement J. Zablocki, represented a strongly anticommunist Polish constituency in Milwaukee and shared the AFV's conviction that leaders like Diem deserved U.S. support. Together with Walter Judd, another AFV sympathizer, Zablocki sharply questioned Colegrove and criticized the negative tone of his stories. Moreover, Zablocki inserted letters and articles that contradicted Colegrove's allegations, including O'Daniel's note to Stone, into the record of the testimony.[66]

The AFV's fears that Colegrove's accounts would undermine public support for aid to Vietnam never materialized, but the stories did create problems for the organization. Two conservative national committee members, Governor J. Bracken Lee of Utah and Representative William Jennings Bryan Dorn of South Carolina, resigned from the group because of its strong endorsement of foreign aid.[67] Another consequence of the Colegrove affair was Diem's decision to cancel a visit to the United States by Nguyen Ngoc Tho, the RVN's vice president, which was to have included an appearance at the AFV's October conference. Wolf Ladejinsky told Gilbert Jonas that the Vietnamese "are absolutely boiling-mad" about the articles and that their publication was directly responsible for the cancellation of the trip.[68] The cancellation deprived the AFV of an opportunity to gain wider recognition for its work because it forced the organization to shelve plans to invite Richard Nixon, Tho's American counterpart, to the meeting.[69]

The Colegrove articles marked an end to a period of AFV accomplishments in portraying Diem's regime as worthy of U.S. support. The AFV had won the favorable attention of prominent and reputable private citizens and government officials, and its members had little trouble publishing laudatory assessments of Diem's leadership in national newspapers and journals. Moreover, they frequently rebutted or allayed doubts and criticisms of the Saigon administration. They were particularly successful in preventing leading figures of America's anticommunist Left from speaking out against Diem's policies. According to Jonas, the telegrams objecting to Ho Huu Tuong's death sentence forestalled open protests by American socialists, and the reassurances of an individual with left-wing credentials like those of Joseph Buttinger prevented public expressions of concern about the RVN's reported human rights abuses.[70] This assertion is borne out in a letter in which Norman Thomas thanked Buttinger for sending a "long and careful, and, to me, convincing reply" concerning Vietnam's problems in the spring of 1958.[71]

Much of the AFV's success in promoting and defending the Diem regime can be attributed to the unusually favorable environment in which it operated. Since conditions in South Vietnam were relatively calm in the late 1950s, the American press and public paid little attention, and the AFV faced, as Gilbert Jonas put it, "literally no organized force" to challenge its positive assessment of Diem's leadership.[72] The AFV had little trouble in presenting its views to academics, journalists, politicians, and officials who shared the group's conviction that communism must be stopped in Vietnam and that Ngo Dinh Diem could do this with American help. Few Americans objected to the U.S. presence in Vietnam, and critics such as Colegrove often called for more effective measures to shore up Diem's government, not an American withdrawal from Vietnam. In testimony before the Senate Foreign Relations Committee, Colegrove declared that Diem had "accomplished a miracle" in creating a functioning government and that assistance to the Republic of Vietnam "is essential to the defense of America and the free world."[73]

Despite the overall success of its work, the AFV did face limits to its influence. As the organization campaigned for American investments in Vietnam, it received complaints from business executives and government officials that the Diem government regarded foreign firms with suspicion and manipulated "a paternalistic system which has controls for everything."[74] Moreover, AFV officers heard that Saigon had no coherent economic policy and that, as Harold Oram concluded after a visit to Vietnam, "there is no plan for investment."[75] The Diem regime periodically kept hopes alive by pledging its assistance to interested companies and by setting up such bureaus as the Industrial Development Center to aid private enterprise, but it failed to follow through on its promises. By the summer of 1958, even one of Diem's most fervent admirers, General O'Daniel, admitted that it "has been quite a problem to pin down just what the Vietnamese want as to Foreign Investment."[76] One of Diem's senior advisers later concluded that the AFV's attempt to create a business interest in Vietnam "brought limited or absolutely no practical results."[77]

Several factors played roles in the AFV's failure to attract American investors to Vietnam. Fears of renewed warfare deterred many firms, but Saigon's policies did a great deal more to keep them away. Diem wanted outside help to develop the RVN's economy, but at the same time he retained a strong Confucian prejudice against commercial activities and was determined to dominate any group that might threaten his political power, including foreign businesses. As a result, his government pursued a contradictory policy of promising assistance to U.S. and European companies while imposing bureaucratic controls that frustrated any firm that wished to do business in Vietnam. Moreover, the regime began to rely heavily on another source of income that obviated any need to deal with foreign investors—the Commercial Import Program (CIP). Designed to pay for the maintenance of the RVN's security forces and bureaucracy, this American-financed project generated revenues for Saigon through the sale of import licenses and the imposition of customs duties. The CIP gave Diem the funds he needed to run his administration, but it stifled Vietnamese industrial production by putting locally manufactured goods at a disadvantage in competing with frequently cheaper U.S. imports and thus discouraging all but the most determined entrepreneurs from investing in Vietnam's industry.[78]

Another difficulty the AFV faced in the late 1950s involved media accounts of the shortcomings of the Diem regime. Many journalists and editors agreed with the AFV's optimistic view of the RVN's development, but many periodicals also printed criticisms of Diem's government. Although AFV members frequently had opportunities to respond to attacks against Diem, there were occasions when editors paid no attention to the AFV's objections and backed the conclusions of their writers. The most striking instance occurred when Roy Howard, the owner of the Scripps-Howard papers, angrily replied to O'Daniel's attack on the Colegrove articles. Howard asserted that O'Daniel had made "intemperate and baseless accusations" and that Colegrove "has earned and enjoyed our highest confidence." Howard not only refused to disavow Colegrove's stories, but he sent another reporter to Saigon to substantiate their allegations.[79]

A final problem that became a constant source of trouble for the AFV was a shortage of funds. The association's financial records are very fragmentary and incomplete, but available evidence indicates that the AFV obtained most of its money from appeals to members and potential donors two or three times a year. Annual income averaged nearly $31,000 a year in the late 1950s, and most of the money came from individuals, not corporate sponsors.[80] Speaking to the executive committee in November 1958, Gilbert Jonas told the officers that "approximately 95 percent of our funds come from private individual contributors and only five percent from corporations." Jonas thought that "a more desirable ratio should be 50–50," but the AFV never came close to reaching that balance or winning the steady support of a major benefactor.[81] Ironically, the AFV's leaders attributed this failure partly to the Diem regime's apparent success in the late 1950s. The relatively peaceful condition of South Vietnam, Jonas observed, had eliminated "the crisis atmosphere which makes fund drives so successful."[82]

Another, and more serious, source of difficulty was the federal government's refusal for four years to give the AFV tax-exempt status. The association had applied for tax-exemption in the spring of 1956, but Internal Revenue Service officials turned down the request because they correctly regarded affairs such as the AFV's economic conferences as activities that had the political objective of "aiding the state or government of Vietnam."[83]

AFV officers repeatedly blamed the IRS ruling for shortfalls in fund-raising operations in the late 1950s.[84] They made constant efforts to reverse the decision but met with no success until they finally agreed to amend the AFV's certification of incorporation with a pledge to refrain from "carrying on propaganda or otherwise attempting to influence legislation."[85] Although the AFV finally received tax-exemption in the spring of 1960, its difficulties in winning it may have prevented the association from establishing a secure financial base in its early years.

By the time the AFV won tax-exempt status, the situation in Vietnam had dramatically changed. Accounts of growing unrest in the country appeared with greater frequency as a communist-led rebellion against Diem gained momentum. These stories disturbed not only the general public, but also some of Diem's most devoted supporters in the American Friends of Vietnam. These individuals publicly voiced their confidence in Diem's leadership, but they privately expressed growing misgivings about reports of Diem's authoritarian policies and the resistance they provoked. This uneasiness grew worse as violence in the South escalated. By the end of 1960, many of the AFV's most active members were losing all confidence in Diem's ability to lead the South Vietnamese state.

chapter 5
Losing Faith in Diem, 1959–1961

Although they vigorously supported Ngo Dinh Diem in public, some of the AFV's leading figures began to entertain serious doubts about his abilities by 1960. Active members such as Joseph Buttinger, Wolf Ladejinsky, Gilbert Jonas, Leo Cherne, and Wesley Fishel were frustrated by the president's unwillingness to heed their advice and dismayed by the growing influence that Ngo Dinh Nhu and his wife exercised over Diem. They also became alarmed by the government's inability to stem the spread of the communist-led insurgency in South Vietnam. Nevertheless, they did not openly criticize Diem. They still hoped that he would, as he had in the past, act boldly to assure his survival, and they feared that Diem's downfall would pave the way for a communist victory in the South. When it became apparent, however, that Diem would make no serious effort to reform his administration, influential figures in the AFV's leadership began to turn against him.

Diem's inability to govern effectively became increasingly clear as reports of mounting unrest in South Vietnam multiplied in the late 1950s. Since his accession to power in 1954, Diem had alienated virtually every segment of the RVN's population by building up a family dictatorship that failed to address the country's economic and social problems. Resentment against the regime had become particularly strong in the countryside, where Diem's officials treated the peasants they were supposed to serve in an arrogant and abusive manner. The government angered the South's large population of tenant farmers, more than a million households, by implementing an inefficient land reform program that failed to satisfy many tenants who wanted land of their own. The Viet Minh cadres remaining in the South exploited this discontent by launching a guerrilla campaign against Saigon in 1957, and they soon received important assistance from their comrades in North Vietnam who began sending supplies and agents (many of whom were southerners returning from the DRV) to the RVN. This aid gave greater strength to a rebellion that withstood Diem's heavy-handed attempts to suppress it. By 1960, the insurgency was making rapid gains throughout the South.[1]

Reports of repression and unrest in Vietnam had troubled some AFV members as early as 1955. Eugene Gregory, the former USIS official who had drawn Justice Douglas's attention to Diem, had complained that Diem's followers resorted to communist tactics of intimidation and fraud in generating support for the president during the election campaign against Bao Dai. Such methods, he worried, could lead to the establishment of a dictatorship with "no free press, no representative assembly, no vigilant civic groups to check the use of power by the government."[2] Another early note of criticism was sounded by William Henderson in a 1957 issue of *Foreign Affairs*. He praised Diem for preserving South Vietnam's independence and speculated that history "may yet adjudge Diem as one of the greatest figures of twentieth century Asia," but nevertheless faulted the president's "archaic, mandarin temperament." Moreover, Diem "has ruled virtually as a dictator" and had transformed the Republic of Vietnam into "a quasi-police state."[3]

Some of the AFV's senior officers also became concerned about the course of events in Vietnam. Joseph Buttinger later claimed that he experienced uneasiness after he exchanged letters with Diem in 1955 and 1956. In a lengthy message to Diem, Buttinger discussed the regime's hostility toward Vietnamese critics who nevertheless seemed to share Diem's anticommunist and anticolonialist convictions. Buttinger deferentially asked the president why he silenced people whose views seemed to coincide with his own. After a delay of several months, Diem sent a reply that simply dismissed his opponents as self-serving and "very mediocre" troublemakers whose behavior threatened South Vietnamese unity in the face of an "implacable" communist menace.[4] Diem's American visit in 1957 did nothing to allay Buttinger's disquietude. While in New York, Diem upset Buttinger by turning down a request that he release Ho Huu Tuong, the Vietnamese Trotskyite, from prison and by denying at a press conference that the RVN held any political prisoners. Moreover, the RVN's leader brushed off warnings about the use of force against dissidents and simply invited Buttinger "to come to Saigon in order to see what his government's policy could and ought to be."[5]

Buttinger did have an opportunity to travel to Vietnam in the summer of 1958, and the experience apparently assuaged his uneasiness for a brief time. He did hear reports of discontent, and Vu Van Thai, whom many AFV members esteemed as an honest and intelligent public servant, remembered telling Buttinger that the Diem regime had reached a point where "it could either evolve towards a paternalistic but free system of government or become a bad and inefficient copy of [a] communist dictatorship."[6] Such comments troubled Buttinger, but when he returned to the United States he made few remarks about Diem's problems and instead emphasized the administration's accomplishments. He later cited "complex and personal" reasons for his willingness to back Diem despite "great misgivings."[7] Nevertheless, contemporary evidence indicates that the visit convinced Buttinger that most of Diem's opposition was confined to "a small group of urban intellectuals" who did not represent the rural majority.[8] Furthermore, Buttinger told his colleagues that many of the charges directed against Diem "were not capable of substantiation" and decided that "the positive factors conclusively outweigh whatever negative criticisms could be made."[9]

Although Buttinger temporarily reassured his associates, a few AFV officers still worried about developments in Vietnam. Wolf Ladejinsky, one of the AFV members who resided in Saigon, shared his misgivings with Gilbert Jonas when the latter visited Vietnam in the spring of 1959. A Jewish refugee from the Soviet Union, Ladejinsky had been hired by the U.S. Department of Agriculture after studying economics and history at Columbia University. His service in Washington involved the study of Asian agrarian problems, and his expertise in this area gave him the opportunity to formulate major land reform programs in postwar Japan and Taiwan. That work played an important role in ensuring the survival of the pro-American governments of these countries, but it did not shield Ladejinsky from a security investigation that led to his abrupt dismissal from the Department of Agriculture at the end of 1954. Ladejinsky's impressive record of success, however, had attracted the favorable attention of such powerful figures as Secretary of State Dulles and Representative Walter Judd. He soon found employment in Saigon—first as an ICA official and then as Diem's personal adviser until 1961. As Diem's assistant, Ladejinsky dealt with land reform issues and drafted plans for the redistribution of holdings in the South. He also acted as a go-between for Diem and the Americans regarding their various plans and concerns.[10]

It was in his capacity as an intermediary between Diem and the Americans that Ladejinsky told Jonas of his anxiety about the situation in Vietnam. Deeply grateful to Diem for employing him at a time when he faced trouble from his own government, Ladejinsky affectionately called the president "my Chief" and "the Boss," and he usually emphasized the regime's achievements in public forums and private correspondence.[11] The spreading communist insurgency and Diem's heavy-handed attempts to put it down nevertheless troubled him. He told Jonas that Diem "places too much weight on security—at least [the] military part" and overlooked its political and economic dimensions. Ladejinsky also said Saigon had not won the trust of the southern Vietnamese and that many southerners were willing to collaborate with local communist cadres. Jonas also heard reports from Vu Van Thai about Diem's problems, especially his dependence on subordinates who flattered him and never questioned his orders. The oppressive behavior of these men, Thai warned, could generate a popular discontent whose "cumulative effect can become major."[12]

Jonas later said he tried to bring these concerns to Diem's attention but met with little success. Diem spoke to Jonas and Ladejinsky at a meeting in mid-April that, according to Ladejinsky, "established an all-time record— it lasted *five* hours." Ladejinsky told Harold Oram that Diem behaved in a "most gracious, considerate" manner as he spoke to Jonas in a "spirit of confidence" and made "extremely complimentary" remarks about the Oram firm's work for the RVN.[13] Despite this friendly atmosphere, Jonas remembered that he made little headway in discussing the regime's troubles with Diem and that he was "stunned" when Ladejinsky himself remained "mute" throughout the conversation. When the meeting came to an end, Jonas realized that "we got nowhere with Diem and I was very depressed at the idea that he just would not listen."[14]

Although he returned to the United States convinced that he had "totally failed to make a dent on Diem's adamant views," Jonas thought the advice of other AFV members might have a greater impact on Diem. He concluded that Leo Cherne might have the best chance of success.[15] Some of Jonas's AFV colleagues, including Buttinger and Wesley Fishel, as well as such senior Vietnamese officials as Thai and Vice President Nguyen Ngoc Tho, concurred. They told Cherne that Diem had a special regard for him, apparently because of the IRC's early and effective refugee work in Vietnam. Despite these expressions of confidence in his abilities, Cherne hesitated, believing that Diem's problems "were inherent in the character of the individual and the culture of the country" and that they "could not be solved in the foreseeable future." He finally agreed, however, to a personal meeting with Diem and told Jonas of his intention to go to Saigon a few months after the AFV's October conference.[16]

Cherne finally went to Vietnam in February 1960, ostensibly to accompany his colleague from the Research Institute of America, Carl Hovgard, on a tiger hunt. He spent most of his time, however, discussing the regime's problems in four meetings with Diem. In a letter to Harold Oram, Ladejinsky wrote that Cherne made an outstanding presentation and that while

Cherne was "never offensive, never using a sledge hammer, . . . there was no doubt in the President's mind what he was talking about." Moreover, Diem "did not take offense to any of this" and expressed his high regard for Cherne.[17] Cherne recalled that Diem seemed to be greatly impressed by what he heard and that he asked Cherne to repeat his comments in Nhu's presence, which Cherne did. At an interview attended by Diem, Nhu, Ladejinsky, Hovgard, and a U.S. Army interpreter, he gave a talk that "led remorselessly to the conclusion" that Nhu had undermined what had been "an inspiring and courageous beginning" for the Diem regime. Nhu then made what Cherne called a "remarkably moderate" reply that characterized many of the criticisms leveled against him as exaggerated and distorted, but he nevertheless agreed that, since there were so many negative perceptions of his influence, needed changes would be made. By the time Nhu finished talking, Cherne had the impression that Nhu would in fact be willing to go into exile.[18]

Cherne remembered that he left Saigon "with the absolute conviction that, in fact, a miracle had been performed" and that sweeping reforms would take place in Diem's administration. Subsequent events soon demonstrated that his trip had accomplished nothing.[19] When Gilbert Jonas mentioned Cherne's "successful" visit in a letter to Wolf Ladejinsky, Ladejinsky quickly replied with a bleak assessment.[20] "Leo . . . did a magnificent job, but he was not successful. Nobody is."[21] In a subsequent note, he stated that "nothing is being done to correct the situation" and that "no advice is accepted from the most devoted friends—Leo was *no* exception."[22] Cherne himself ruefully confessed failure three years later. "Nothing took place, except the required departure of several of Nhu's critics from government."[23]

Cherne was not the last AFV officer who expressed concern about the state of the Diem regime. Wesley Fishel had been one of Diem's earliest backers, but when he made a trip to Vietnam in the summer of 1959, Fishel, like other AFV members, heard disturbing accounts of Diem's troubles with an insurgency that seemed to be making rapid strides. Before leaving the RVN, Fishel asked Diem to answer a series of questions about reported guerrilla activities in the South. Fishel did this, he later told Diem, in order to obtain information for "a serious, authoritative article" on the RVN's security problems that "would convince officials and scholars in the Free World that you continue to fight a war against the Communists even today, and that you deserve to be supported." Diem, however, never replied, and Fishel decided to raise the matter again in a letter to Diem at the end of April 1960.[24]

In his letter, Fishel outlined his worries about reports of violence in the

RVN and criticisms of the regime. He wrote of the need to obtain an accurate picture of security in the South, especially since critics of the Diem regime, such as the scholar Bernard Fall, seemed to be receiving accurate news about the progress of the insurgency. "It is a matter of some pain to us who are your *friends* that your *enemies* are better able to secure detailed information about what is happening in your country than we are . . . !" Fishel complained. He also told Diem that his reputation had suffered in America because of a growing perception that he had chosen "sycophants" as subordinates and that many of these men engaged in "dishonesty, corruption, graft, and other self-seeking activity." Finally, Fishel told Diem of growing discontent with Diem's domestic policies and informed the president that he had been "questioned sharply about the 'dictatorship' in Vietnam" at recent meetings of the Association of Asian Studies.[25]

Although increasingly troubled by Saigon's policies, Fishel and his colleagues in the AFV saw no alternative to Diem and continued supporting him. They rallied to Diem when eighteen Vietnamese politicians and officials criticized the regime at a meeting held in Saigon's Caravelle Hotel on April 26 and called for a sweeping reform of the administration. In a postscript to his lengthy April letter to Diem, Fishel recommended that Saigon take steps to expose "the iniquities of the petitioners" by providing the American press with information highlighting the protestors' past ties to the Japanese, the French, and Bao Dai.[26] The Oram group also tried to discredit the dissenters, who became known as the Caravelle Group, by drawing up a memorandum impugning their motives and alleging that their political influence "is highly negligible."[27]

As some of its officers rallied to Diem in his confrontation with the Caravelle Group, the AFV itself did little in the months immediately following the incident. It continued its deliveries of supplies to schools and hospitals in Vietnam and hosted a delegation of Vietnamese legislators who visited New York in late August. When the U.S. presidential campaign gained momentum in the late summer, Louis Andreatta, the executive secretary, suggested that the AFV send letters asking John F. Kennedy and Richard M. Nixon, the Democratic and Republican nominees, about their positions on Vietnam. O'Daniel, apparently mindful of past IRS charges that the AFV had engaged in political activities, vetoed the idea and told Andreatta that the organization should "stay clear of anything that might have to do [with] or be given the suspicion of politics."[28]

The association also made tentative arrangements for a conference on American-Vietnamese collaboration in the spring of 1961. Some members worried that if conditions in the South continued to deteriorate, the symposium could be transformed into a forum for attacking Diem's government; but in a series of meetings in August, the officers planning the affair agreed that any criticisms of Diem's policies that might arise would be "moderate, constructive and for the most part in perspective." The AFV, however, later suspended, then canceled, the conference as resistance to Diem intensified and became ever more violent.[29]

By the autumn of 1960, the communist rebellion had gained greater momentum and some of Diem's own soldiers had turned against him. The ranks of the insurgents steadily expanded, and the communists eventually created a formal resistance organization to lead the struggle against Saigon—the National Liberation Front of South Vietnam (NLF). As the NLF won more and more adherents, some of Diem's officers concluded that only drastic changes could save the RVN. They made a desperate bid to revitalize the regime by staging a coup on November 11. Marines and paratroopers, Saigon's elite soldiers, surrounded the presidential palace as their leaders sent a set of demands to Diem that called for a dramatic reform of the government. Trapped in the palace, Diem opened negotiations with the dissidents while secretly ordering loyalist forces to Saigon. The ruse worked, and on the morning of November 12 the uprising rapidly collapsed when units backing the regime arrived in the capital and forced the rebel formations to surrender.[30]

Although Diem thwarted the coup, the events of November 11–12 revealed the depth of resentment against his government. The president, however, did virtually nothing to mitigate this discontent and instead intensified repressive measures against his opponents. Despite his promises to inaugurate sweeping reforms in the week following the revolt, Diem took no action until February 6, 1961, when he announced the creation of new government ministries and very tentative steps toward electing village councils.[31] He displayed greater alacrity in dealing with his enemies by arresting most of the signatories of the Caravelle Manifesto in the days following the coup. Diem also tightened his control over an army he already had corrupted and politicized by favoring officers who had unquestioningly supported the regime. Finally, the president became more reluctant to accept American advice, especially since the U.S. embassy had encouraged a negotiated settlement to the coup, an action Diem regarded as an attempt to put the rebels on an equal footing with himself.[32]

Most members of the American Friends rallied to Diem in the greatest crisis he had faced since his 1955 confrontation with the sects. In a telegram sent on November 14, O'Daniel, Duke, Buttinger, Cherne, Fishel, and Henderson expressed satisfaction that "the national army and the people have again, as they did five years ago, vindicated your faith in them." They nevertheless expected Diem to unite the country and "lead the Vietnamese people toward greater freedom, justice, and prosperity than they have ever before known." By doing this, the president would lead his people in destroying "the forces of reaction and the communist menace which still jeopardize their hard-won independence." The cable ended with the reassurance, "As you march forward on the path of progress, we and our countrymen stand with you to the end."[33] Not every member of the AFV, however, agreed with the sentiments voiced in the telegram. Assuming that the organization's entire leadership had endorsed the message, Louis Andreatta placed "American Friends of Vietnam" after the signatures, but soon received reprimands from Gilbert Jonas and Diana Lockard for doing so.[34]

Unaware of these divisions within the AFV, Diem capitalized on the cable and expressed his gratitude for the AFV's backing. The president, according to one critic, proceeded to "splash the message on the front pages of his newspapers."[35] Tran Van Chuong told the association that its "understanding and support at such crises and trials are fully appreciated." He then declared, "In all these years, they have inspired the President and helped him solve many difficult problems."[36] Diem's reaction to the message can also be seen in a note recording Wesley Fishel's conversation with Diem's secretary:

> WF talked to Vo Van Hai—
> jubilant
> Diem on top,
> stronger than ever,
> reforms fast & furious
> But [the] thing that could have happened—
> Diem stronger than he thought he was
> 'moved by telegram—
> 'understood fully implications . . .[37]

Although publicly pleased with the coup's failure, the AFV's members disagreed among themselves over its significance. When Gilbert Jonas referred hopefully to "sweeping changes" in a note to Wolf Ladejinsky, Ladejinsky replied that the coup attempt "has given rise to NO new attitudes with respect to a host of issues that call for reconsideration."[38] Some AFV officers shared Ladejinsky's pessimism, but others voiced far greater optimism about Diem's chances. In a radio discussion chaired by Christopher Emmet on

November 18, William Henderson suggested that the revolt and the communist insurgency reflected "some kind of failure on the part of the regime to win solid support for itself." Emmet also saw the event as "a warning," but Kenneth Young, who had joined the AFV after leaving the State Department in 1958, disagreed. Conceding that the government faced serious difficulties, Young expressed admiration for Diem's ability to display "the courage, the guts, and the skill to sit this one out and come out on top." Joseph Buttinger, another participant in the discussion, generally supported Young's optimistic appraisal. He thought that Saigon's population had exhibited no enthusiasm for the coup, and he voiced confidence in Diem's ability to defeat the communists.[39]

Privately, however, Buttinger expressed greater pessimism about the situation in the South. He had no sympathy for the coup leaders, whom he regarded as "a bunch of very incompetent people," and he affirmed his faith in Diem by writing, "I believe that the continued existence of the country requires this man."[40] Nevertheless, Buttinger lamented "the absence of a permanent and live contact between government and people" and doubted the sincerity of Diem's promises to carry out reforms.[41] In a letter to Diem, Buttinger wrote that the November 11 revolt "reflects certain grave signs of increasing dissatisfaction" and "is a manifestation of several concerns shared even by your closest friends here." He also warned that the uprising might prompt the incoming Kennedy administration to reconsider America's commitment to Vietnam. "The liberal views of the new President and his foreign policy associates," he declared, "could predispose them to view the attempted coup as a final warning signal for American policy in Vietnam."[42] Buttinger's message, however, never reached Diem because some AFV leaders refused to sign it. Among them were O'Daniel, a strong supporter of Diem, and Henderson, who feared that "it may even antagonize the President, in view of all the advice and adverse comment he's already had on the situation."[43]

Buttinger's frustration also could be seen in his reaction to an article in *The Nation* that condemned the Diem regime and attacked the AFV as "a Diem propaganda outfit."[44] Jonas asked Buttinger to compose a rebuttal to the essay, but the latter declined on the grounds that he considered it to be a "clever and effective" piece whose "political argument cannot be easily refuted." Moreover, Buttinger expressed his disappointment with Diem's recently announced administrative reforms. "The President condescends," he complained, "to let his ministers do some of the work (and perhaps also make some of the decisions) he formerly reserved for himself, but for those outside the government, for those who have been stirring up a chorus of criticism all over the world, he has no word or gesture." Buttinger believed that only "decisive political action in Saigon" could counteract the criticism of the regime reflected in the article. If the government did nothing, the Republic of Vietnam might survive, "but it will be lost as a cause for seriously concerned liberals."[45] Jonas accepted this decision but suggested that Buttinger had been "unduly pessimistic." Jonas had recently seen Young, Ladejinsky, Fishel, and Henderson and had reached "a much more optimistic conclusion" about the situation in the South.[46]

The confidence of Jonas and his associates rested on their expectations for the RVN's upcoming presidential elections. Jonas hoped that if the balloting took place under "truly free" conditions, "it would appear that things are getting back on the right track again."[47] Diem, however, ran against two sets of obscure candidates in a contest that was essentially meaningless. Nguyen Dinh Quat, a wealthy businessman, headed a ticket that included a retired Cao Dai military commander, Nguyen Thanh Phuong, as the vice presidential candidate. The other slate featured two men who had not been active in Vietnam's political life since the 1940s: Ho Nhut Tan, a seventy-five-year-old "practitioner of Oriental medicine," and Nguyen The Truyen, a chemical engineer in his sixties. Although Diem faced no serious challenge, his officials encouraged maximum voter participation as a way to reflect the government's ability to control the people. Despite NLF threats to sabotage the election, balloting took place under relatively peaceful conditions on April 9, 1961. Diem won the election with 78 percent of the vote.[48]

Despite the farcical nature of the election, some of the AFV's leading figures publicly regarded the event as a positive sign of democratic growth in the RVN. A letter sent to the *New York Times* over O'Daniel's signature cited the two opposition candidates and Diem's promised reforms as "evidence of Vietnam's progress toward ultimate democracy." The note went on to call for American understanding and support of the RVN and denounced the communists for waging "the hottest war of 1960" against the Diem regime's "progressive economic and social policies."[49] O'Daniel's views also appeared in a column written by Irene Corbally Kuhn, a well-known foreign correspondent who was a personal friend of the general. Kuhn accepted O'Daniel's assertion that communist attacks had escalated in the South "because all other efforts to overthrow Ngo's government had failed," and she chided Diem's critics for "lint-picking from ignorance."[50]

Leo Cherne also made a positive assessment of developments in Vietnam in an article he wrote for the *New York Times Magazine* on April 9, the day of the election. Although dismayed by Diem's disregard of advice he had given the year before, Cherne had a greater fear of the consequences of a communist victory in Vietnam because "communist strategists in Asia" saw Vietnam as "a keystone without which empire, wealth and breathing space cannot be achieved." Cherne admitted that the RVN could not be considered a democracy "by our standards" and that it "is still a long way from becoming one." He nevertheless added, "President Ngo was as emphatic in his commitment to democratic ideals during my recent conversations with him as he was when I first met him only days after he assumed the seemingly impossible burden of restoring a broken country in 1954." He also praised Diem's programs for developing the country but said the insurgency had kept pace with these measures and had transformed Vietnam into "the one living laboratory in the world where we can observe the daily use of the entire spectrum of Communist assault—economic, political, psychological, military."[51]

The AFV's expectation that the voting in Vietnam marked a step forward in South Vietnam was expressed in a telegram sent to Diem. O'Daniel, Buttinger, Cherne, Fishel, Ladejinsky, and Henderson signed a message congratulating Diem and Vice President Tho on their victory. "Our respect and admiration for courage and wisdom of Vietnamese people," they told the president, "reinforced by outcome this momentous election." They then voiced their belief that Diem's next five-year term would see the "greatest strides toward freedom, justice, prosperity in Vietnam history."[52] In reality, however, this declaration reflected a rather forlorn wish that Diem would soon implement significant reforms. When these were not forthcoming, most of the AFV's leaders finally turned against the regime.

Although suffering from growing doubts about Diem's abilities, AFV members clung to what Joseph Buttinger called a "desperate hope that Diem would at the right moment initiate reforms we had kept urging on him."[53] Even though his resistance to their advice frustrated them, Diem's American backers remembered his previous success in suppressing the sects, resettling the northern refugees, and avoiding the elections called for in Geneva. Memories of these early achievements sustained expectations that Diem once again would act decisively in dealing with troubles besetting the South. Buttinger reflected this faith in Diem when he wrote, "The man has surprised us already several times and may yet have to reveal the full scope of his leadership abilities."[54]

Diem himself took certain steps to keep American trust in him alive. He had a talent, Gilbert Jonas observed, for knowing "what were the right things to say to each audience."[55] Although he often disregarded the advice he received, the president rarely voiced his outright opposition and thus gave his interlocutors the impression that he might act on their suggestions. When Buttinger expressed his concern about the regime's policies in the late 1950s, Diem gave evasive replies but rarely dismissed Buttinger's worries out of hand. He also seemed to pay serious attention to the remarks Leo Cherne made about the malevolent influence Nhu exercised over the RVN's government and indicated that he would address them. Moreover, Diem's implementation of his land reform program, as flawed as it turned out to be, seemed to provide convincing proof that the Vietnamese leader had made a serious commitment to reforming the South's economy and society.

Even after it became evident that Diem would not act on their advice, AFV members remained reluctant to break with him and instead ascribed the regime's ills to the influence of Nhu and his ambitious wife. Wesley Fishel thought Diem's efforts to establish his government on a firm institutional basis had been "balanced out and eventually negated by the increasing influence of Mr. and Mrs. Nhu," while Wolf Ladejinsky regarded Nhu as "the 'evil genius' dominating the scene."[56] The AFV members thought Diem might make significant progress if he could be persuaded to circumscribe or eliminate the Nhus' influence. They tried to convince Diem that Nhu should be dismissed, but the president, bound by strong family loyalty to his brother, refused to do so. As opposition to his government intensified, Diem relied even more heavily on Nhu's skill at repression because, as Buttinger wrote, "Diem knew that his brother's instruments of coercion—his spies, secret services, Special Forces, political parties, as well as his talent for corruption and terror—were indispensable to the regime."[57]

The hope that Diem eventually would make needed changes and the tendency to blame the Nhus for the regime's shortcomings were not the only factors contributing to the AFV's unwillingness to turn against Diem. Another factor, Buttinger wrote, was "the fear that open attacks on Diem might hasten a Communist victory and such attacks were therefore harmful." This concern is reflected in a letter from Ladejinsky to Buttinger. "While I am just as entitled to righteous indignation vis-a-vis the regime as any other fellow on the Executive Committee of the Friends," Ladejinsky stated, "we must temper it with the thought that Vietnam does face the danger of a Communist takeover."[58] The AFV thought that none of Diem's noncommunist opponents—figures considered unreliable because of their past ties to the French, the sects, and Bao Dai—would be as effective as Diem in combating the communists. Although disquieted by Diem's repressive policies, most AFV members thought his overthrow would "create a vacuum into which the Communists would march with flying banners within a few weeks."[59]

Therefore, while privately trying to persuade Diem to change direction, the AFV's officers did not voice their misgivings in public.

Finally, the AFV tolerated Diem's dictatorial behavior because many of its members believed that Vietnam did not have a political tradition that would enable a democratic society to function. "It has never known a Western-style democracy," O'Daniel asserted. "It may never experience it in the future."[60] Fishel voiced a similar opinion. "From the standpoint of the history of thought, the people of Southeast Asia are not, generally speaking, sufficiently sophisticated to understand what we mean by democracy and how they can exercise and protect their own political rights."[61] Many of the organization's leaders hoped that the Republic of Vietnam eventually would evolve into an open society and urged Diem to take steps to encourage this development, but they thought that the Vietnamese would accept Diem's government as long as it satisfied their basic economic and social needs. "For 90% of the Vietnamese people," Buttinger claimed, "an effective and competent administration is infinitely more important than a 'liberal' administration . . . and I am certain that in this respect he [Diem] is closer to the people than his critics."[62]

Information concerning Diem's attitude toward the AFV is far less extensive than that on the AFV's view of Diem, but the material that is available suggests several reasons why the president ignored the advice and warnings of AFV leaders. To some extent, Diem was influenced by Nhu, who, according to Vu Van Thai, considered the AFV to be "a group of well-intentioned, naive idealists with little political impact." Diem's confused and chaotic administration of his own government also played a role. Thai recalled that, although Diem "greatly esteemed" the AFV, he seemed to have no clear idea of the political philosophy of its members or of its potential use as a lobbying organization. Diem's failure to work effectively with the association could be seen when the regime sent Thai as a representative to an AFV symposium without giving him any instructions. Thai later wrote: "At the conference, I gave an address presenting my own view on a concept of development for Vietnam as if it was the official one. Upon my return to Saigon I did not produce a report of my mission and nobody asked me. When I saw President Diem I conveyed to him the greetings from those participants who asked me to do so and the President asked news of the other members of the executive committee and that was all."[63]

Even if he had tried to make more effective use of the AFV, Diem would have faced trouble from his own embassy in Washington. The RVN's ambassador, Tran Van Chuong, was related to the Ngo family through the marriage of his daughter to Nhu, but previous service in Bao Dai's government and the promptings of an ambitious wife had given him a desire for high office that his assignment to Washington did not satisfy. Moreover, Chuong, a wealthy landowner, had been unhappy with the regime's agrarian reform policies, and as a Buddhist he resented the favoritism Diem showed toward Vietnamese Catholics.[64] Diem was aware of Chuong's hostility and he once told Ladejinsky that he did not regard Chuong as an "effective . . . advocate for Viet-Nam," but he did not remove Chuong from his post.[65] It is not clear why he did nothing, but Diem may have thought that the dismissal of his representative to the United States would have embarrassed him in American eyes. Furthermore, Chuong had been, as Buttinger put it, "deprived of any meaningful function whatever," and Diem may have calculated that the ambassador would cause fewer problems for the regime by staying in America.[66]

Diem paid a heavy price for keeping Chuong in office because the ambassador took steps to undermine the work of the regime's American supporters. In private conversations with Oram, Jonas, and Fishel, Chuong "tore apart the land reform program as a fraud," and in public forums he claimed that "landlords like himself have been terribly treated."[67] Chuong also interfered with the Oram firm's efforts to respond to press coverage of events in Vietnam. He verbally told Jonas "to do nothing further" on Diem's agrarian reform policies and blocked or delayed the company's attempts to distribute materials concerning South Vietnam's internal security problems and the protests of the Caravelle Group.[68] Despite this obstructive behavior, Chuong remained in Washington and acted in a way that, as Fishel told Diem in 1960, "has virtually succeeded in destroying the organization of your friends in America."[69]

Diem's self-concept as the South's leader also played a part in his failure to use or listen to the AFV. "Diem believed," Frances Fitzgerald observed, "that the Hand of God, or the will of Heaven, supported him."[70] Moreover, as one study notes, conservative Vietnamese like Diem thought that "the very fact that they have prevailed would be an indication that their mode of politics is correct," and that they therefore had no need of winning popular support.[71] Guided by this thinking, Diem expected obedience from the people he ruled and could not comprehend American suggestions that he had to implement reforms to assure their backing. This attitude also made him quite willing to employ repressive measures against anyone who might challenge his regime and thus throttle any movement toward democracy that the Americans favored.

The inconsistency of its members' behavior also contributed to the ineffectiveness of the AFV's advice to Diem. While privately warning the president to liberalize his regime and undertake major reforms, leading figures in the group such as Buttinger, Fishel, Cherne, and Ladejinsky continued praising Diem in public. They usually rallied to his defense whenever he faced major crises such as the meeting of the Caravelle Group or the November 11 coup attempt, and they sent him congratulatory telegrams that, despite their veiled warnings, gave the overall impression that he would retain their unwavering support. The AFV's behavior, in this regard, paralleled that of the U.S. government, whose officials often strongly urged Diem to overhaul his administration while publicly voicing full confidence in his abilities. In both cases, Diem apparently concluded that he would enjoy continued American backing even if he disregarded American advice. This private and official support nevertheless began to unravel when Diem's inability to rule the South became all too apparent.

chapter 6
AFV Policy Disputes and American Escalation, 1961–1962

In the first two years of his presidency, John F. Kennedy dramatically increased America's support for the government of Ngo Dinh Diem. The new administration raised the number of American servicemen in South Vietnam from approximately 750 in early 1961 to more than 11,000 troops by the end of 1962. It also stepped up the flow of military supplies. The American Friends of Vietnam, which had repeatedly called for a greater commitment to the RVN in the past, made few public comments about this development. Most of the organization's leading figures agreed on the necessity of averting a communist victory in Vietnam, but by the early 1960s they held sharply differing opinions of Diem's ability to defeat the National Liberation Front and the wisdom of continued support to his regime. The AFV's officers argued bitterly over the association's posture toward Diem, and as a result the AFV remained silent about the crisis in Vietnam as the United States involved itself ever more deeply in that country's affairs.

Divisions within the AFV became apparent when the group's officers spoke to a State Department official in the spring of 1961. This meeting was requested by Joseph Buttinger in an April letter to Secretary of State Dean Rusk. A talk with AFV representatives, Buttinger averred, would be worthwhile because "some of us have acquired a familiarity with the complex affairs of Southeast Asia that is uncommon among private citizens" and had a "capital of experience" that the American government "should not disregard."[1] William Henderson supported Buttinger's request in a letter sent to Walt W. Rostow, the assistant to McGeorge Bundy, Kennedy's national security adviser. "Members of the Executive Committee," he informed Rostow, "feel increasingly alarmed over the steady deterioration of the situation in Laos and South Vietnam, and believe that the country [the United States] is prepared to support a much more vigorous stand in this area than has hitherto been taken."[2]

Rusk himself did not see the AFV officers, but the State Department made arrangements for an interview with U. Alexis Johnson, the deputy under secretary of state for political affairs, on May 25, 1961. AFV members attending the meeting included Buttinger, Henderson, Christopher Emmet, Franklin Leerburger, Frank Trager, and Wesley Fishel.[3] Gilbert Jonas remembered participating in the discussion as well and said that General O'Daniel also was present. According to Jonas, the AFV representatives delivered a confusing message to Johnson because they expressed differing opinions on how to deal with Diem. Much of this trouble stemmed from O'Daniel's disagreement with pleas to persuade Diem to reform his regime. "We were trying to prevail upon U. Alexis Johnson," Jonas recalled, "to rein Diem in and not give him free rein and O'Daniel kept undercutting us through the whole meeting." Jonas thought that this contradictory advice must have given Johnson "the weirdest view of this group because we'd say, 'You can't—We still want to work with this guy [Diem], but you can't let him go too far.' "[4]

By the time of this unproductive interview, Washington had made major new commitments to Diem's survival. The escalating war in Vietnam, as well as crises in Cuba, Berlin, and Laos, convinced the Kennedy administration, one of the president's advisers later recalled, that communism "was on the offensive" and that this aggression "must now be met solidly."[5] Moreover, Kennedy worried that a failure to take a strong stand in Vietnam would expose him to charges that he had "lost" the country to communism, claims that could could seriously jeopardize his chances of reelection in 1964. In the face of these pressures, the president took steps to bolster Diem's government by approving plans for the expansion of Saigon's security forces and by sending U.S. military advisers to Vietnam to train the Vietnamese in counterinsurgency warfare. Kennedy informed Diem of these measures in a letter affirming America's willingness "to join with you in an intensified endeavor to win the struggle against Communism and to further the social and economic advancement of Viet Nam."[6]

While Kennedy and his advisers concluded that Diem needed greater American support, many of the AFV's leading members voiced growing doubts about Diem's ability to solve the crisis in the South. The misgivings evident during the State Department interview in May had gained such force by the summer of 1961 that they sparked a protracted debate over the AFV's policies. Buttinger initiated this dispute in a letter sent to O'Daniel on August 27, 1961. Buttinger announced his intention to resign as chairman of the group's executive committee. He claimed that he could no longer devote sufficient attention to the AFV's activities but then went on to cite another concern. "In the course of the last year," he told O'Daniel, "there has developed a fear in the U.S., which is shared also by many of our members, that the policies of President Ngo Dinh Diem are no longer adequate for the appalling task of defeating the Communist attempt to conquer South Vietnam through political subversion and military aggression." Buttinger strongly recommended that the American Friends of Vietnam examine the premise of "unreserved public support" for the Diem regime at its next executive committee meeting.[7]

When ten of the executive committee's fifteen officers, including O'Daniel, Buttinger, Henderson, Jonas, Trager, and Harold Oram, gathered in New York on September 27, 1961, Buttinger submitted his resignation as chairman, and a lengthy discussion of the AFV's aims and activities followed. According to the minutes of the meeting, a number of sharply differing views emerged, "with some members advocating continued support for the policies of the Vietnamese government, as in the past, others advocating a period of inactivity pending developments in Vietnam, with still others proposing a shift in emphasis to humanitarian activities." No clear decision had been reached by the time William Henderson put forth a resolution calling for a compromise. His proposal recommended that the executive committee stress "the social, educational, and humanitarian aspects" of the AFV's work for an "indefinite period" and determine the organization's future course of action "in the light of unfolding events in Vietnam." After the presentation of Henderson's suggestions, Buttinger closed the debate by announcing that he would postpone his resignation until the executive committee reached an agreement about the resolution at its next meeting.[8]

A few of the AFV officers expressed uneasiness about Henderson's proposal. O'Daniel thought that refraining from commenting on Vietnam's political situation undermined Diem's position. "I just can't see," he complained, "our becoming silent about the man we have mentioned so often."[9] Another AFV member, however, felt that a refusal to speak out on Diem's domestic policies only reinforced the president's refusal to undertake reforms. Franklin Leerburger, an engineer who served on the executive committee since 1958, compared Diem's position to that of Fulgencio Batista, the Cuban dictator overthrown by Castro. In a letter to Buttinger, Leerburger declared, "If the hearts and minds of the South Vietnamese, are not sympathetic with the regime because of its paternalistic and dictatorial and 'Mandarin' orientation, I doubt that we will eventually gain any more than we did from Batista's Cuba and for the same reason."[10]

Although these objections were discussed when the executive committee met again on October 12, 1961, most of the panel's members approved the major points of Henderson's resolution. They agreed that the AFV should call attention to Diem's struggle against the communist insurgency, and to "emphasize, for an indefinite period, the educational and welfare aspects of the organization's work." They also asked Buttinger to draft a letter to Diem expressing their "fears and apprehensions concerning the present situation, together with assurance of the Committee's undiminished support of South Vietnam's fight against Communist aggression."[11] As a result of this settlement, Buttinger withdrew his resignation. O'Daniel, who could not attend the October 12 meeting, registered his approval of its outcome by telling Buttinger, "I am glad to be with you in doing what we can to help save Vietnam from the Communists."[12] This agreement, however, put only a temporary halt to the AFV's internal disputes. Differing opinions on Diem's leadership resurfaced in a few months.

The AFV's policy debate took place shortly after the Diem regime had cut its ties with the group's close collaborator—Harold Oram's public relations firm. Both Oram and Gilbert Jonas believed that the Central Intelligence Agency persuaded Diem to terminate his contract with the company.[13] According to Jonas, the CIA acted at the behest of the U.S. ambassador in Saigon, Elbridge Durbrow, who had received complaints from Diem about American news coverage of the 1960 coup attempt. Durbrow also heard that Oram's organization had presented Diem with a "very frank analysis" of press reaction to the revolt, and he decided to contact the group through the State Department.[14] Jonas claimed that he went to Washington and informed Durbrow of the contents of the Oram firm's commentary. The firm, according to Jonas, had bluntly told Diem that the American media's favorable treatment of his regime had come to an end and that the president could remedy this situation only by initiating major reforms. Angered by this advice, Durbrow retaliated against the Oram firm by getting "the CIA to sit down with Mme. Nhu and say, 'What you need is a better—better PR.'"[15]

Diem abruptly broke the RVN's tie with Oram's company in May 1961 and turned to the public relations firm of Kastor, Hilton, Chesley, Clifford, and Atherton. He agreed to pay this group $100,000 a year, nearly three times the $36,000 annual fee Oram's organization had received for the previous six years.[16] Oram received word of this decision from Ambassador Chuong, who wrote a letter expressing feelings of "regret" and "melancholy" about the end of a relationship in which Oram and his associates had "actively, intimately and successfully" aided the RVN's diplomats "in our efforts to promote a better understanding of Viet Nam in the United States."[17]

It is difficult to determine the accuracy of the charges Oram and Jonas made about the roles Durbrow and the CIA played in persuading Diem to break his contract with the Oram firm. Durbrow himself had told Diem to reform his regime on several occasions, and it is logical to assume that he would have wanted to alert Diem to the fact that this matter was becoming a major concern of the American press. Durbrow's frank advice had placed such a strain on the ambassador's relationship with Diem that the Kennedy administration replaced Durbrow with Frederick E. Nolting, an amiable and soft-spoken Virginian who received instructions to deal more tactfully with Diem, in the spring of 1961.[18] Moreover, in a paper written by an AFV member in 1965, no reference is made to U.S. government pressures to force Diem to terminate his relationship with Oram's company. The document merely states that "Jonas and Oram were fired for their criticisms."[19]

Other documentary evidence, however, shows that Diem had been encouraged to turn to another group. In a talk with the president a month after the November 11 coup, Durbrow suggested that Diem "hire [a] good foreign public relations expert in order to develop better press relations," but the ambassador seemed to be referring to a representative hired to work in Saigon and not to the services of an overseas concern.[20] Other sources, however, contain recommendations that Diem seek the assistance of a company other than Oram's. Writing to Diem in September 1960, Edward Lansdale advised, "I have long believed that you need a good, private American public relations firm to help you." He then proposed that Diem secure the services of King and Maheu Associates in Washington.[21] A similar suggestion came from Samuel T. Williams, O'Daniel's successor at the Military Assistance and Advisory Group in Saigon. Discussing the matter in a note to Father Raymond de Jaegher, Williams thought that Diem should employ "a high caliber public relations man" who would contact prominent editors and reporters and supply them with "*good* news items each day."[22] Although sketchy, such correspondence suggests that Diem may have indeed responded to American pressures to change his public relations counselors.

The South Vietnamese embassy may also have been responsible for Saigon's break with Oram. In September 1961, Tran Van Chuong emphatically told the AFV's executive secretary that "the change had been made without his knowledge," but he had in fact created serious problems for the Oram firm in the past.[23] Writing to Oram in the spring of 1960, Wolf Ladejinsky stated that word of Oram's troubles with Chuong had reached Saigon, and that he had been informed that the ambassador "misses no opportunity to stick a pin in" when discussing the Oram company's work.[24] Jonas mentioned the group's difficulties in a letter and speculated that Chuong was trying to terminate Oram's contract with Saigon. "As things now stand," he wrote, "it would seem that we are being eased out while our Washington colleagues attempt to build a case for this step."[25] Tensions between the firm and the embassy abated in the summer of 1960, but the problems may have convinced Diem that a change in public relations representatives should be made.[26]

As Diem tried to improve his image overseas by changing American consultants, his fortunes in Vietnam steadily declined; Washington responded by adopting new measures to bolster his regime. NLF guerrillas launched a series of devastating attacks throughout Vietnam in the autumn of 1961, and some of Kennedy's advisers concluded that the NLF's gains could be stopped only by U.S. ground troops. Kennedy sent a special mission headed by General Maxwell Taylor, his personal military adviser, to meet with American and Vietnamese officials in Saigon. After Taylor and his associates finished their trip in early November, they recommended that the United States enter a "limited partnership" with the Vietnamese that would involve the expansion of military and economic assistance programs and the deployment of U.S. infantry and engineering units to back the Army of the Republic of Vietnam (ARVN). Kennedy, who worried that the commitment of ground forces would boost Vietnamese morale only temporarily, turned down the troop request, but he did authorize more American advisers and more allocations to aid projects. In the year following this decision, more than 11,000 U.S. servicemen went to Vietnam to help the Diem regime crush the NLF insurgency.[27]

Many of the AFV's officers, meanwhile, became increasingly pessimistic about Diem's ability to cope with the troubles besetting the South. The resignation of Vu Van Thai, esteemed by many AFV members for his competence and integrity, as the RVN's director of the budget and foreign aid reinforced these doubts. Thai had steadily lost influence in the regime because of his concerns about the direction of its economic policies and his disputes with the Nhus over the expenditure of government funds. By the fall of 1960, worried that the Nhus would punish him, he submitted his resignation. Diem did not accept it, however, and kept Thai in Vietnam. An opportunity to flee Saigon arose in the summer of 1961 when Jonas, stopping in the city while doing some work for the Peace Corps, met Thai and informed journalists, including Tillman Durdin and Stanley Karnow, of Thai's plight. He also talked to officials in the Vietnamese embassy in Washington, and he made it clear to Thai "how upset our friends here in the States were over your difficulty in obtaining approval for your resignation."[28] Finally,

Jonas threatened to organize a rally on behalf of Thai in the United States. These activities, Thai believed, saved him from any reprisals by the Nhus and finally led to his departure from Vietnam.[29]

After leaving Vietnam, Thai traveled to France and then the United States, where he secured a position in the United Nations' Technical Assistance Program in early 1962. Before going to work for the United Nations, Thai spoke out against Diem's policies and received assistance from leading figures in the American Friends of Vietnam. Joseph Buttinger hosted an AFV reception for Thai in New York on November 9, 1961. Gilbert Jonas called the event a "delightful" affair that was attended by such noted liberals as "Roger Baldwin, Leo [Cherne], the Durdins, the Teddy Whites, etc." in an effort, as Buttinger told Norman Thomas, "to demonstrate our dissatisfaction with the way President Diem is running the affairs of his country."[30]

Jonas also helped Thai make arrangements for meetings with staff members of the Senate Foreign Relations Committee.[31] Thai also spoke to American journalists and appeared with Leo Cherne on a televised discussion of Southeast Asian affairs hosted by Eleanor Roosevelt. These activities, Thai believed, influenced the views of the AFV membership and some American correspondents. He nevertheless concluded, "I had no impact whatsoever on American policy towards Vietnam," a judgment borne out in a telegram Dean Rusk sent to Saigon in November 1961.[32] Referring to critical comments made by Thai in an interview with a *Washington Post* reporter, Rusk instructed Ambassador Nolting to disavow any administration connections with Thai and to "assure Diem that no one in [the] USG [United States Government] inspired these stories and we regret their appearance."[33]

One of the AFV's most active officers shared Thai's gloomy views when he visited Vietnam in January 1962. After traveling throughout the country and speaking to a number of American and Vietnamese officials, Wesley Fishel "said he was so depressed . . . that he almost wished that he had not come to visit Viet-Nam."[34] The professor wrote of his dismay in a letter to John B. Hannah, president of Michigan State University. "For the first time in seven and one-half years," Fishel lamented, "I have become a pessimist about the fate of South Viet-Nam. In the two and one-half years since my last visit to that country there has been a most profound and distressing deterioration there, politically, socially, and psychologically. . . . The hopes and aspirations of 1954 and 1955 have been allowed to die, and a miasma of apathy pervades the atmosphere."[35]

Fishel attributed many of the South's ills to "the 'evil influences'" Nhu and his wife exercised over Diem. Nhu's policies had "failed miserably . . .

to mobilize the hearts and loyalties of the people." Because of this, the rapid build up of American aid helped only to "warm the fingers and toes" of an ailing regime. Fishel wrote, "Unless what I have termed the 'evil influences' are removed from the scene, in one way or another, Ngo Dinh Diem's government is not going to make the grade."[36] Nevertheless, when asked by an embassy officer what would be needed to shock Diem into making drastic changes, Fishel "remained discreetly silent," leading the official to conclude, "It comes very hard for him to put forth suggestions adverse to the political fortunes of Diem to whom he has been close for so long."[37]

Although reluctant to break with Diem, Fishel saw his personal relationship with the president deteriorate during this visit. In a meeting with Diem and Nhu, Fishel informed the two men that the AFV "is virtually defunct" and went on to tell Nhu that "he and his wife had killed it."[38] Fishel, in turn, was attacked by the two brothers. They held him partially responsible for the publication of articles by Michigan State University professors who criticized the regime after visiting Vietnam, a development that led to Diem's decision to terminate his government's contract with MSU.[39] They also identified Fishel as the source of a news report outlining the pessimistic views of an American visitor to Vietnam. Fishel's opinions had indeed served as the basis of the story, but he claimed that he did not want them to be made public. In a letter to Harold Oram, Fishel said he had expressed his bleak appraisal of the situation in a conversation with Ambassador Nolting, who promised to keep the discussion confidential. Nolting, however, then went on to repeat some of Fishel's conclusions in a talk with embassy staff members that eventually was leaked and reported by Keyes Beech, a correspondent for the *Chicago Daily News*.[40]

In the month after Fishel's visit to Saigon, Diem became the object of what journalist Stanley Karnow called "an aborted aerial assassination." Two Vietnamese air force pilots, disgusted with the regime's corruption and its incompetent direction of the war, changed course from an assigned bombing mission and instead attacked the presidential palace on February 27, 1962. The bombs missed their intended target, but Mme. Nhu suffered a broken arm, and three guards and servants were killed. One of the assailants flew on to Cambodia, while the other was shot down and captured, but survived his imprisonment. Diem attributed his own survival to "divine providence," but the attempt on his life made him ever more suspicious of his subordinates and dependent on family members like Nhu.[41]

Father Raymond de Jaegher, an AFV member who admired Diem, also called the president's survival a providential event. Working in Saigon as the director of the Free Pacific Association, an anticommunist news agency he founded in the mid-1950s, the priest was driving by the palace when the raid began and witnessed the attack. He described his relief over Diem's escape in a letter to Louis Andreatta. "The death of the President," he told the AFV's executive secretary, "would have mean[t] very soon the communistic control of Free Vietnam left without a strong and courageous leader."[42] Andreatta thanked de Jaegher for his note and assured him that observers in America had followed news of the assassination attempt "very closely." He also told de Jaegher that copies of his letter would be circulated to members of the AFV's executive committee.[43] Unlike its response to previous crises, however, the AFV did not send Diem a message congratulating him on his survival. The organization's silence on this occasion reflected the deep dissatisfaction many members felt about Diem's government.

While refraining from any public comments about the Diem regime's troubles, the AFV kept active by undertaking a variety of assistance and information programs. Some of these projects, such as the shipment of books and supplies to the University of Hue, had been going on since the 1950s. Others were more recent. In 1960, Canadian missionaries asked the organization to provide supplies to help mountain tribes at Fyan, a village near the highland city of Dalat. The AFV responded by making arrangements for the delivery of medicines, blankets, and school kits. It gave similar assistance to leprosaria in Vietnam and raised more than $26,000 to help victims of the 1961 floods in the Mekong Delta. In addition to sending aid to Vietnam, the AFV continued hosting receptions for dignitaries from Vietnam and assisting Vietnamese students studying in the United States. Finally, the association distributed literature about Vietnam, including reprinted articles, an occasional newsletter about economic developments in Vietnam, and promotions of books written by AFV members such as Fishel, Buttinger, and O'Daniel.[44]

The above activities, however, did little to allay the misgivings some individuals had about the AFV's silence on the political crisis in Vietnam, leading to another internal policy dispute in the spring of 1962. Buttinger helped precipitate the debate by once again announcing his intention to resign as the executive committee chairman, this time in a letter to O'Daniel on March 15, 1962. Buttinger based his decision on his disillusionment with Diem and went on to tell the general:

> Briefly, I no longer believe that the regime of President Ngo Dinh Diem, whose public support has been the main object of our activities, is capable

of defeating the Communists without drastic political reforms, which the President and his advisers refuse to permit. Furthermore, I have become convinced that President Ngo Dinh Diem does not believe in democracy and can therefore no longer be regarded as an exponent of the principles that justify the efforts and sacrifices made by the US and Vietnamese army to defend South Vietnam against Communism.

Adding that he did not regret his early backing of Diem, Buttinger nevertheless voiced his disappointment at the Vietnamese leader's failure to understand that "a people cannot fight, and will not fight, if freedom is precisely what it lacks."[45]

Buttinger submitted his resignation to the AFV's board of directors on April 26, 1962, but they postponed the choice of a new chairman until the next executive committee meeting. On June 21, eight members of the panel met in New York. William Henderson served temporarily as the executive committee chairman, and O'Daniel, Buttinger, Jonas, Oram, Emmet, Leerburger, and Diana Lockard participated in the discussion. The meeting proved to be what Christopher Emmet called a "harrowing and exhausting" affair, as the AFV officers debated the organization's future policy for three and one-half hours. The minutes don't provide a clear idea of the positions taken by the participants, but letters written by Emmet a few weeks later indicate that O'Daniel, Oram, and Emmet wanted to avoid or mute any unfavorable comments about Diem's policies, while Buttinger, Jonas, Lockard, Leerburger, and Henderson favored a more critical stance.[46] In the end, the executive committee accepted a compromise put forth by Jonas that outlined a statement of principles declaring the AFV's support for American and Vietnamese efforts to defeat the NLF but urging Diem's government to "undertake all necessary political and other measures" needed to win popular support. It also included a proviso that the group would "speak frankly and, if necessary, critically, on the above principles in order to help fulfill them." Most of those taking part in the discussion agreed to abide by the compromise until a panel appointed by Henderson drafted a final set of policy guidelines.[47]

Despite the executive committee's approval of Jonas's statement, frustration over the inconclusive outcome of the debate led two officers, Franklin Leerburger and Diana Lockard, to resign from the AFV. Leerburger regarded the June 21 meeting as "a clear signal that the American Friends of Vietnam are so deeply split as to make action in any direction almost impossible." He then declared his intention of quitting the AFV after writing to Henderson, "All things considered, I believe that we have plumbed the depths and explored the fields of possible agreement without reaching more than an expression of pious hopes."[48] Lockard decided to leave the association because she thought its assistance programs failed to provide a "sufficient *raison d'etre* for the American Friends of Vietnam." Since the AFV had not undertaken a project that it could operate "more effectively than, or at least as effectively as, any other group," she saw no reason for remaining.[49] These departures, however, did not alarm the other leaders of the AFV; some even declared that they were happy to hear of Leerburger's withdrawal. Emmet thought Leerburger's criticisms of Diem had become "utterly unreasonable," and when O'Daniel received word of the resignation, he remarked, "That should be a help."[50]

Determined to keep the organization active, the AFV's remaining officers reached a policy settlement on October 4, 1962. They accepted two sets of guidelines—a statement drafted by Emmet and an amended version submitted by O'Daniel. Both affirmed the need to preserve the Republic of Vietnam and called for the requisite American assistance and the Vietnamese reform programs. Emmet's analysis, however, occasionally expressed a more pessimistic appraisal of the Vietnamese situation than O'Daniel's. When discussing the impact of American military aid, for example, Emmet said it merely enabled the RVN to "barely hold the line." O'Daniel's draft, on the other hand, claimed that the influx of U.S. troops and military supplies "has sufficiently heartened the Vietnamese military to the extent that any deficiencies in the Vietnamese political situation in Saigon will have [a] diminishing effect on the struggle in the countryside." Despite these differences, the AFV's leaders found the two statements to be sufficiently compatible to serve as the principles needed to chart the group's future course of action.[51]

Although the executive committee meeting of October 4 enabled the AFV to continue its work, it did not effectively settle disagreements over a common policy toward Diem, a failure that prevented the AFV from speaking publicly at a time when the United States was rapidly committing itself to the survival of the Diem regime. The AFV's officers did not question the premise that a communist takeover of Vietnam should be averted, and they backed American efforts to assist Saigon. They sharply disagreed, however, about Diem's ability to cope with the insurgency in the South. By 1962, Jonas, Buttinger, Fishel, and Leerburger concluded that the RVN's president not only was incapable of defeating his enemies, but had pursued a course of action that made their triumph all the more likely. In their view, Diem's unwillingness to carry out effective land reforms, collaborate with other anticommunist Vietnamese politicians, and curb the corrupt and tyrannical behavior of his family circle was undermining the regime. Jonas, speaking at Columbia University, claimed that Diem's failure to implement political reforms "brings a Communist victory closer to success in South Vietnam," while Buttinger thought Diem's policies prevented the "full mobilization of the country's fighting power against the Communists."[52] These AFV critics did not yet call for a complete break with Diem, but they had reached the point where they believed that the RVN would not survive unless strong American pressures compelled Diem to inaugurate far-reaching reforms.

Other AFV officers thought Diem could cope with the NLF, or that the massive buildup of American troops and supplies would compensate for his regime's deficiencies. O'Daniel emerged as the most vocal defender of Diem, but he received the backing of other members, including Christopher Emmet, Frank Trager, and Monsignor Harnett. Returning from a trip to Southeast Asia in May 1962, Trager declared that the scale of American support for Diem would make Saigon's political troubles seem irrelevant. Harnett concurred and told O'Daniel: "I do not think that an organization such as the American Friends of Vietnam should quibble or allow itself to be misled by partisan political attitudes. This is not meant to condone any political injustices. It is meant to throw light on the fact that the complete human welfare of the members of any state far outweigh some of the political variables."[53] Diem's defenders in the AFV steadily dwindled over time, but he retained enough adherents in the early 1960s to prevent the group from adopting a more critical stance toward his regime.

Ironically, the inability of its leaders to formulate a common political policy left the AFV with little to do except devote most of its energies to work that, according its charter, was meant to be the organization's primary concern—educational and charitable projects in Vietnam. This did not mean that political messages disappeared entirely from the AFV's literature in the early 1960s. Appeal letters condemned the "Communist invaders" who launched attacks "in a desperate effort to overwhelm the Vietnamese who are defending their homeland."[54] The group nevertheless refrained from praising Diem in its publications and no longer sent the president congratulatory messages.

Instead of addressing political issues, the American Friends of Vietnam concentrated on direct aid programs to Vietnamese educational and medical institutions. In a three-year period from April 1, 1960, to March 31, 1963, the AFV procured more than $227,000 worth of material, much of it from pharmaceutical companies who donated dated but usable stock, and shipped it to Vietnam.⁵⁵ According to a paper summarizing AFV activities from 1960 until 1961, the group's success in obtaining this assistance could be attributed to the IRS grant in March 1960 of tax deductibility for contributions to the organization.⁵⁶ This favorable development was reinforced by what Gilbert Jonas called "the concentrated efforts by the staff" in direct aid projects.⁵⁷ The growth of the AFV's charitable work, however, may also have reflected the failure of the group's leaders to agree on a common stance toward the Diem regime that would have enabled them to pursue an active political program. As a result, the AFV could focus its energies only on noncontroversial humanitarian aid projects.

Despite its impressive success in obtaining goods in kind, the AFV had little luck raising cash in the early 1960s. Contributions dropped from nearly $31,000 in the late 1950s to $20,587 in the 1960–61 fiscal year. The AFV suffered a slight drop in revenues the following year to $20,317, then underwent a sharper loss in 1962–63, when it received only $18,901.⁵⁸ The reasons for these decreasing revenues are not entirely clear, but the AFV's records indicate that one cause was a decline or mistiming in the mailing of appeal letters. AFV officers attributed the lower income in 1961–62 to the distribution of only two letters that year, and they also noted that another message was sent out during a vacation period when few people were likely to respond.⁵⁹ The escalating violence in Vietnam and the AFV's internal disagreements about the Diem regime may also have contributed to the association's financial difficulties. The board of directors speculated that the fall in income "may have been due to increasingly unfavorable publicity on the situation in Vietnam" or "a lack of strong political policy by AFV."⁶⁰ The problem grew even worse as unrest in Vietnam gained greater momentum in 1963.

Even if its leaders had succeeded in formulating a political policy, especially one more critical toward Diem, the American Friends of Vietnam would have had little influence on a government determined to bolster the Diem regime. Kennedy and his advisers, like the Eisenhower administration, knew that Diem had serious flaws, but they thought no one else could replace him as the head of an anticommunist Vietnamese state. They often found Diem's resistance to American advice to be infuriating, and the members of the Taylor mission even considered supporting an attempt to overthrow him. For the moment, however, they drew back from such a step. Arguing against American assistance to a coup against Diem in their report to Kennedy, General Taylor and his associates said, "It is by no means certain that we could control its consequences and potentialities for Communist exploitation." Moreover, they believed that greater American involvement in a program of "limited partnership" would compensate for Diem's weaknesses by creating "de facto changes in Diem's method of administration."[61] Finally, America's difficulties in other parts of the globe, especially in Cuba, Laos, and Berlin, convinced many officials that the United States had to demonstrate its firmness against communism, and that Vietnam presented the best opportunity for doing this. As a result, they displayed no enthusiasm for fostering tensions with a government whose help they needed in making such a stand.

Since Kennedy and his advisers decided to throw their support behind Diem, AFV members who voiced misgivings about the RVN's president received few positive responses from official quarters. McGeorge Bundy thanked Michigan State University president John Hannah for a copy of Fishel's pessimistic letter and called it an "informative and useful" document, but there is no indication that Fishel's views influenced a government rapidly building up its commitment to Diem.[62] Others displayed greater hostility toward critical opinions expressed by those in the AFV. Leo Cherne wrote that some officials "tenaciously resisted and dismissed" criticisms of Diem, and an AFV paper claimed that some members had become "*persona non grata* with the State Department" because of the doubts they had expressed.[63] The administration, encouraged by reports from Saigon that optimistically assessed the impact of its new commitments to the RVN, disregarded criticisms of Diem until the regime revealed its self-destructive character in a crisis that led to an ultimate break with its American supporters and to the overthrow and death of its leaders.

chapter 7
The AFV and the Fall of Diem, 1963

In the spring of 1963, Ngo Dinh Diem, who had been desperately struggling to crush a communist insurgency in South Vietnam, was also confronted with an assertive Buddhist protest movement. His brutal attempts to suppress the Buddhists failed, and demonstrations and riots soon swept across the cities of the South as thousands of Vietnamese who resented Diem's dictatorship joined the ranks of the dissenters. This crisis forced the U.S. government to reconsider its support of Diem and eventually led to American approval of Vietnamese military plans to overthrow the president in the autumn of 1963. The turmoil in Vietnam also compelled the American Friends of Vietnam to reexamine its own policies. Despite an earlier agreement to avoid discussing controversial issues concerning Vietnam, many AFV leaders concluded that the escalating tensions in the RVN made such a stance impossible, and that the AFV must forcefully criticize Diem's repressive actions. Internal policy disputes and organizational disarray, however, prevented the AFV from responding rapidly to the fast-breaking events in the South, and the association consequently played the role of a concerned, but powerless, bystander to the tumultuous events of 1963.

Because of an executive committee decision in October 1962, the AFV itself refrained from addressing any troublesome questions dealing with Vietnam. Its members, however, were free to express their own opinions about developments in the country. AFV officers who had lost all faith in Diem became quite critical of his regime and paid closer attention to his adversaries than they had in the past. In early 1963, Jonas, Buttinger, Fishel, Henderson, and Cherne met with Nguyen Ton Hoan, a conservative opponent of Diem. Some of them had had contacts with Hoan years before, but they had dismissed him, as Buttinger once wrote, as "a rather weak and confused man" whose integrity had been compromised by his collaboration with the sects.[1] They showed a greater willingness to listen to Hoan once they became disillusioned with Diem. Gilbert Jonas, informing an aide of Senator Mike Mansfield that Hoan had "considerably impressed several knowledgeable Americans," made arrangements for Hoan to see State Department representatives and staff members of the Senate Foreign Relations Committee in Washington, thus giving a critic of Diem an opportunity to put his views before American officials.[2]

As some AFV members introduced Diem's opponents to Washington, others criticized Diem in correspondence with government officials. Wesley Fishel sent a lengthy analysis of the regime to Edward Lansdale, who had been dealing with counterinsurgency and covert operations in the Pentagon since 1957. Fishel praised Diem for overcoming a formidable set of obstacles in his first year in office, but he then condemned the president's subsequent failure to govern his country wisely. Since the late 1950s, many of Diem's virtues had become crippling weaknesses. "His determination," Fishel asserted, "has become stubbornness; his strength of character has become as a shining shield behind which he has hidden his face and refused to see the evil his courtiers have done; his patriotism has turned into a rejection of outside ideas and influences in favor of the comforting 'Vietnamese' suggestions and flattering members of the presidential entourage." Fishel concluded that, after ruling the South for eight and one-half years, Diem had provided it with no effective guidance, and that the "Vietnamese people are waiting for leadership."[3]

Lansdale found parts of Fishel's critique, especially the character sketches of Diem's family, to be "rather good," but he rejected Fishel's conclusion that Diem had utterly failed.[4] Many of Diem's policies, especially his reliance on Nhu, had disturbed Lansdale, but the former CIA agent could not bring himself to break with the man whom he had done so much to support and who served as "Lansdale's conduit to influence."[5] Moreover, Lansdale thought Diem's Vietnamese critics had little to offer in the way of a constructive alternative to Diem's rule and that Diem's overthrow would undo whatever had been accomplished in Vietnam. In a reply to Fishel, Lansdale disputed the Michigan State University professor's judgment. "My concern continues to be for the Vietnamese people. Thus, the question is not so much 'What is the status of the regime' as it is 'What can we, with some real wisdom, do to help the people construct a more hopeful future?' How about turning those big brown eyes of yours on this part of the problem?"[6]

By early 1963, many of Lansdale's colleagues in the government no longer shared his confidence in Diem's leadership, and events in Vietnam soon reinforced these doubts. Diem's inability to destroy the NLF with massive outlays of American aid became dramatically clear when communist guerrillas defeated a superior ARVN force at the village of Ap Bac in January 1963. Within a few months of the Ap Bac debacle, Diem faced trouble on another front. Vietnamese Buddhists, who resented the favoritism that the president showed toward his fellow Catholics, began protests against the regime after Diem's police shot and killed Buddhist demonstrators in Hue on May 8. The shootings set off a wave of riots throughout the South that gained even greater force the following month when Buddhist monks and nuns expressed their opposition to Diem's policies by burning themselves to death. By late June, tensions in Vietnam had reached the point where virtually no compromise was possible between a regime that did virtually nothing to placate its opponents and dissidents who had grown increasingly militant.[7]

Diem's confrontation with the Buddhists shocked and disturbed public and government opinion in the United States. For many Americans, the upheaval in the South provided the first evidence of the depth of resentment against Diem. Criticisms of Diem rapidly multiplied, especially when Mme. Nhu derisively called the Buddhist suicides "barbecues" and declared, "Let them burn, and we shall clap our hands."[8] Influential papers like the *New York Times* warned that if Diem "cannot genuinely represent a majority then he is not the man to be President," and the first stirrings of an antiwar movement became evident as American citizens picketed the RVN's diplomatic offices and placed newspaper ads condemning the Diem regime's "unjust, undemocratic, and unstable" character.[9] The turmoil in Vietnam also alarmed U.S. officials, who tried to persuade Diem to resolve the crisis through negotiations with the dissenters. Diem's refusal to heed this advice angered the Americans and convinced some of Kennedy's subordinates that if Diem did not make peace with the Buddhists, the United States would be "compelled publicly to disassociate itself from the GVN's [Government of Vietnam's] policy."[10]

The turmoil in the South also troubled members of the American Friends of Vietnam. Joseph Buttinger, who had lost all faith in Diem by the spring of 1963, sponsored a meeting of American and Vietnamese scholars on June 29 to discuss the crisis in Vietnam and possible solutions. Conference participants decided that the RVN could be saved only by Diem's removal from office and his replacement by a government that would carry out the reforms needed to undermine the appeal of the communists. Buttinger wrote a memorandum outlining these conclusions and sent it to the conferees and to State Department officials who requested copies.[11] Wesley Fishel also became involved with opposition to Diem by forwarding plans for a coup against the

Vietnamese leader to Washington. Fishel had spoken to a former official of the regime who proposed seizing power by taking Diem and his entourage as hostages but needed American financial assistance to ensure the success of his plot. In writing to Washington, Fishel said some of his interlocutor's ideas "may be considered risky, or even hare-brained," but he noted that the man had a reputation for honesty and intelligence and that "the reward of success would be great."[12]

The Buddhist crisis had convinced most AFV members that Diem would have to be ousted, but a few individuals continued supporting the president. Journalist Norbert Muhlen, who sat on the AFV's national committee, worried that the "American Friends of Vietnam does not want to defend Diem" and outlined his concern in a letter to the group's officers.[13] In this note, Muhlen cited sympathetic Catholic publications that presented the "true facts" of Diem's troubles with the Buddhists and urged the organization to counter attacks on Diem "immediately and forcefully."[14] The association, however, gave Muhlen little satisfaction. Henderson, the head of the executive committee, sent a reply claiming that the AFV's "non-partisan" character prevented it from speaking out on the events taking place in Vietnam and that the AFV could distribute only materials that "present all responsible sides" of the controversy.[15]

O'Daniel, as he had in the past, continued backing Diem and voiced growing anger with AFV officers who attacked the regime. He expressed his indignation in replying to a letter from Lansdale complaining of the AFV's failure to follow through on suggestions Lansdale had made about participating in an assistance program for strategic hamlets. Lansdale told the general that some of his colleagues in Washington had concluded that the AFV "is too anti-VN [Vietnam] and anti Diem to be of any real help in the proposed effort." Referring to the AFV's leaders as "Madison Avenue eggheads," Lansdale declared that "it gets me as mad as hell to have a group of dillettantes [sic] confuse what sounds cute at a cocktail party with the reality of needs today in Vietnam."[16] O'Daniel warmly agreed with Lansdale's sentiments and denounced the unwillingness of the AFV's officers to back Diem. "The majority of our executive committee," he lamented, "are overly cautious in making any decisions re action in support of Diem. They are afraid of being wrong. I have argued with them until blue in the face that everything goes in warfare but they shy from it."[17]

Events in August, however, convinced all but the most committed advocates of Diem that he would have to go. On August 21, Ngo Dinh Nhu ordered troops under his personal control to attack pagodas throughout

Vietnam in an effort to crush the Buddhist revolt. Instead of quelling the unrest, this brutal assault merely fueled popular anger against Diem. Demonstrations continued in the South's cities, and some of the regime's most prominent figures registered their disapproval of the raids by quitting their posts, including Vu Van Mau, the RVN's foreign minister, and Tran Van Chuong, Mme. Nhu's father and the RVN's ambassador to the United States. An even more significant expression of discontent came from Vietnamese military officers appalled by the savagery of the crackdown and angered by Nhu's attempt to implicate the ARVN in the attacks by dressing the assailants in army uniforms. On August 23, the RVN's senior commanders approached U.S. intelligence agents and, after disavowing the ARVN's involvement in the repression, asked about American reaction to a possible attempt to oust Nhu.[18]

Kennedy's advisers, outraged by the pagoda raids, responded favorably to this inquiry. On August 24, senior Washington officials, including the president himself, gave their hasty approval to a State Department message telling the embassy in Saigon that the "US government cannot tolerate [a] situation in which power lies in Nhu's hands" and that "we are prepared to accept the obvious implication that we can no longer support Diem" if Diem refused to break his ties with Nhu.[19] Second thoughts about this course of action soon surfaced as members of the administration complained that they had endorsed the telegram without adequate consultation. However, they eventually agreed to stand by the policy after a lengthy, and at times acrimonious, debate. This decision effectively committed the United States to Diem's overthrow, but the conspirators in Saigon had trouble mustering the forces needed to stage a revolt. By the end of August, they had canceled their plans for a coup.[20]

While the Kennedy administration began taking a harder line toward Diem, the American Friends of Vietnam groped for an appropriate response to the pagoda raids of August 21. Most AFV officers thought the association should suspend its aid program to the University of Hue to protest the Diem regime's punishment of faculty members and students who had demonstrated against the government. Besides this gesture, many AFV leaders favored a sweeping condemnation of the attacks on the Buddhists. Jonas believed that the assaults made the "pursuit of the war against the Reds virtually impossible" and declared that the AFV must vigorously denounce them if it "is to make any impression at all."[21] Buttinger threatened to quit the AFV if the group did not issue a declaration criticizing the raids. Another member, Elliot Newcomb, warned of his intention to resign as well. In Newcomb's view, Diem's harsh treatment of the Buddhists demonstrated that the president "has lost the support of the people irretrievably," and any continuing support of Diem "would only induce the weakening of the people's resistance to communism."[22]

A few individuals nevertheless opposed a hasty response to the raids or simply objected to doing anything at all. Christopher Emmet favored suspending the assistance program to the University of Hue but wanted no release of a general policy statement until a meeting of the AFV's executive committee.[23] General O'Daniel continued backing Diem and resisted any effort to condemn his policies. He blamed "a political group within the Buddhists" for triggering the turmoil in the South and argued that "religious differences are being used as a weapon by the Communists." O'Daniel thought Diem would eventually settle his differences with the dissidents and urged other AFV officers to refrain from making any declaration about the crisis in the South. "I believe," he told the executive committee, "we should make the best of the situation and do our damnedest toward winning the war." If the organization decided to criticize the regime, O'Daniel warned, he would resign as the AFV's national chairman.[24]

O'Daniel's threat did not prevent the AFV's officers from voting to suspend aid to the University of Hue, but the organization's leaders reached no agreement on issuing a statement dealing with the wider crisis in Vietnam. At an emergency meeting of the executive committee convened by Henderson on September 10, only four of the group's fourteen officers showed up—Jonas, Oram, Emmet, and Henderson. Correspondence with other AFV members enabled these individuals to reach a decision on the assistance program to Hue, but the board did not have the quorum needed to set new policy guidelines. As a result, discussion of the AFV's stance toward the rapidly changing developments in Vietnam had to be postponed for a few more weeks.[25]

Although generally inconclusive, the September 10 meeting led to the resignation of two AFV officers. Angered by the sparse attendance at the gathering, William Henderson decided to resign as the executive committee chairman. In a note to Louis Andreatta, the association's executive secretary, Henderson wrote, "It seems fruitless to continue guidance of the AFVN, in very trying circumstances, if I cannot even gain the courtesy, much less the cooperation of other members of the Executive Committee."[26] O'Daniel quit his post as the AFV's national chairman a few days later because of his unhappiness over the decision concerning the University of Hue. He thought the group's intention to stop sending aid to the school "can only play into the hands of the Communists" and "give more ammunition to Hanoi in its fight against South Vietnam."[27]

In the weeks following the departures of Henderson and O'Daniel, the association became more openly critical of Diem. The resignation of O'Daniel, Diem's strongest advocate in the AFV, contributed to this development, as did Henderson's replacement as executive committee chairman by Joseph Buttinger, who had been advocating Diem's overthrow since the spring of 1963. The organization's new stance became evident in early October, when it assisted a prominent Vietnamese critic of the regime, Tran Van Chuong. The AFV sponsored a luncheon to honor the former ambassador and to counter publicity then being given to Chuong's daughter, Mme. Nhu, who had just arrived in America to defend the policies of her husband and brother-in-law in a nationwide speaking tour. At the luncheon at New York's Harvard Club on October 8, Chuong called for "selective" cuts of aid to Diem's government and claimed that a victory over the NLF would be impossible as long as Diem and his family ruled the South.[28] AFV members also made arrangements for Chuong to speak at the Overseas Press Club on October 17 and provided him with copies of a letter written by a former administrator of the University of Hue stating that Hue's population "had been living in deadly terror" since the pagoda raids of August 21.[29] This talk marked the beginning of a three-week speaking tour designed to take Chuong to seventeen American cities and university campuses.[30]

The AFV's leaders also considered making a policy statement sharply attacking Diem. At a meeting on October 9, 1963, the executive committee discussed the group's future course of action and agreed to examine a new set of guidelines to be drafted by Buttinger.[31] Buttinger sent copies of the draft to the AFV's officers in late October. The document admitted that the AFV had enthusiastically backed Diem in his early years in power but went on to condemn the president for failing to take the measures needed to win popular support. Instead of rallying the South's population to his government, Diem had transformed the Republic of Vietnam into "a state run by a secret political party and a secret police." As a result, the Vietnamese people had turned against Diem's administration, and the RVN's collapse seemed certain unless a "fundamental change in policy" took place. The American Friends of Vietnam, the draft concluded, demanded that "the present regime give way to a government of national union." The association would further this objective by opposing continued American assistance to Diem, creating a climate of opinion that would encourage the United States to take "constructive action" in settling the crisis in Vietnam, and giving encouragement to Diem's "democratic opposition" in Vietnam.[32]

As the AFV moved slowly toward an open break with Diem, Kennedy's advisers reviewed their options and consulted some of the AFV's officers in their deliberations. Paul Kattenburg, the deputy director of the State Department's Office of Southeast Asian Affairs, remembered having "many agonizing discussions" with Wesley Fishel in which Fishel reluctantly concluded that "Diem had to go."[33] According to Gilbert Jonas, Fishel also assisted the State Department's Intelligence and Research Bureau in drafting a paper outlining the choices Americans faced in dealing with Diem. This document concluded, "The generals . . . would be welcome to take over from Diem." Jonas, who said he helped Fishel compose the memorandum, remembered that both men worried that Diem would not survive a coup, but that "there was no other thing you could do" because Diem would not take the steps, especially breaking his ties to Nhu, needed to stay in power.[34]

The Americans were presented with another opportunity to oust Diem in October, when Vietnamese officers renewed their plans for a coup. Approaching a CIA operative who had close ties to the Vietnamese officer corps, General Duong Van Minh, Diem's senior military adviser and the leader of the plotters, asked how the Americans would react to an attempt to overthrow Diem. Henry Cabot Lodge, a prominent Massachusetts Republican who succeeded Nolting as ambassador in August, turned to Washington for guidance. He soon received a reply stating that, though the United States "had no wish to stimulate a coup," it would not "thwart a change of government or deny economic or military assistance to a new regime" willing to work with the Americans in defeating the communists.[35] In addition to relaying this information to the dissident generals, the Kennedy administration signaled its approval of a coup by recalling the CIA station chief, an individual who had close ties to Diem and Nhu, and by instituting selective cuts in the Commercial Import Program, the economic bulwark of Diem's government. Encouraged by these gestures, the conspirators proceeded to draw up their plans for rising against the regime.[36]

The plotters launched their coup on the afternoon of November 1, 1963, and rapidly seized control of most of Saigon. Only Diem's guard battalions offered any significant resistance, but insurgent forces trapped these troops on the grounds of the presidential palace. Diem and Nhu frantically tried to rally support from commanders around the country but found that most of the ARVN's leaders had sided with the rebels. Diem also turned to the

U.S. embassy for help. Ambassador Lodge, however, offered no support and simply expressed concern for Diem's personal safety. When it became apparent that the uprising could not be crushed, Diem and Nhu escaped from the presidential palace and fled to Cholon, the Chinese district adjoining Saigon. There, the two brothers eventually decided to surrender to the victorious generals on the morning of November 2, after receiving promises from the junta of safe conduct. Some officers, however, fearful that Diem or Nhu would somehow stage a comeback, decided that the two men should be killed once they were captured. As a result, Ngo Dinh Diem, once hailed by his American backers as the "dynamic leader of a new political force in Asia," died with his brother in the back of an armored personnel carrier in the streets of Saigon.[37]

With the deaths of Diem and Nhu, the structure of their regime quickly disintegrated. The organizations Nhu had so painstakingly constructed—the Can Lao Party, the various security services, and the youth, women's, and civil service associations—collapsed overnight. Three members of Diem's family, Archbishop Thuc, Mme. Nhu, and Ambassador Ngo Dinh Luyen, escaped the vengeance of the rebels because they were abroad at the time of the coup. Another brother was less fortunate. Ngo Dinh Can, who ruled Central Vietnam on Diem's behalf until the onset of the Buddhist crisis, fled to the American consulate in Hue after the revolt began. Ambassador Lodge later turned Can over to the new government upon receiving assurances that he would be treated "legally and juridically." The junta tried Can on charges of murder, extortion, and abuse of office in the spring of 1964, found him guilty, and condemned him to death. On May 9, 1964, Can died before a firing squad in Saigon.[38]

The AFV's leaders reacted to news of the coup and the killings of Diem and Nhu with mixed feelings of relief and dismay. Referring to the deaths of the two brothers years later, Leo Cherne said he "regretted it deeply," but went on to state, "I would not have shed many tears had the action that was taken focused its lethal consequences on Nhu, but not Diem."[39] Joseph Buttinger claimed he also had been troubled by the turn of events. "I was deeply disturbed by the politically unnecessary and despicable murders of Diem and his brother Nhu."[40]

Correspondence at the time of Diem's overthrow, however, indicates that while Buttinger may have been distressed by the assassinations of Diem and Nhu, he fully backed the coup. Responding to a letter asking the AFV to protest the executions of the two men and the failure of the Americans to protect them, Buttinger replied that, although he had been "shocked" by the killings, he thought the rebellion had been relatively bloodless compared to similar events elsewhere in the world, and that he believed that most of the dissident generals had regretted the fate of the two brothers. Buttinger also absolved the U.S. government from responsibility for the murders by making the questionable assertion that it had "very little to do" with the events that had transpired in Saigon. At the conclusion of his response, Buttinger declared that the new regime in Vietnam should be backed if it promised to improve prospects for "the fate of the country and the well being of its population."[41]

Besides supporting the coup in private correspondence, Buttinger expressed his public approval along with other AFV officers. On November 3, two days after Diem's overthrow, Buttinger sent a supportive telegram to the new regime on behalf of the American Friends of Vietnam. "We feel certain," the message declared, "that the new leadership of the Republic of Vietnam provides an opportunity for all the Vietnamese people to unite both in this struggle and in the efforts to insure freedom under a government responsive to the deepest needs and aspirations of your compatriots."[42] Buttinger voiced similar confidence in a fund-raising letter written two weeks later. Although regretting the death of Diem, "a patriot in his own right," Buttinger said the deceased president had "progressively alienated every major group and institution in South Vietnam." The administration that succeeded Diem's, he averred, "offers a decisive alternative to the dangerous situation which had preceded the coup." He concluded the appeal by requesting the money needed to support the AFV's activities. "The Vietnamese have now done what was necessary to put their house in order," he told his readers. "Our duty is to support them until they have won full freedom and lasting peace."[43]

Although most of the AFV's officers joined Buttinger in backing the RVN's new government, a few did not and instead quit the organization. Reporter Sol Sanders, who had supported Diem since the early 1950s, had become increasingly unhappy with the AFV's criticisms of Diem. When the association cabled its best wishes to the RVN's new government, he asked the AFV to remove his name from its letterhead.[44] General O'Daniel, who had remained on the AFV's executive committee after resigning as its chair, also broke all ties with the group. "What has happened is infamous," he declared, calling Diem's overthrow "the destruction of a fine ally and anticommunist fighter."[45] The general lamented the demise of the Diem regime in an article entitled "When I Think of Ngo Dinh Diem," which appeared in southern California newspapers and indirectly attacked the AFV. "I think of a respected American organization," O'Daniel wrote, "that openly criticized Ngo Dinh Diem, when it could have used its influence to better advantage."[46] Two weeks after the AFV publicly endorsed the new government, O'Daniel announced his decision to quit the association in a terse letter that read, "Herewith please accept my resignation from the American Friends of Vietnam."[47]

The AFV accepted O'Daniel's resignation, and some members felt relieved that the AFV was rid of an individual whose stubborn defense of Diem had done so much to complicate the group's policy decisions. Shortly before O'Daniel's resignation, Buttinger wrote, "I would be much happier if he stuck to his threat to resign also from the Executive Committee."[48] The AFV's officers nevertheless directed Buttinger to write a note to O'Daniel expressing gratitude for the general's "outstanding work" on behalf of the AFV and "the sincerity, integrity and devotion which you have brought to the organization."[49] O'Daniel's departure from the AFV received a far more favorable comment from Mme. Nhu, who thanked the general for a letter of condolence on the deaths of her husband and brother-in-law: "You did well, General O'Daniel, to resign, from the 'American Friends of Vietnam,' for those people went so far in their crime as to incite my parents to betray the Ngos without the least reason and even to break with me. But now their crime to all is their shame, and it would be justice and a lesson for posterity when they are all recalled in our History for what they truly are, false friends and traitors."[50]

The killings of Diem and Nhu had upset another member of the AFV as well, but President Kennedy, unlike others in the group, bore a far heavier responsibility for bringing about the events leading to the assassinations. When he first received word of the deaths on the morning of November 2, Kennedy was conferring with his senior advisers about the coup in Saigon. One of the participants in this meeting, General Maxwell Taylor, remembered that, upon hearing of the murders, Kennedy "leaped to his feet and rushed from the room with a look of shock and dismay on his face which I had never seen before."[51] Another assistant, historian Arthur M. Schlesinger Jr., wrote that the president had not been "so depressed and shaken since the Bay of Pigs."[52] One of Kennedy's friends tried to console him with the thought that Diem and Nhu had, after all, been tyrants, but the president disagreed. "No, they were in a difficult position. They did the best they could for their country."[53] Within three weeks of Diem's murder, Kennedy himself fell before an assassin's bullets in Dallas, Texas.

The deaths of Kennedy and Diem marked the end of one of the most crucial episodes in America's prolonged, and ultimately futile, effort to shape Vietnam's destiny. By approving, if not actively encouraging, the plot against Diem, the Kennedy administration had deepened American involvement in Vietnamese affairs and committed the United States to ensuring the survival of the governments that succeeded Diem's. Despite the importance of the coup and the crisis that preceded it, the American Friends of Vietnam played a small part in shaping the turbulent events of 1963. American officials did seek the opinions of some of the AFV's leading figures, including Buttinger, Fishel, and Jonas, but developments in Vietnam such as the Buddhist uprising, the pagoda raids, and the decision of Diem's generals to stage a coup played a far greater role in determining American policy than the views of the AFV's leaders.

The AFV also exercised little influence on American public opinion during the last months of the Diem regime. Its sole pronouncements during this period consisted of press releases announcing the suspension of aid to the University of Hue and General O'Daniel's resignation as the AFV's national chairman. A State Department summary noted that several observers regretted the halt in assistance programs to Hue, but Andreatta, the AFV's executive secretary, reported that none of the New York media outlets that received these releases reported the AFV's action. He added that only one radio station had approached the AFV for comments on the situation in Vietnam, but that it never broadcast the interview.[54]

The AFV's feeble performance during the Diem regime's final crisis can be attributed to a number of factors. As in previous years, internal disputes troubled the organization. No one in the group questioned the assumption that a viable South Vietnamese state could be established and that its independence represented a vital American interest. By the spring of 1963, however, most of the AFV's officers concluded that the Republic of Vietnam had no chance of surviving as long as Diem and his family remained in power. Nevertheless, a vocal minority of AFV members resisted any open break with the regime. O'Daniel, the national chairman, would not countenance any public disapproval of Diem's policies. Others, such as Emmet and Oram, reluctantly agreed that Diem's position had become desperate, but insisted on a full discussion of the situation by the AFV's leadership before taking any action. The executive committee eventually overrode O'Daniel's objections to any public strictures against Diem by deciding to suspend aid to the University of Hue, and the AFV became more openly critical of the president after O'Daniel's resignation by assisting such opponents of the regime as Ambassador Chuong. The group moved slowly, however, in its deliberations on a general policy statement, and drafts of the document were still circulating among the AFV's leaders when the Vietnamese generals launched their coup against Diem.

The AFV's internal disputes also prevented the group from drafting the appeals needed to raise the money to fund its activities. The association sent out a fund-raising letter in March 1963, about two months before the beginning of the Buddhist crisis, and did not send out another appeal until November 19, 1963, nearly three weeks after Diem's overthrow. As a result, the AFV had virtually no money to engage in any significant activity at the time the turmoil in the South had reached its height in the fall of 1963. When William Henderson called for the emergency executive committee meeting of September 10, Andreatta had to inform O'Daniel that the AFV had only $50 in the bank and could not pay for the general's trip from his San Diego home to New York.[55]

Despite these difficulties and the marginal role it played in Diem's overthrow, the American Friends of Vietnam remained active in the months following the regime's collapse. Its leaders voiced a fresh hope and optimism that the coup of November 1 had "created a new opportunity for the cause of freedom" in Vietnam.[56] Although many members had become bitterly disillusioned by Diem, they did not waver in their belief that a viable anticommunist state could be established in South Vietnam. In their eyes, Diem's failure simply proved that his government had become "the main obstacle to victory over the Viet Cong [NLF]."[57] With the establishment of a new administration in Saigon, the AFV believed that a significant step had been taken in ensuring the survival of the Republic of Vietnam. It therefore continued its policy of supporting a southern regime and any American efforts to bolster it in its struggle against the communists.

chapter 8

The AFV and the Escalation of the War in Vietnam, 1964–1965

The American Friends of Vietnam continued its efforts to generate support for the Republic of Vietnam in the months following the November 1 coup. The organization, however, suffered from financial troubles that forced it to suspend its operations in the spring of 1964 and remained inactive until a new crisis in Vietnam led to a resumption of its activities. This emergency, the Saigon government's imminent defeat at the hands of the National Liberation Front, prompted President Lyndon B. Johnson to commit American military forces to a major ground war in Vietnam in order to avert a communist victory. The AFV backed this policy and became an emphatic defender of America's involvement in the escalating conflict in Vietnam.

Taking notice of the AFV's support, the White House turned to the American Friends in an attempt to counter the protests of antiwar critics. Nineteen sixty-five marked the AFV's closest collaboration with the government, as government officials obtained money for the AFV and the association's officers informed White House staff members of the programs they sponsored. Although receiving valuable help from Washington, the AFV was plagued by financial and organizational problems that limited its effectiveness; as 1965 drew to a close, the group faced an uncertain future as its contacts with the White House diminished.

In the aftermath of Diem's overthrow, the AFV reorganized its leadership by replacing officers who had quit the group during the Buddhist crisis. Leo Cherne and I. Milton Sacks returned to the executive committee after having left the board in the 1950s. New members also took seats, including Kenneth T. Young, a former diplomat who had dealt with the AFV in the Eisenhower years, and Robert Shaplen, a correspondent for the *New Yorker* magazine who had considerable experience in Asian affairs. Wesley Fishel filled O'Daniel's post as the head of the AFV in May 1964, while Gilbert

Jonas became the vice chairman, and Joseph Buttinger still led the executive committee.[1]

Changes took place in South Vietnam's leadership as well, but with far more serious consequences for the future of the Republic of Vietnam and the AFV. In the wake of the Diem regime's collapse, a military revolutionary council commanded by General Duong Van Minh worked with a civilian cabinet headed by Nguyen Ngoc Tho, Diem's former vice president, in running the country. However, bitter infighting among the groups that formed this government prevented it from functioning effectively. Moreover, the new government showed little enthusiasm for prosecuting a vigorous campaign against the NLF, which disturbed American officials. Within three months of the November 1 coup, a group of disgruntled officers led by an ambitious general named Nguyen Khanh toppled Minh's government. The Americans who initially dealt with Khanh were favorably impressed by the RVN's new leader, and Ambassador Henry Cabot Lodge declared that Khanh "is able" and "has got a lot of drive."[2] Khanh's accession to power, however, inaugurated an era of instability that plagued the RVN for more than a year as he and his political opponents struggled bitterly for control of South Vietnam. Their rivalry not only created chaos in Saigon but also crippled the campaign against the NLF; military officers often used their troops to further their personal ambitions instead of fighting the guerrillas. The situation in the RVN consequently deteriorated rapidly throughout 1964.[3]

The turmoil in Saigon had an adverse effect on the AFV as well. Speaking at an executive committee meeting on February 6, 1964, Buttinger told AFV officers that Khanh's coup "had upset the organization's political position, which was one of cautious support of the ruling junta," and made "a sensible fund appeal extremely difficult."[4] Cash contributions declined from $18,901 in the 1962–63 fiscal year to $17,853 in 1963–64. The AFV tried to overcome this problem by sending appeals emphasizing "welfare efforts to benefit the Vietnamese people," and cutting expenses by reducing the schedule of Louis Andreatta, the executive secretary, to a three-day workweek in March. But attempts to raise money remained unsuccessful, apparently because of the public's disenchantment with the continuing unrest in the South and its general "apathy towards events in Vietnam."[5] By May 1964, the AFV's financial situation had become so dismal that Andreatta submitted his resignation as executive secretary, a position he had held since November 1958. With Andreatta's departure the following month, the AFV effectively ceased functioning.[6]

The AFV suspended its activities as a new president, Lyndon Baines Johnson, made an ever deeper commitment to the Republic of Vietnam. A forceful and shrewd Texas politician determined to make his mark on American history, Johnson worried that an NLF victory would encourage communist aggression and trigger "a mean and destructive" debate over responsibility for South Vietnam's collapse.[7] Anxious to prevent such a debacle, Johnson shored up the Saigon government by stepping up the flow of supplies and raising U.S. troop levels to more than 20,000 servicemen. He also applied military pressure to the Democratic Republic of Vietnam in an attempt to stop northern support for the NLF. The measures included American reconnaissance activities in the DRV's waters and airspace and U.S. sponsorship of OPLAN 34-A, an operation that coordinated South Vietnamese commando raids against the North.[8]

Events in the summer of 1964 soon gave Johnson the opportunity he needed to take even stronger action against the DRV. In August, North Vietnamese torpedo boats responding to OPLAN 34-A attacks clashed with U.S. destroyers in the Gulf of Tonkin. Johnson retaliated by ordering air strikes against the DRV's naval bases. Moreover, he sent a bill to Congress authorizing the president "to take all necessary measures" to protect American servicemen and to deter aggression in Southeast Asia.[9] The Gulf of Tonkin Resolution received the overwhelming approval of both the House and the Senate and served as the legal basis for subsequent American escalation of the war. Johnson, preoccupied with the presidential election campaign of 1964, made no immediate use of his new powers, but he did permit the drafting of plans for air raids against the DRV and gave final approval for a more aggressive campaign against the North after winning a crushing electoral victory in November.[10]

While Johnson considered proposals to bomb the North, the American Friends of Vietnam resumed its work in the final weeks of 1964. The reasons for the AFV's revival are unclear, but the available record indicates that Wesley Fishel, the AFV's chairman, played a key role. In doing so, Fishel probably received Washington's encouragement. He told the AFV's officers that many government officials thought the AFV was "the only legitimate organization dealing with Vietnam and that it has been influential and worthwhile in the past." Members of the administration had apparently apprised Fishel of their intentions as well. He informed the association's leaders that "the intensification of some activities" in Vietnam was likely.[11]

Fishel spoke to his colleagues in December 1964, the first time the AFV's leaders had met since the previous May. Buttinger, Cherne, and Jonas attended these gatherings, as did William Henderson, who returned as a member of the executive committee. A new officer also appeared—Colonel Charles T. Bohannon, a reclusive figure who had worked closely with Lansdale in the Philippines and Vietnam in the 1950s. After discussing the association's future course of action, the executive committee agreed that "the American Friends of Vietnam still has a potentially vital role to play" and that it "should make one more sustained effort during 1965 to help bring about the decisions needed to secure a viable and stable Free Vietnam."[12]

One of the first activities of the revived AFV was seeking interviews with administration officials in order to present the group's views to the government. This effort met with success when AFV members conferred with William P. Bundy, assistant secretary of state for Far Eastern and Pacific affairs and the brother of presidential adviser McGeorge Bundy. Fishel, Shaplen, and Christopher Emmet saw Bundy at the State Department on December 8, 1964.[13] The AFV's officers gave Bundy a memorandum outlining a six-step program for Vietnam. The plan, which incorporated several ideas that Kenneth Young had outlined in a few essays, called for the inauguration of national and rural "resurgency" campaigns that would "win the allegiance of the rural people on their own terms." This would involve the promotion of social and economic reforms in Vietnam, the deployment of SEATO forces "to insulate Vietnam and the Mekong Valley from communist aggression by seepage," and the initiation of a "Johnson Plan" to develop the Mekong River basin.[14] Fishel later told the executive committee that the AFV's suggestions had been "favorably received" by Bundy, a judgment shared by James C. Thomson, a staff member of the National Security Council who attended the meeting.[15] Thomson called the interview "a rather profitable discussion" and the paper submitted to Bundy "a thoughtful memorandum."[16]

AFV officers also tried to see the president. On December 5, Fishel sent a letter to Johnson asking the president to meet the AFV's board of directors in mid-December. "As the only group in the United States whose interest and activities focus on Vietnam," Fishel told Johnson, "we believe that we are in a unique position to offer professional assistance" in developing public support for the administration's Vietnam decisions.[17] Thomson backed Fishel's request, noting that "we are badly lacking in friendly private organizations" to endorse the government's policy and this need "might well be served by giving the group a boost."[18] Johnson refused to see the delegation, but the AFV tried again in January. This time, they wanted to give the president a revised version of the paper Bundy had received the previous month. In a memorandum to Johnson, staff members of the National Security Council advised the president to see the AFV representatives and that the State

Department believed "a gesture of support by you . . . would be helpful in meeting our public information problem on Vietnam here at home." Johnson, however, turned down the AFV's second request as well.[19]

The date on which the president's rejection is noted, February 1, provides a likely explanation for his refusal. On that day, Johnson presided at a meeting of the National Security Council and told the participants that he would send McGeorge Bundy to Saigon to assess the situation in Vietnam. He made this decision after receiving warnings from Bundy that the administration faced a "disastrous defeat" unless it moved decisively in Vietnam.[20] Bundy, who received the backing of Defense Secretary Robert McNamara, favored more forceful measures. Johnson was receptive to this advice but refrained from taking any action until Bundy made a trip to Saigon. Facing the prospect of making a dramatic new commitment to the RVN, it is doubtful that the president would have wanted to focus attention on his administration's deliberations by meeting with a group advocating firm American support for the Republic of Vietnam.[21]

Within a week of his refusal to see the AFV delegation, Johnson dramatically escalated America's participation in the war as events in Vietnam forced him to make rapid decisions about U.S. policy. Bundy left for Vietnam on February 2, and as he conferred with political and military leaders in Saigon, the NLF staged a major attack against a U.S. military base at Pleiku, a town in Vietnam's Central Highlands. The guerrillas killed eight servicemen and wounded more than 100 others. The Americans retaliated by bombing the North on February 8. Bundy, who regarded the assault on Pleiku as an opportunity to take stronger action against the DRV, returned from Saigon with the recommendation that the United States initiate sustained air strikes against the North. Johnson accepted this advice and authorized ROLLING THUNDER, the code name for the bombardment of the North, on February 13. The deployment of U.S. ground forces to Vietnam took place within weeks of ROLLING THUNDER's commencement; two marine battalions arrived at an air base near the port of Da Nang in early March. General William Westmoreland, the commander of American troops in Vietnam since 1964, asked for reinforcements that could assist the ARVN and conduct aggressive operations against the NLF. After conferring with his senior advisers, Johnson agreed to the deployment of additional combat and support units to Vietnam, a decision that virtually made the United States a full-fledged participant in the war.[22]

The American Friends of Vietnam gave early support to Johnson's escalation of the war, having applied pressure for forceful measures when they thought that the administration was hesitating. The group's leaders had been considering a wide-ranging program designed to save the RVN since the AFV's revival in late 1964 and made preparations to release a policy statement in February 1965.[23] Wesley Fishel informed the government of the imminent distribution of this paper on February 11, a few days after the attack on Pleiku. Speaking to Lewis Sarris, an official in the State Department's Intelligence and Research Bureau, Fishel declared that the AFV's executive committee had unanimously called for a "strong stand" against the communists in Vietnam and was proposing several steps to ensure the RVN's survival, including air strikes against North Vietnam and the deployment of U.S. ground troops to the South. Fishel asked Sarris to inform National Security Council staff members, including Bundy, of this statement, and he finished his conversation with a threat. If the government "did not respond favorably to these proposals," Sarris reported, "his group, all of whom he described as experts and prolific writers on South Vietnamese affairs, would proceed publishing highly critical articles on US policy in South Vietnam."[24]

The AFV, of course, did not carry out Fishel's threat because Johnson decided to bomb the North. The group's position paper, released on February 23, called the air strikes "an appropriate response" to the "increased external, Communist intervention in South Vietnam." It said the bombardment would destroy military targets, "provide a lift to morale in Free Vietnam," and convince the Vietnamese and other Asian peoples that "we mean to stay and help, no matter what risks we must incur." The statement recommended that the U.S. government consider sending combat troops ("perhaps as many as two brigades") to the South to act as a firefighting force or a military "cordon sanitaire" across Vietnam and Laos to block communist supply lines to the South. Other measures proposed by the AFV included the creation of an Asian-American International Voluntary Corps to work in the Mekong River basin, and the formation of a "North Vietnam Liberation Front" to wage psychological and paramilitary operations against the DRV.[25]

The paper placed much of its emphasis, however, on a "Johnson plan" to develop the Mekong River valley, a project it outlined in visionary terms. This enterprise, the document averred, would have "as much potency and promise for success" in Southeast Asia "as the Marshall Plan did in Europe and the Tennessee Valley Authority in the United States." The program would make the generosity of America's intentions in Vietnam "crystal clear" to the rest of the world and would "infuse new energy into the Vietnamese" struggling against the NLF. Finally, it would give the countries of Southeast Asia "a genuine opportunity to harness nature, enlarge justice, extend life, eradicate the scourges of illness and illiteracy and enable long-suffering peoples to reap the fruits of their soil and the permanent benefits of national independence."[26]

The proposal of a "Johnson plan" apparently was an attempt by the AFV to attract the favorable notice of a president already considering the notion. Johnson had been acquainted with the idea since May 1961, when Arthur Goldschmidt, an old acquaintance who worked for the United Nations, told Johnson of UN proposals to develop the Mekong River valley. After he became president, Johnson responded positively to aides who made suggestions about a Mekong Valley project.[27] Kenneth Young, the AFV officer who promoted modernization of the region in several essays, had served as ambassador to Thailand during the Kennedy administration and was familiar with the plans because they involved Thailand as well as Vietnam. Although there is no available documentary evidence linking the AFV's proposals with those of the government, it is likely that Young was aware of Johnson's interest in the Mekong River program and that this knowledge shaped the drafting of the AFV's position paper.[28]

The reaction to the AFV's policy statement was generally favorable. In a letter to Buttinger in early March, Jonas wrote, "We are now being called upon by people in State, Congress, the press, etc. to draw up the detailed proposals for each aspect of our general manifesto."[29] John V. Lindsay, a liberal Republican congressman from New York, called the steps outlined in the paper "thoughtful recommendations."[30] Clement Zablocki, the Wisconsin Democrat who had been receptive to the AFV's opinions in the past, wrote that he had been "happy to have your organization's views on the matter."[31] One representative, however, was more circumspect. James Scheuer, a New York Democrat who became an early critic of the war, called the statement "an interesting document with a number of productive ideas" but thought it proposed "a great deal of wishful things as to possibilities."[32]

The AFV received few responses from the White House, however, until other Americans began questioning the administration's course of action. Opponents of Washington's policy formed an antiwar movement that included pacifists, politicians, academics, journalists, clergymen, civil rights leaders, and student activists. This loose coalition voiced its opposition to the war in letters to editors and political leaders, newspaper advertisements, visits to officeholders, and street demonstrations. The most novel tactic these early dissidents employed was the teach-in. Developed by professors who had been influenced by the civil rights movement, the first teach-in took place in March, when more than 3,000 students and faculty members of the University of Michigan attended campus lectures, debates, and discussions concerning Vietnam. This form of protest spread to more than 100 U.S. colleges and culminated in a "national teach-in" in Washington on May 15. There, 5,000 young people heard from both supporters and critics of the war, while more than 100,000 students listened to television and radio broadcasts of the proceedings.[33]

Johnson and his advisers initially paid little attention to the antiwar movement, but they began to take steps to counter its influence as protests mounted in the spring of 1965. Johnson tried to defuse criticisms of his policy by delivering a major address at Johns Hopkins University in which he called for "unconditional discussions" with the DRV and proposed a major international effort to develop the Mekong River valley, the project advocated by the AFV.[34] The White House also had its staff members meet with delegations of protestors and sent a team of representatives from the State Department, Pentagon, and Agency for International Development to present the administration viewpoint on college campuses. These attempts, however, generally met with little success, and some of Johnson's subordinates became "very frustrated with the sense that the shrill, anti-Vietnam faction on the campus was sort of taking charge by outshouting, outshoving, and outmaneuvering the groups who felt that Hanoi was not necessarily the great saints [sic] of this century and the South Vietnamese were not necessarily the devils incarnate."[35]

Anxious to stem the small but rapidly growing chorus of protest, the Johnson administration sought the help of private citizens and groups who supported its policies. Thus began its collaboration with the American Friends of Vietnam. One of McGeorge Bundy's assistants, Chester L. Cooper, served as the White House liaison to the AFV. A CIA official, Cooper had been dealing with Vietnamese affairs since 1954, when he attended the Geneva Conference as a member of the American delegation. Assigned to the National Security Council staff in 1963, Cooper handled matters concerning Asia and became involved in the government's attempt to counter opposition to the war.[36] He discussed this work in an April 1965 memorandum to Jack Valenti, one of Johnson's most devoted assistants. "The basic difficulty," Cooper asserted, "is that our supporters are largely silent and either unorganized or dis-organized. The *problem* is to encourage and assist the moving spirits in the pro-group without, at the same time, creating the impression that the Government is sponsoring its own pressure group." Cooper proposed the creation of "a non-official speaker's bureau and clearinghouse" and the development of a "people-to-people" assistance program for Vietnam. He told Valenti that Wesley Fishel had expressed the AFV's interest in both projects but that the group needed "a modest sum (say $25,000) to work up a battery of unofficial speakers." Cooper had asked the Bureau of the Budget about possible funding, but was informed that the government could provide no money. He concluded that "someone has to put the bite on well-motivated private individuals."[37]

The Johnson administration quickly found a willing contributor in Sidney Weinberg, an immensely successful financier known as "Mr. Wall Street." A partner at the investment firm of Goldman, Sachs, Weinberg had served as an unofficial adviser to presidents since the New Deal and had organized business support for Johnson's candidacy in 1964.[38] Valenti helped Weinberg get in touch with Fishel, who told Weinberg that the association needed $55,000 in order to work effectively. Weinberg responded by obtaining donations for the AFV from the Ford Motor Company Fund, the Beinecke Foundation, the Procter and Gamble Fund, and the Cabot-Saltonstall Trust. These contributions totaled $27,000, far short of the goal set by Fishel.[39] Fishel nevertheless voiced gratitude for the money the AFV did receive and told Weinberg that his assistance would help the group in its "vital educational function."[40] The White House also expressed its appreciation to Weinberg. Speaking on behalf of Johnson and the White House staff, Valenti wrote, "I just want you to know how grateful we all are for your instant response regarding the American Friends of Vietnam."[41]

In addition to securing financial backing for the AFV, the Johnson administration helped Fishel organize a rally at Michigan State. Cooper saw the event as "an exceptional opportunity" to counter the teach-ins and thought that government representatives "could anticipate a generally favorable and open-minded audience." He recommended that Carl Rowan, a reputable black journalist who headed the U.S. Information Agency, and either UN ambassador Adlai Stevenson or Vice President Hubert Humphrey appear as administration spokesmen. Such speakers, he argued, would win wide media coverage and have a strong impact on young people concerned with both the civil rights movement and Vietnam.[42] The White House heeded Cooper's advice and sent Humphrey and Rowan to speak at MSU on June 1. The vice president delivered what Cooper called a "vigorous exposition of our Vietnam policy," and Rowan urged his audience "to involve themselves constructively in one of the great causes of our time, specifically our effort to preserve Vietnamese independence." Cooper regarded the event as a great success and reported that the MSU students had given a "friendly and receptive" hearing to the speakers.⁴³

The White House also tried to secure AFV participation in a publishing venture to support administration policy. On May 1, Cooper had made arrangements for a meeting between Fishel and Trevor N. Dupuy, a retired army colonel who headed the Historical Evaluation and Research Organization (HERO), a private research group that provided services to the government. During their discussion, Fishel and Dupuy considered plans for a newsletter offering "informed, objective and constructive editorial commentary" on developments in Asia, especially Vietnam.⁴⁴ After seeing Fishel, Dupuy sent a note to the professor outlining plans for drafting the newsletter, which would be jointly sponsored by HERO, the AFV, and the Asia Society. Its editorial board would include AFV members Fishel, Frank Trager, and Kenneth Young, who was also the president of the Asia Society, and professors George McT. Kahin, Norman Parmer, and David Wurfel. Each would receive a $1,000 honorarium if he agreed to serve.⁴⁵ HERO sent out a draft of the first issue in early May "in the hope that distribution can begin before the coming May 15 'teach-in' in Washington."⁴⁶

Within a few days of sending out copies of the first newsletter, however, Dupuy began expressing second thoughts about the project. In a memorandum discussing the difficulties the program faced, he cited a number of financial, organizational, and editorial problems. Dupuy also voiced misgivings about HERO's involvement in "what can be labelled as a political activity." He worried that the groups sponsoring the periodical would be discredited once it became known that they had consulted with administration representatives in launching the venture. "The Government might find, despite the gratitude of individual officials, that it could not in the future make such use as it has of these organizations," he wrote. Still considering the newsletter a good idea, Dupuy recommended that the AFV sponsor a meeting to discuss the matter, but HERO withdrew from the undertaking.⁴⁷

On June 3, 1965, the AFV's board of directors agreed to print an occasional newsletter concerning Vietnam and appointed Fishel, Trager, William Henderson, Young, and Roger Hilsman, who had served in the State Department during the Kennedy administration, to staff an advisory committee dealing with the newsletter. The officers also discussed activities to encourage "American popular involvement with Vietnam," especially by organizing student groups.⁴⁸ Fishel informed Cooper of the AFV's decisions shortly after the meeting, also noting that the association still needed money to continue its work. Cooper, however, told Fishel that Weinberg's assistance had been "a one-shot operation" and that the AFV had to find a way of raising enough money to become financially self-sufficient. Fishel said he would make renewed efforts to obtain a secure source of funding for the AFV.[49]

Most AFV members backed Johnson's escalation of the war, but a few who did not quit the AFV as its support of the government's policies became more outspoken. The resignation of Joseph Buttinger, the AFV's founder and executive committee chairman, was the most notable departure. Buttinger had become increasingly pessimistic about the South's prospects since Diem's overthrow and began to voice doubts about America's ability to save the RVN.[50] When the AFV endorsed Johnson's decision to bomb the North in February 1965, Buttinger announced his intention to step down as the executive committee chairman. In a letter to Fishel, Buttinger declared:

> There was a chance to defeat communism in South Vietnam with political means, but this chance has been thrown away in ten years of reactionary policies and neglect of social reforms. . . . Without a profound political and social transformation of the South, which it would now be utopian to expect, a military victory would oblige the United States to permanently occupy the country, for the purpose of preventing the Communists from taking over, and in order to keep a police regime in power—a prospect which would mean the political bankruptcy of the West in Asia.[51]

Apparently in response to pleas by Gilbert Jonas and others to stay, Buttinger remained in the AFV for a few more months. He finally decided to leave after debating his colleagues at an executive committee meeting on July 8, 1965. At this gathering, he expressed his opposition to the bombing of the North on the grounds that it had not stopped the flow of supplies to the NLF and that it had not forced the DRV to the negotiating table. Moreover, he had become "more and more aware of military analogies with French military failures," and he asked what purpose the air strikes served.[52]

The other AFV officers present, Fishel, Charles Bohannon, Leo Cherne, Christopher Emmet, Jonas, and Trager, responded by defending ROLLING THUNDER. Bohannon, who had initially expressed misgivings about the bombing, argued that the raids against the North had "significantly improved" morale and had served as a warning to the Chinese.[53] Others said the raids had caused "acute distress" in the North, that the Soviet Union and the People's Republic of China had been "embarrassed" by the air strikes, and that the United States "is breaking up the standard pattern of Communist insurrectionary takeovers." These arguments did not convince Buttinger, who, believing that "the main question remains political," said, "We are divorcing our military effort from our political program."⁵⁴ Buttinger decided to leave the AFV shortly after this meeting, despite attempts by Fishel and others to persuade him to stay. Fishel, who said Buttinger's "leadership and guidance have led the organization through countless crises," regretfully accepted the resignation.⁵⁵

Buttinger's departure from the AFV took place just before Lyndon Johnson irrevocably committed the United States to a major war in Vietnam. Johnson's decision was prompted by an NLF offensive that threatened to topple the Saigon regime in the summer of 1965. With the RVN facing imminent defeat, General Westmoreland called for massive American reinforcements to save the South and give the United States and its Vietnamese allies "a substantial and hard hitting offensive capability on the ground" that would convince the communists that "they cannot win."⁵⁶ Westmoreland's request set off a round of lengthy deliberations in Washington that ended when Johnson decided to send a large ground force to Vietnam in late July. The president worried that the deployment of U.S. combat units to Vietnam might trigger Soviet or Chinese intervention, as well as jeopardize congressional approval of his cherished Great Society reform program—"the woman I really loved." He therefore downplayed the significance of his decision by announcing it in a low-key manner at a midday press conference on July 28.⁵⁷ Johnson thus temporarily calmed U.S. public opinion and bought time for his legislative agenda, but he also set the stage for resentment against his administration once the costs and duration of the war became apparent.⁵⁸

The AFV issued no immediate statement concerning the American escalation of the war, but in the weeks following Johnsons's decision, AFV members backed administration policy in the media and in public forums. One of its most notable efforts was the appearance of several AFV officers at informal hearings convened in August by William Fitts Ryan, a New York congressman who criticized American intervention in Vietnam. Six AFV representatives—Fishel, Cherne, Trager, Robert Shaplen, Kenneth Young, and Gerald Steibel—spoke before Ryan's panel. Although they criticized certain American actions, especially a tendency to emphasize the military aspects of the conflict at the expense of its political and social dimensions, they voiced no doubt about the legitimacy or morality of America's presence in Vietnam. Shaplen told legislators that the United States had "lost numerous opportunities to encourage and foster the development of a free and democratic Vietnam," but added, "I firmly believe that we can still play a useful role there."⁵⁹ Young declared that the American intervention in Vietnam "will promote the national security of the United States" and "will deter war."[60] In a letter to the White House, Gilbert Jonas expressed his satisfaction with the AFV's performance at the hearings and claimed that the group's witnesses did "very well, generally overpowering the opposition."[61]

The AFV also hired a national field coordinator to direct its work, especially in making contacts with student groups across the country in an effort to counter the antiwar movement. Two men with previous experience in the National Student Association held this post. Seymour Reisin, who taught in the New York City school system, served as the coordinator in the summer of 1965. When Reisin resumed his teaching duties in September, a former president of the student association, Gregory Gallo, replaced him. Reisin and Gallo sent letters to student and youth organizations informing them of the AFV's willingness to provide literature and speakers. Recipients of this material included the Young Democrats, Young Republicans, the United States Youth Council, the Student Division of the NAACP, and the Hillel and Newman clubs. The two men also met with representatives from these associations in order to generate student support for the war effort and to provide AFV members with forums to present their views.[62]

A few AFV officers kept the White House regularly informed of these activities in letters that outlined both the organization's accomplishments and its problems. Financial difficulties still troubled the AFV, and Fishel told Chester Cooper that the group's executive committee had decided to scale down operations unless the association obtained needed funds. The American Friends, he declared, "can not function indefinitely on a day-to-day basis and must have *immediate* cooperation and reciprocal evidence of good faith in order to carry on effectively."[63] Cooper discussed the AFV's predicament in a memorandum outlining the AFV's programs and requirements. The AFV, he reported, "cannot be supported through its own fund raising ability." At least another $25,000 was necessary, and either Fishel or Frank Trager, the AFV's treasurer, could be contacted on the matter of contributions.[64]

The White House tried once again to help meet the AFV's financial needs. A memorandum by the AFV's executive secretary shows that the group received money through the help of Edwin Weisl Sr. and Arthur Krim, two of Johnson's closest supporters. Weisl, characterized by one AFV member as "a powerful friend of powerful people," was an influential New York lawyer who had backed Johnson since the late 1930s and became the New York State representative on the Democratic National Committee with Johnson's support.[65] Krim was president of United Artists Corporation in New York City and struck up a close friendship with Johnson after working as a fund-raiser in the 1964 campaign.[66] Johnson himself evidently took part in the AFV effort; he saw Weisl and Krim a few days before the two men made arrangements for the donation of $20,000 to the AFV in September and October. The AFV warmly appreciated this help. In a note to Cooper in early October, Trager wrote, "This keeps us in action until we can turn about for what I hope will be a bigger and more certain 'umbrella.'"[67]

Besides assisting the AFV in obtaining needed funds, the White House aided the group in printing and distributing literature. The AFV finally carried out plans to issue a journal entitled *Vietnam Perspectives* in the fall of 1965. The articles, although occasionally criticizing certain American or Vietnamese policies, strongly backed the American intervention in Vietnam. Frank Trager, who served on the editorial board, regarded *Vietnam Perspectives* as "an intended answer to *Viet Nam Report* put out by the 'Teach-in' crowd."[68] The White House agreed with this judgment and took steps to ensure the journal's success. Cooper made arrangements for Morris I. Leibman, a prominent Chicago lawyer whom the administration enlisted in an effort to win support for its policies, to buy and distribute 5,000 copies of *Vietnam Perspectives*.[69] NSC staff members also put the AFV in contact with Nicholas Kissberg of the New York City Teamsters union ("the reputable ones," as one memorandum put it) in order to secure free printing services. The Teamsters agreed to reproduce short articles for the AFV, and the association once again benefited from valuable administration assistance.[70]

The help given by the White House enabled the AFV to continue its work into the autumn of 1965. Much of this activity simply continued earlier projects such as establishing ties with student groups backing the war effort and disseminating the views of AFV members through speeches, newspaper columns, magazine articles, and broadcasts.[71] It also involved the sponsorship of special programs aimed at generating support for the war. One such undertaking tried to attract the approval of the academic community with a petition drafted by Stanley Rothman, a government professor at Smith College. The petition conceded that the United States had made "important mistakes" in Vietnam but backed the American commitment to the RVN on the grounds that a communist victory "will spell disaster for millions of South Vietnamese and other millions in Southeast Asia."[72] The AFV eventually printed the statement, which carried the signatures of nearly 200 professors from New England colleges, in the *New York Times*. It also planned to distribute the statement again in order to win the approbation of thousands of academics across the country.[73]

In another project, the AFV extended its assistance to five Vietnamese students who traveled to the United States in October and November. The Saigon government, which was then led by Generals Nguyen Cao Ky and Nguyen Van Thieu, sent these young men to America in an effort to counter the antiwar critics. The United States Youth Council and the AFV helped them make visits to California, Wisconsin, Illinois, Connecticut, and New York. Most of the AFV's work involved making arrangements for the delegation's public appearances in the New York area, including a talk at Columbia University, a press conference at the Carnegie International Center, and an hour-long interview with Edwin Newman of the National Broadcasting Corporation. When this trip ended in early November, Jonas called it "a tremendous success" that had received "saturation coverage on all medias."[74]

For the American Friends of Vietnam, 1965 marked the zenith of the organization's ability to procure funds and carry on a wide-ranging program of activities. The AFV's backing of Johnson's Vietnam policies had played the key role in attracting the notice of an administration desperately seeking the support of private citizens and groups. Of the more than $75,000 the AFV raised during its 1965–66 fiscal year, nearly two-thirds, $47,000, came through the help of individuals with close ties to Johnson—men like Weinberg, Weisl, and Krim.[75] This money gave the AFV the wherewithal it needed to defend America's involvement in Vietnam, and some of its work won national attention. The publication of *Vietnam Perspectives* received a favorable notice from *Time* magazine, which called the journal's essays "well-researched articles."[76] Gilbert Jonas exulted in the media coverage of the Vietnamese students' visit to New York, and the AFV's sponsorship of Stanley Rothman's petition merited a front-page story in the *New York Times*.[77]

Nevertheless, by the end of 1965, as the group received diminishing support from the White House, it became evident that the AFV's success would be short-lived. The executive branch had provided the AFV with valuable help, but it did not, as historian Melvin Small notes, "pull out all of the stops for the AFV," and it tried to "keep the organization at arm's length." The administration may have done this, as Small suggests, "for appearance's sake," or because it had "a degree of sensitivity to such operations," but such reservations did not prevent the administration from attempting to form its own support group two years later.[78]

A more likely explanation for the reluctance of the White House to give unrestricted aid to the AFV is that its staff members came to the conclusion that the group had only a limited influence on public opinion. Chester Cooper, who had the most extensive contacts with the AFV, raised this matter in a memorandum to some of Johnson's senior aides in December 1965. Worried that public approval of the government's policies "may be more superficial than it is deep and committed," Cooper wondered whether the administration could even build on the support it already had, and he doubted that private organizations like the AFV could do the job because they "are too small to have much of an impact."[79] The association's chronic financial problems reinforced this impression of its weakness, and Cooper later remembered that he felt that the AFV was not "terribly effective."[80]

The AFV found its fiscal difficulties to be particularly troubling. Because of the group's failure to find a secure source of funding, much of its work in 1965 would be characterized by what Gilbert Jonas called "an inordinate amount of wasted effort and wasted money." Jonas also complained that a number of the group's projects had been "subsequently scrapped by [a] lack of funds before they could be fully implemented."[81] The attempt to print an expanded version of Rothman's petition became one of the major casualties because the AFV could not raise the money to purchase space in the *New York Times*.[82] Fiscal difficulties also undermined the AFV's student programs. Gregory Gallo, the national field coordinator, declared that the AFV had to forge a "personal contact" with friendly student groups across the country in order to have any impact. He nevertheless did not see this happening. "It seems unlikely that the organization will ever have the necessary resources to do this."[83]

The AFV's monetary problems also led to a rapid turnover of secretaries and activity directors who quit the AFV when it became apparent that they could not count on a steady source of income. This "revolving door of staff," Jonas lamented, forced the AFV "to start from scratch to train new persons and to educate them about Vietnam only to find them leaving just as they have become fully productive."[84] The AFV leaders also failed to set priorities for what the organization should do, a matter Fishel regarded as the AFV's worst problem. When he resigned as the national field coordinator in March 1966, Gregory Gallo wrote that the AFV's officers had not yet reached any consensus on a course of action and that the AFV "as presently constituted is incapable of doing the hard thinking necessary to effectively implement its goals."[85]

Perhaps the most striking example of the disarray afflicting the AFV was the group's response, or lack of one, to a bitter attack against it in the summer of 1965. The association was denounced by a young journalist named Robert Scheer in a booklet published by the Center for the Study of Democratic Institutions, a liberal think tank founded by the former university president Robert Maynard Hutchins, and in an article printed in *Ramparts*, a liberal Catholic magazine whose editorial policies took on a radical tone as the 1960s progressed. These essays examined the origins of the American involvement in Vietnam, and Scheer had interviewed some of the AFV's officers while researching the topic. The AFV had helped Scheer contact these people, but one of the AFV members who spoke to Scheer, Leo Cherne, expressed misgivings about the journalist's attitude. "I told him quite frankly," Cherne wrote in a letter to the AFV's executive secretary, "that I had some reservations about the possibility of bias."[86]

Cherne's apprehensions were borne out by Scheer's harsh criticisms of the American Friends of Vietnam. He identified the AFV as the formal organization of the Vietnam Lobby, "a small and enthusiastic group of people... who maneuvered the Eisenhower Administration into supporting the rootless, unpopular and hopeless regime" of Ngo Dinh Diem.[87] This clique, Scheer charged, not only had secured America's backing of Diem, but made strenuous efforts to commit the United States to a massive aid program on Diem's behalf.[88] It did so by claiming that most Vietnamese rejected communist rule and by arguing that South Vietnam had made "rapid strides towards political stability and economic independence" under Diem's leadership.[89] When Diem employed repressive measures against his opponents, Scheer asserted, the lobby formulated "an ideological framework to explain away the uncomfortable facts that occasionally found their way into the mass media as 'a necessary reaction to the Communist menace' confronting Diem."[90] He noted that, although many AFV members eventually lost confidence in Diem, "the myths that they created—that we were 'asked' to step in by the Vietnamese people, that we were protecting 'democracy' by blocking elections—remain long after Diem to haunt the State Department White Paper and President Johnson's speeches."[91]

Scheer's writings, which were marred by a number of inaccuracies and greatly exaggerated the AFV's influence, angered many AFV members, but the association made no formal reply. Scheer made several errors in discussing the circumstances of Diem's exile from Vietnam and his first meetings with his American supporters. He also exaggerated the AFV's influence in pressuring the U.S. government to commit itself to South Vietnam's defense and to blocking the 1956 elections. The AFV, however, made no effort to point out these flaws in a public rebuttal. An AFV officer, probably Jonas, drafted some notes that questioned Scheer's qualifications, cited factual errors, and accused the journalist of trying to "fit the facts into... [his] thesis, eliminate the facts which did not fit into the thesis, and to fabricate 'facts' where none were available."[92] The AFV, however, did not use this draft to rebut Scheer's claims. Fishel called for a response at a meeting of the board of directors in November, but, as William Henderson noted several months later, "No one had been willing to work on it."[93] Cherne, who had been "appalled" by what he called the "misstatements, total lies, distortions" made by Scheer, tried to organize a reply in 1967, but he, too, discovered that "nobody seemed to regard this as a particularly useful activity."[94] The reasons for the association's failure to counter Scheer's attack are not clear, but AFV officers may have worried that a forceful response would simply have given the charges wider attention. They may also have concluded that the essays would have convinced only a relatively small, if highly vocal, group of antiwar protestors. Their inaction, however, allowed Scheer's account to become the standard interpretation of the AFV's work and influence for years to come.

By the end of 1965, the AFV's monetary and organizational troubles once again threatened to bring it to a halt. Its ability to win indirect financial support from the government proved to be a temporary success that would not be repeated. As the new year began, contacts between the AFV and the White House dwindled, and by late February 1966, an officer of the group reported that the American Friends "do not seem to be doing much—they have never received the promised funds."[95] Although it remained considerably active for a few more years, the American Friends of Vietnam would never again be able to carry out the wide range of programs it had undertaken in 1965.

chapter 9
The AFV and the American War in Vietnam, 1966–1968

In the two and one-half years following his decision to commit ground forces to Vietnam, Lyndon Johnson tried to break the will of the Vietnamese communists by sending more American troops and escalating the bombing campaign against North Vietnam. This effort ultimately failed and instead led to increasing discontent within the United States. A growing number of Americans questioned America's involvement in Vietnam, while others wanted the government to take forceful measures that would lead to a military victory. The dissatisfaction with the conduct of the war exacted a growing toll on the administration's popularity and credibility.

The leaders of the American Friends of Vietnam, however, defended Johnson's actions in the belief that they avoided the extremes of capitulation to the communists or a dangerously expanded conflict. The association tried to generate public support for the president by organizing a publishing program and a speakers service. It also worked with government and Vietnamese officials and with other private groups that backed the war effort. The AFV carried out these activities on a modest scale since it no longer received White House assistance in securing funds, but it obtained enough revenue to continue its operations and even raised a large sum of money in 1967. This progress came to a sharp halt in 1968, when the communists launched a major offensive that shattered public confidence in the administration's policy and led to peace talks with the Democratic Republic of Vietnam. These sudden changes marked the beginning of a swift decline in the AFV's fortunes, and the organization faced the prospect of closing down by the end of 1968.

The AFV supported Johnson's policies as the fighting in Vietnam rapidly escalated and opposition to the war increased throughout the United States. American troop strength, which totaled 23,000 servicemen in early 1965, approached 500,000 by the end of 1967. The Americans fought well, but they did not break their enemy's determination to continue the struggle in the South. Moreover, success on the battlefield could not remedy the chronic weakness of governments in Saigon, which retained the corrupt and repressive character that had alienated millions of Vietnamese in the Diem era. Stalemate and frustration in Vietnam contributed to a growing disenchantment with the war in the United States. The antiwar movement grew larger and became more organized as it drew attention through repeated protests. The dissidents were regarded by many Americans as disruptive and even treasonous, but Johnson and his advisers could draw little comfort from this because many of the people who condemned the protestors also criticized the administration for waging a half-hearted war effort. By July 1967, the Gallup poll reported that Johnson's handling of the war had received only a 33 percent approval rating.[1]

Although Johnson came under fire from many quarters, the American Friends of Vietnam never joined the ranks of critics. It maintained its support of the administration even as some of the oldest members withdrew from the AFV and a new set of leaders took their place. Wesley Fishel stepped down as the AFV's chairman in the spring of 1966 and left the organization the next year, claiming that professional and family obligations in Michigan had made his responsibilities in the AFV "too heavy" a burden "for me to carry."[2] Gilbert Jonas had quit the AFV after his public relations firm signed a contract with the Saigon regime at the end of 1965. In a letter to Fishel, Jonas wrote, "I care so deeply about the work of the American Friends, but the new circumstances dictate the propriety of this decision." Jonas nevertheless kept in touch with the AFV in his capacity as the RVN's public relations representative. These contacts came to an end only when his company's agreement with Saigon expired some time in late 1966.[3]

As individuals like Jonas and Fishel dropped out of the AFV, other members began to exert greater influence. Two officers, William Henderson and Frank Trager, had been active in the organization since the mid-1950s. In 1965, Henderson succeeded Joseph Buttinger as the executive committee chairman while Trager became the group's treasurer, positions that gave each man a strong voice in setting the AFV's policies. A few newcomers also emerged as dominant figures in the AFV. Dr. George K. Tanham, a student of guerrilla warfare who worked for the Rand Corporation, a research institution affiliated with the Air Force, took Fishel's place as the AFV's national chairman in the spring of 1966. Two other members, Murray Baron and William Ward, joined the AFV's board at the same time. Baron, a political activist who had participated in the struggle to form labor unions in the

1930s and had been one of the founding members of New York's Liberal Party, became one of the AFV's busiest speakers and most valuable fundraisers. Ward, an executive in the business information firm of Dun and Bradstreet and a senior officer in the army reserve, would head the AFV in its final years.[4]

The emergence of new leaders marked a hardening of the AFV's attitude toward the war as the group gave virtually unqualified support for Johnson's policies. The association had been formed initially to secure American backing for the RVN and it had never challenged South Vietnam's legitimacy or American efforts to sustain it. Nevertheless, in the first decade of the AFV's existence, some members had questioned certain American and Vietnamese actions, especially in the last years of the Diem regime. Such misgivings seldom surfaced after the conflict escalated in 1965. Moreover, the AFV's leadership, perhaps mindful of the bitter disputes that had plagued the organization in the early 1960s, concluded that the AFV should not try to attract a broad following "because of the difficulties of controlling policy direction."[5] This decision may explain the declining number of names on AFV letterheads after 1965. The AFV listed more than ninety names in the 1950s and early 1960s, but the number dropped to between fifty and sixty in the years following 1965. This development troubled at least one staff member, who thought the AFV should try to shape the debate on the war "rather than echoing President Johnson or attacking groups opposed to the war," but the complaint received an unsympathetic hearing from officers who placed the AFV squarely behind the administration.[6]

This shift in the AFV's stance reflected the views of the men who headed the organization in the mid-1960s. Some members, especially Baron and Trager, had battled the communists since the 1930s and, as a former AFV officer once said, "carried that animosity to their graves."[7] Baron had particularly bitter memories of combating communist efforts to infiltrate the labor movement in the 1930s, and he concluded that the behavior of his opponents had been guided by "perfidy and unbounded treachery."[8] The AFV's officers also compared Chinese and Soviet support for the insurgency in Vietnam to the belligerence of the Axis powers and argued that it merited a firm response from the United States. Frank Trager regarded "wars of national liberation" as the "contemporary hallmark of communist aggression" while Murray Baron applauded America's intervention in Vietnam as an act of "remarkable anticipation" and "far-sightedness" that would deter future attacks.[9]

Although their past convictions played a major role in shaping their support for Johnson's policies, the ties that some of the AFV's officers had formed with the U.S. government also influenced their views. Close bonds had been forged between Washington and academic circles during the Second World War as various departments and agencies employed the skills of university professors, especially those trained in the social and hard sciences, in the struggle against the Axis. This relationship flourished with the onset of the Cold War and some of the AFV's most active members had benefited from it. In the mid-1950s, Wesley Fishel collaborated closely with the Eisenhower administration in establishing the Michigan State University program that aided the Diem regime. In subsequent years, he frequently gave advice to officials in Washington and Saigon. George Tanham, Fishel's successor as the head of the AFV, also had accepted government assignments, serving on the Pentagon's Vietnam Task Force in 1961 and as the deputy director of the AID mission to the RVN in 1964. Finally, Frank Trager worked as a foreign aid official in Burma in the early 1950s and later acted as a consultant for Washington in the 1960s.[10]

Academics like Fishel, Trager, and Tanham who collaborated with the government hoped to shape American policy, but, in many respects, their employers in Washington had a greater influence on them. They shared many of the views of the officials with whom they worked, including an intense hostility toward communism, a confidence that economic development would bring prosperity and freedom to Asian societies, and a strong belief in the need for American leadership in the world. As a result, they rarely questioned the premises guiding the actions of the U.S. government. Moreover, as the British journalist Godfrey Hodgson notes, these scholars discovered that they "tended to be influential only in proportion as their ideas fitted in with the needs, fears or preconceptions of their new patrons."[11] As a consequence, academics who served as consultants for Washington, including such senior AFV officers as Fishel, Trager, and Tanham, frequently became the partisans of the policies they supposedly were assessing.[12]

Guided by a leadership that had committed itself deeply to the success of the war effort, the AFV employed a variety of arguments to justify American intervention in Vietnam. As it had in the past, the group regarded the Republic of Vietnam as an independent state threatened by outside attack. The activities of the NLF, Wesley Fishel asserted, had been "directed and controlled by the North Vietnamese Communist Party resident in Hanoi."[13] The DRV's aggression was unusual, according to a pamphlet published by the AFV, because it had been waged in a "subtle and piecemeal" manner that "exploited local grievances." The brochure went on to assert, however, that this campaign could still be seen as "an external effort to overthrow a sovereign government."[14]

The AFV also repeated its earlier claims that the Vietnamese people strongly opposed communist rule. In the 1950s, it had based this assertion on the massive refugee flight from the North; in the 1960s, it pointed to national elections in the RVN as evidence of southern anticommunism. Commenting on the presidential contest of 1967 won by General Nguyen Van Thieu, a fund-raising letter declared, "Clearly, the Vietnamese are determined to participate in their own government, and just as clearly, the vast majority want nothing to do with the Communists on any basis."[15] When some critics raised the issue of the RVN's avoidance of the referendum of 1956, the AFV's officers reiterated the old charge that the dictatorial character of the northern regime and its larger population base made any fair election impossible.[16] The AFV's leaders concluded that the United States had a "moral obligation" to help "the beleaguered South Vietnamese . . . choose their own way of life by the ballot box instead of the bullet."[17]

While repeating earlier arguments about the RVN's sovereignty and the strength of Vietnamese anticommunism, the AFV also emphasized events that had gained greater public attention as the war intensified—atrocities committed by NLF and North Vietnamese troops. The association's literature asserted that many Vietnamese civilians were "victims of deliberate cruelty."[18] One brochure featured an article from *Time* describing the killing of more than 200 refugees by communist troops who "incinerated" their terrified victims with flamethrowers. The pamphlet called this massacre "a horrifying example of the use of terror and assassination to achieve political ends."[19] Another leaflet, which highlighted communist executions of more than 1,000 civilians at Hue in 1968, declared that this bloodshed reflected the "callous disregard of the Viet Cong for the lives and property of those they seek to 'liberate.'"[20]

The AFV's most effective pamphlet, "The Innocent Suffer," featured photographs of Vietnamese killed or wounded in guerrilla attacks and an excerpt of an article written by novelist John Steinbeck. While visiting Vietnam in early 1967, Steinbeck recorded his impressions of the war, including a report outlining the NLF's use of terror to control the South's population. Claiming that the NLF "has much the same selfless impulse, the same gentle democratic direction . . . as the Mafia," Steinbeck charged that its cadres aimed at "domination of the land and the minds of the poor people" and that they would "stop at no horror, no lie, no trick to achieve it."[21] The AFV's executive director found "The Innocent Suffer" to be the group's most effective brochure and stated, "The wide distribution of this item has brought our name to the attention of thousands of people who would otherwise never have heard of us."[22]

In addition to distributing pamphlets, the AFV devoted considerable attention to printing and selling the association's own journal—*Vietnam Perspectives*. The group made plans to publish the periodical on a quarterly basis and ten issues would appear by 1968. But some members, including Fishel, argued that "other activities of the organization should not be sacrificed to the magazine" and worried that the cost of publishing *Vietnam Perspectives* "would wipe us out financially." The AFV's board of directors overrode these objections in September 1966 and decided to give precedence to publication of the journal.[23]

Fishel's apprehensions about *Vietnam Perspectives* proved to be well founded since the magazine "never made any money" for the AFV.[24] In fact, the association's executive director estimated that the AFV took a $3,200 annual loss in printing *Vietnam Perspectives*. The problem can be attributed partly to the AFV distributing dozens of free copies to academics, politicians, journalists, and student leaders. It made no systematic attempt to get paid subscriptions for *Vietnam Perspectives* until late 1966, when a former Foreign Service officer named Hugh O'Neill became the AFV's executive director and began updating the group's files and subscription lists.[25] A more serious shortcoming of the periodical lay in its narrow focus of support for Johnson's policies. "There was no real diversity in it," Jonas recalled. He said that, when the magazine first appeared in 1965, he had warned Fishel that it "could not succeed if he made it one point of view." The editorial board of *Vietnam Perspectives* apparently disregarded such admonitions since the articles it published raised few serious questions about Johnson's conduct of the war.[26]

The AFV enjoyed greater success in sending its members to address gatherings concerning Vietnam. These representatives usually participated in debates and discussions about the war on college campuses, but they also appeared before political clubs, church groups, and radio and television audiences. At times, their presentations simply involved lectures outlining their views on the situation in Vietnam. On other occasions they debated such antiwar activists as Norman Thomas, Allard Lowenstein, the poet William Stringfellow, and William Sloane Coffin, the Yale chaplain.[27]

The AFV members claimed that many listeners were receptive to their arguments, but they also remembered running into difficulties. Murray Baron asserted that many of the people organizing the presentations opposed the war. He frequently "had the experience of coming to a four panel discussion on TV or radio, [and] I was the only one defending our policy," a situation that enraged Baron, who thought he had been used as "a fig leaf" to mask the biased character of these proceedings.[28] On other occasions, AFV members were subjected to verbal and physical abuse by protestors. One officer, William Ward, said he had been hit on the head by a rock thrown by an individual whom he sarcastically called a "sweet, young nineteen-year-old pacifist."[29] Despite such troubles, the AFV's leadership spoke of the "high importance of the Speakers Service" and continued sending members to gatherings.[30]

In carrying out its activities, the AFV collaborated with government representatives, Vietnamese diplomats, and private groups that backed the war. Although the Johnson administration gave the AFV no more financial help after 1965, it provided other forms of assistance. White House and State Department staff members advised people who sought speakers supporting government policy to contact the AFV. They also supplied the organization with materials and information it requested, including photographs of communist atrocities, which appeared in the AFV's brochures. AFV officers traveling to Washington usually had an opportunity to speak to officials on an informal basis. These contacts, although not as frequent and close as those of 1965, continued throughout Johnson's presidency and into the Nixon administration.[31]

The AFV's dealings with the Vietnamese government became sporadic after the RVN broke its contract with the Oram firm in 1961 and most of the AFV's leaders had turned against the Diem regime. The Vietnamese made a brief attempt to reestablish ties with the AFV after the RVN's agreement with the Kastor-Hilton company expired in 1962. At one point, the embassy's counselor, Nguyen Phu Duc, even showed an interest in an AFV proposal to organize a conference in 1963, but this plan collapsed when the Buddhist crisis erupted. The organization occasionally corresponded with Vietnamese officials in Saigon and Washington after Diem's overthrow, and when the fighting began to escalate in 1965, it agreed to publicize the Saigon regime's request for refugee assistance. These contacts did not take place on a sustained basis, however, until the end of 1965.[32]

The AFV began working more closely with the Vietnamese after Saigon selected Vu Van Thai, and then Bui Diem, as its representative in Washington. A former economic adviser to Ngo Dinh Diem, Thai won the respect of many Americans for his intelligence and honesty. An editorial in the AFV's *Vietnam Perspectives* hailed Thai's 1965 appointment as "testimony to his confidence in the present regime's motives and his confidence in the future."³³ Thai actually disliked most of the South's military leaders, but he nevertheless hoped for the eventual formation of "a viable political system able to withstand communist subversion" and accepted the post in Washington. After a year as ambassador, Thai quit his position when it became apparent that no meaningful reforms would take place and that the growing U.S. military presence would only sharpen hostility between the Saigon government and the Vietnamese people.³⁴ Thai's replacement, Bui Diem, began working for the Saigon regime in 1965. A member of the badly splintered Dai Viet Party, Diem had won the confidence of Nguyen Cao Ky, the flamboyant air force general who served as the RVN's premier from 1965 until 1967. Diem initially acted as Ky's assistant for planning and foreign aid and then moved on to the RVN's foreign ministry. Ky designated Diem as Thai's successor in December 1966, and Diem left for Washington at the end of the year.³⁵

Both Thai and Diem had previous experience in dealing with the AFV and worked well with the organization once they arrived in the United States. By the mid-1960s, Hugh O'Neill recalled, the South Vietnamese "were kind of looking around for all the friends they could find." They provided the AFV with informational material and occasionally sent a representative to fill a speaking request the association had received.³⁶ Thai and Diem also saw AFV members who traveled through Washington and sometimes invited the group's officers to the Vietnamese embassy for a meal and a review of the situation in Vietnam.³⁷ The AFV members, in turn, showed a readiness to help the Vietnamese and occasionally agreed to embassy requests to present Saigon's case to congressional representatives.³⁸

Although willing to aid the RVN's diplomats, the AFV also expressed its concerns and criticisms. In contrast to their approach during the Ngo Dinh Diem era, the association made few efforts to persuade the RVN's later rulers to undertake major reforms. But AFV officers mentioned certain troubling issues such as reports of continuing infighting among the South's leaders and human rights abuses by Saigon's forces, and they urged the Vietnamese to "clean up their act."³⁹ Thai and Diem reported these concerns to Saigon, but they had minimal influence on developments in Vietnam. Individuals such as Ky and Thieu concluded that the rapid military buildup signified America's willingness to give unconditional support to the RVN. "To my regret," Diem later recalled, "Saigon didn't understand that well this problem of the necessity of having a public relations campaign or program dealing with the U.S. public opinion."⁴⁰

The American Friends of Vietnam cooperated not only with American and

Vietnamese officials, but also with private groups, especially those on college campuses. One of the organizations it worked with, the Young Americans for Freedom (YAF), had a large membership of 28,000 young men and women in the mid-1960s and received valuable political guidance and financial assistance from prominent conservatives. It became, as one account has stated, "a militant, active, and imaginative voice in support of the war," and it used literature printed by the AFV in an effort to shape student opinion.[41] The American Friends also collaborated with two other associations that had ties to the YAF—the Student Committee for Victory in Vietnam and the Student Coordinating Committee for Freedom in Vietnam and Southeast Asia. The AFV gave pamphlets to the former group and helped the latter by providing it some of the money it needed to send a delegation to Vietnam.[42]

Despite such gestures, the AFV did not work closely with these organizations. Its dealings with them were sporadic and, in many cases, the students initiated the contacts. The American Friends simply lacked the staff and resources needed to collaborate with other supporters of the war on a sustained basis. It even found the little help that it could provide to be taxing. When he sent some literature to the Young Americans for Freedom in 1967, O'Neill asked for contributions, explaining that "we are an extremely small-budget operation" that worked "on a shoestring."[43]

O'Neill's remark reflected the AFV's constant inability to raise adequate funds for its activities. In the spring of 1966, the association asked the foundations that had helped it at the behest of the White House to renew their grants of financial aid, but it met with no success since Johnson's aides no longer encouraged donations to the AFV. The group's chaotic administrative situation did not help matters. Hugh O'Neill noted that "contributions were not posted upon receipt in 1965 and 1966" and the AFV therefore missed the opportunity of adding the names of new donors to its list of supporters.[44] The AFV tried to attract fresh sources of income by persuading Henry Cabot Lodge and General Maxwell Taylor to serve as its honorary chairmen, but its fortunes did not improve. In September 1966, William Henderson informed the board of directors that "the financial resources of the organization have dwindled alarmingly." In a letter written a few months later, an outside observer described the AFV as "a low budget operation, or better still, one surrounded by a sea of poverty."[45]

Certain developments in 1966, however, enabled the AFV to continue its work and set the stage for a modest recovery in 1967. In April, the association received $3,000 from the Pew Foundation, a group that the AFV's executive secretary called "a rather hard line anti-communist outfit." The Pew Foundation, which insisted that these donations be kept confidential, renewed this grant in 1967 and 1968.⁴⁶ The AFV also received funds from the conservative *Reader's Digest* magazine and its publishers, DeWitt Wallace and his wife, Lila Acheson Wallace. In the fall of 1966, the Wallaces sent $1,000 to the AFV and their endowment agency, the *Reader's Digest* Foundation, gave another $1,000. Mrs. Wallace presented the AFV with $1,000 in 1967 and the *Reader's Digest* Foundation gave the AFV a total of $2,000 in 1967 and 1968.⁴⁷ The arrival of new personnel also helped the American Friends of Vietnam. Murray Baron secured several large donations, and O'Neill updated files and lists that had been neglected during two years of almost constant staff changes.⁴⁸

The AFV built on these achievements in 1967 by launching its most successful fund-raising drive. In a campaign inaugurated in the spring, the AFV raised $23,000, more than half of the group's $43,000 income for the 1967–68 fiscal year.⁴⁹ O'Neill attributed this achievement to a growing hostility toward the antiwar protestors and to increased public concern about the conflict. A revised and up-to-date list of contributors also helped, but O'Neill gave most of the credit to "The Innocent Suffer"—the brochure featuring Steinbeck's article on the brutal behavior of the NLF. "I would like to make use of Mr. Steinbeck's literary style and reputation every time I raise funds," O'Neill wrote, "but I am not optimistic about that."⁵⁰ In fact, the association never had another opportunity to reprint a piece by Steinbeck, nor was it able to secure a dependable source of income to ensure its future viability. O'Neill accurately summarized the AFV's troubles in writing, "My particular organization has a fiscal existence that is reminiscent of Eliza jumping from ice-floe to ice-floe."⁵¹

The AFV's situation became even more precarious in the closing months of 1967 with the creation of a new administration support group—the Citizens Committee for Peace with Freedom in Vietnam. Steps for forming this association began in the spring of 1967 when Johnson's Vietnam policy came under increasing fire. Although the dissenters faced strong opposition from several quarters, they continued protesting the war and enjoyed new strength and prestige when more prominent Americans joined their ranks. Dr. Martin Luther King Jr. had previously voiced quiet misgivings about the American intervention, but the civil rights leader began speaking more forcefully in February 1967, when he concluded that the war seriously threatened the nation's ability to address its domestic ills. Senator Robert F.

Kennedy, Johnson's most bitter political enemy, also openly opposed the president by calling for an unconditional halt to the bombing of the North. Johnson and his advisers tried countering this dissent in various ways. They called General Westmoreland to Washington for consultations in April, but they used the general's presence in the capital to assure the public that things were going well in Vietnam. The White House also helped sympathetic groups organize parades supporting the American troops in Vietnam, and some of the president's aides suggested sponsoring a telegram-writing campaign to back the servicemen in Indochina. Another, more sinister measure involved Johnson's secret use of the Federal Bureau of Investigation and the CIA to probe the antiwar movement and uncover any ties that it might have with the communists.[52]

In their effort to generate support for administration policy, some of Johnson's advisers suggested "the creation of a national group of 'Names' which would support the war in Vietnam."[53] The White House, however, did not regard the AFV as a suitable vehicle for such an enterprise. Memories of the AFV's marginal impact on public opinion in 1965 and knowledge of its financial problems may have discouraged Washington from resuming a close partnership with the association. Moreover, the AFV itself already had made an unsuccessful attempt to attract several prominent Americans to its national committee in the autumn of 1965. The organization had invited distinguished figures such as former secretary of state Dean Acheson, union leader George Meany, former Harvard president James B. Conant, financier David Rockefeller, and John McCloy, the former high commissioner to Germany, to join its ranks, but it received only letters of regret. There is no available evidence indicating why these people rejected the AFV's offer, but one account suggests that Scheer's articles, which had been published shortly before this effort, had tarnished the AFV's reputation and effectively discouraged people from associating with it.[54]

Instead of relying on the AFV, Johnson's subordinates recommended that a new committee be formed. They began working on the project in May 1967 after the president gave his approval. The responsibility for organizing the group fell to John P. Roche, a political science professor from Brandeis University who acted as a special consultant to the president, and who also served on the AFV's board of directors. Roche informed the president that, in addition to collaborating with other White House aides, he worked with two outsiders in setting up the organization—Clark Clifford, a powerful Washington lawyer who had counseled presidents since the Truman administration, and Murray Baron, another AFV member who "is a real professional, totally committed to you and your objectives."[55] Roche and his associates selected Paul H. Douglas, a former senator from Illinois with a record of strong opposition to communism and a firm commitment to civil rights and labor rights, as the head of the group. Douglas, then acting as the president of a liberal human rights association called Freedom House, agreed to serve the new group after Leo Cherne, chairman of Freedom House's executive committee, assured Roche that he had no objections to Douglas's appointment. Roche told Johnson that he would "leave no tracks" of his own involvement and thus protect the group from charges of acting as a "White House Front."[56]

After a few months of preparatory work, Douglas announced the formation of the Citizens Committee for Peace with Freedom in Vietnam at a press conference in Washington on October 25, 1967. The association had former presidents Harry S. Truman and Dwight D. Eisenhower as its honorary chairmen, and its roster featured the names of several distinguished Americans, including some of the individuals who had refused to join the AFV two years before. Appearing on this list were such figures as Acheson, Conant, Meany, former secretary of state James Byrnes, Senator Leverett Saltonstall, and Generals Omar Bradley and Lucius Clay. A number of AFV members also joined the group, including Murray Baron, Leo Cherne, Christopher Emmet, Wesley Fishel, I. Milton Sacks, and Frank Trager. In a statement to the press, Douglas called the Citizens Committee a "national and non-partisan" organization that favored "a sensible road between capitulation and the indiscriminate use of raw power." He insisted that the idea for creating the association had been his own and that the committee backed no particular administration, although it supported "the office of the Presidency." The new group, Douglas averred, spoke for "the great 'silent center' of American life," and it aimed to make sure "that the majority voice of America is heard—loud and clear" so that the communists would not regard the protests against the war as a sign of national weakness.[57]

The AFV publicly hailed the formation of the Citizens Committee but the new association, which attracted considerable notice from the press, actually posed a threat to the AFV's continued existence.[58] In his remarks to reporters, Douglas said his organization would set up a speakers' bureau and print and distribute pamphlets expressing its views, work that the AFV already had been carrying out. Moreover, the presence of such notable and respected figures as Eisenhower, Truman, Bradley, and Acheson on the Citizens Committee attracted considerable financial support. Within weeks of its establishment, the Citizens Committee had received $30,000, more than two-thirds of the AFV's total income for the 1967–68 fiscal year.[59]

Faced with the prospect of unequal competition for funds and members, George Tanham asked the AFV's leadership to consider the possibility of "terminating the American Friends." The board of directors addressed the issue at a meeting on March 12, 1968.[60] Leo Cherne proposed "consideration of merging with the Citizens Committee for Peace with Freedom in Vietnam," but others objected. Tanham, who was leaving the AFV to serve as an adviser to the U.S. embassy in Thailand, thought the AFV should remain independent, while Baron contended that Douglas's association faced trouble in formulating policy statements because of the "difficulties of clearances with [the] big wheels." These arguments eventually prevailed, and the AFV's leaders agreed that the group should continue its activities.[61]

Events in Vietnam, however, effectively destroyed the ability of the AFV or any other organization to generate support for Johnson's Vietnam policy. On the evening of January 30, 1968, the beginning of Vietnam's lunar new year (Tet), communist forces struck more than 100 South Vietnamese cities and towns in an attempt to trigger a popular uprising against the Saigon regime. This effort failed and the attackers suffered fearful casualties in weeks of savage fighting, but the Tet offensive shocked an American public that repeatedly had received official assurances that slow but steady progress was being made in Vietnam. It also convinced many Americans that Johnson's policies had failed. In the weeks following the attack, Johnson tried to defuse growing unrest in the United States by launching a peace offensive that limited the bombing of North Vietnam and offered negotiations with the DRV. He also stunned Americans in a speech announcing this new policy by declaring, "I shall not seek, and I will not accept, the nomination of my party for another term as your president."[62] After an interval of a few days, the Hanoi regime announced its willingness to begin peace talks with the United States, and on May 13, 1968, American and North Vietnamese diplomats met for the first time in Paris. These negotiations, however, did not signal an end to the war. The struggle in Vietnam would continue for almost another five years as diplomats squabbled in Paris.[63]

The Tet offensive and Johnson's subsequent decision to launch a peace initiative had a devastating impact on the AFV's ability to generate public support for the war effort and to raise money. The organization already had experienced serious trouble when a fund-raising drive launched in the autumn of 1967 ended in failure, but the shock of the Tet offensive and its aftermath created even more serious problems for the AFV. By February 21, O'Neill wrote that if attempts to secure contributions met with no success, "I see little alternative to consideration of going out of business."[64] O'Neill and others attributed the AFV's declining fortunes to the impact of Tet and to "the general disillusionment with Johnson and the disillusionment with the war, which didn't seem to be going well." Reflecting on the AFV's troubles years later, O'Neill said these events marked "the beginning of the end because you couldn't generate much support for anything in Vietnam."[65]

The AFV tried solving its fiscal crisis by turning to the people who had helped it obtain large sums of money in 1965. Sidney Weinberg received a request for a contribution in June, and O'Neill wrote that he would ask another previous benefactor, Morris Leibman, for assistance as well.[66] The AFV devoted most of its energy, however, to getting aid from Jack Valenti, who had left the White House in 1966 to become president of the Motion Picture Association of America. Meeting Valenti in December 1967, O'Neill outlined the AFV's programs and status. Valenti, who seemed to be "favorable [sic] impressed" by O'Neill's presentation, told O'Neill that "he would like to set up a session for me to explain our operations to several people in New York" and asked O'Neill to contact him in January.[67]

The AFV's records do not indicate if this later interview ever took place, but O'Neill eventually saw Valenti again on July 1, 1968. The AFV's executive director reported that this talk "went pleasantly, but could hardly be called a wild success." Valenti informed O'Neill that he had been preoccupied with the campaign to secure Vice President Humphrey's nomination for the presidency, and he expressed reluctance in asking potential contributors to give money to more than one cause. He said the few people he had approached had shown no interest in helping the AFV, and that he had no close relationship with individuals such as Weinberg. Valenti then suggested that O'Neill draft an appeal letter to be signed by Paul Douglas or General Bradley, a remark that indicated he had confused the AFV with the Citizens Committee. Although Valenti promised to get in touch at a later time, O'Neill concluded that nothing more could be expected from Valenti in the immediate future.[68]

Valenti apparently provided the AFV with no further help; the association's financial position steadily deteriorated in the final months of 1968. O'Neill remembered going on half-pay at one point and that by the end of the year "it had become necessary for me to forego my salary for several months." He informed the AFV's chairman that he could no longer afford to do this, and that he would be resigning as the group's executive director in January 1969. Working for the AFV had been a "privilege" and O'Neill strongly believed that "the organization has a useful purpose to serve," but the need to have a steady source of income had become imperative.[69] As 1968 drew to a close, the American Friends of Vietnam faced a bleak and unpromising future.

chapter 10
The Last Years of the AFV, 1969–1975

In its final years, the American Friends of Vietnam led a precarious, fitful existence. Financial troubles continually plagued the organization and many members either quit or stayed on only as names on a letterhead. Those remaining active in the group, however, tried to keep the AFV alive in the hope that its fortunes would improve and in the fear that its dissolution would signal a loss of American confidence in the Republic of Vietnam's future. When a new president, Richard M. Nixon, took office in 1969, the AFV supported his policy of strengthening the Saigon regime while withdrawing American forces from Vietnam. Contacts between the White House and the AFV developed in the early years of Nixon's presidency, but they would not be as extensive or close as those formed during the Johnson administration.

As the American role in the conflict diminished, the AFV faced growing difficulties in operating effectively; with the signing of agreements that ended America's participation in the war in 1973, the AFV became virtually defunct. The organization lingered on for a few more years and engaged in a brief campaign to rally support for the RVN when the Saigon regime faced defeat in 1975. This attempt, however, evoked no response from politicians or a public weary of the struggle in Vietnam. Saigon fell to communist forces on April 30, 1975. The AFV soon followed the Republic of Vietnam into oblivion.

William F. Ward, the business executive who had joined the AFV in the mid-1960s, headed the group in the late 1960s and early 1970s. He had been an officer of the association since 1966, and on March 12, 1968, the board of directors elected him chairman after George Tanham was appointed to serve as an adviser on counterinsurgency to the U.S. embassy in Thailand. Ward took this position at a time when the Tet offensive not only had shattered public confidence in Johnson's Vietnam policy but also had undercut any endeavor to generate support for the war effort. With the AFV's financial situation rapidly deteriorating by early 1969, Ward and his colleagues considered the possibility of dissolving the AFV. After a protracted discussion, however, they agreed that another attempt should be made to keep the organization alive.[1]

In deciding to continue the work of the American Friends, the AFV's leaders appointed an unpaid volunteer to replace Hugh O'Neill, who had resigned as executive director at the end of 1968. They selected a young man who had served in Vietnam, William Brownell, to fill the post. Brownell, whose well-to-do family was related to Herbert Brownell, Eisenhower's attorney general, had been stationed in Vietnam from 1967 until 1968 and had been disturbed by America's conduct of the war, which seemed to "destroy anything we were endeavoring to save." The American influence on Vietnamese society also troubled him; he thought it exposed the Vietnamese to a commercialized culture he regarded as a "Las Vegas style concoction which was of no value to good people." Brownell nevertheless had been strongly attracted by "the embattled nation" and hoped that he could help Vietnam when he returned to the United States in the autumn of 1968. "I wanted to do something for Vietnam," he later recalled, "and in some unconscious way wanted to show what Americans could do for that country." Brownell became the AFV's executive director in February 1969.[2]

Brownell's hopes of helping Vietnam faded soon after he took office. He quickly concluded that the AFV's leaders had no "clear vision of where they were going."[3] He was also discouraged by student and public antagonism toward the war. Before departing for Vietnam in 1967, Brownell had a number of friends in college who backed the commitment to the RVN. When he returned home in 1968, he found that most of this support had vanished. He regarded the students who still endorsed the American effort as "red-eyed fanatics" and concluded that "all the reasonable, coherent" supporters of the war effort "have given up the fight." He also found the war-weariness of the general public to be disheartening. "I failed to realize," he wrote in a letter to Ward, "that by now some 99% of the United States have become either totally apathetic toward Vietnam involvement or they have become distinctly hostile toward it."[4]

Besides being discouraged by popular resentment over the war, Brownell also was disturbed by what he called "a Machiavellian mass of maneuvering all directed towards bringing the American Friends under direct Vietnamese control."[5] Recalling this incident years later, Brownell claimed that a diplomat at the RVN's UN observer mission tried to dominate the AFV by promising the purchase of several thousand dollars worth of materials from the group without requiring their delivery. Given the AFV's troubled financial condition, Brownell found the offer tempting, but he made no commitment to accept it. He did not inform the board of directors of this proposition—partly from a sense of embarrassment and partly because of fears that such an action would rupture potentially useful ties with the Vietnamese. The official from the observer mission made repeated pledges of substantial sums of money, and Brownell began to find this pressure to be "a tad frightening." Anxious to escape this situation and frustrated with the AFV's lack of progress in dealing with public opinion, Brownell abruptly quit his job in the spring of 1969.[6]

The Vietnamese attempt to control the AFV was not the first time that the RVN's diplomats had tried to use the organization for their own purposes, but it represented their most serious effort to do so. Similar episodes had taken place in the Diem era when Nguyen Phu Duc, the first secretary of the RVN's Washington embassy, tried to give orders to AFV officers. Duc's heavy-handed behavior only antagonized the Americans, and the AFV's records indicate that other Vietnamese officials did not repeat Duc's mistakes. Hugh O'Neill nevertheless recalled that, when he became the AFV's executive director in 1966, he received a warning from William Henderson that "the American Friends was not acting on behalf of the Government of Vietnam and that it should be careful not to do anything that would make it look like that we were acting on their behalf in any way."[7] O'Neill himself had no trouble with Saigon's representatives, and William Ward, who headed the AFV during Brownell's brief tenure, also could not recall any difficulties. It seems that Brownell was the only AFV officer subjected to Vietnamese pressure, apparently because some of the RVN's diplomats saw him as a young and inexperienced man who could be easily influenced. Their attempt to manipulate Brownell failed, but it played a major role in prompting him to quit the AFV.[8]

Brownell's sudden departure left the AFV without anyone to administer its affairs. In July 1969, the board of directors moved to fill this gap by placing the management of the AFV in the hands of William Henderson, who had just opened a consulting firm. Upon accepting the responsibility, Henderson told the association's officers that the AFV had raised less than $8,000 in its latest fund-raising drive and that an attempt to keep it functioning would have to be reconsidered if the organization continued leading a "hand-to-mouth existence." With no one objecting to this advice, Henderson began supervising the AFV's activities and continued this work until the association's demise in 1975.[9]

Meanwhile, a new president, Richard M. Nixon, was working to end direct American participation in the Vietnam conflict. Nixon, who succeeded Johnson in January 1969, continued peace talks with the communists in Paris, but he tried to speed up the negotiations by authorizing his national security adviser, former Harvard academic Henry Kissinger, to hold clandestine meetings with DRV representatives. As these discussions took place, Nixon launched a "Vietnamization" program that involved the withdrawal of U.S. ground forces from Vietnam and their replacement by Vietnamese units with extensive aerial and logistic support from the Americans. This effort included providing the RVN's rulers with the funds and advice needed to implement land reform laws, rural reconstruction projects, and the Phoenix Program—a controversial campaign that tried to smash the NLF through the arrest or execution of communist agents. By the end of Nixon's first year in office, all of these projects were well under way, and Nixon, despite the vocal opposition of an ever larger antiwar movement, had convinced many Americans that he had formulated a policy that would lead to "peace with honor."[10]

The American Friends of Vietnam supported Nixon's policies as it had Johnson's, and it forged a new set of ties with the White House. The organization initially gained the administration's attention through the efforts of Frank Barnett, a close friend of Henderson and Trager who headed the National Strategy Information Center, a research and consulting group interested in defense and international affairs. Barnett mentioned the AFV in a letter to Charles Colson, a shrewd but unscrupulous assistant of Nixon's who dealt with private organizations like the AFV. In language that compared the AFV to a business firm, Barnett identified Henderson, Ward, and Trager as the AFV's key figures and encouraged Colson to establish a link with an association that "carries credibility with academics and journalists" and "is one of 6–8 corporations that merit the attention of those interested in a sophisticated and diversified investment strategy." Colson, who at the time had been worrying about dissident efforts to discredit the Vietnamization program, thanked Barnett for his advice in a reply written on January 16, 1970. He wrote that the AFV "sounds very good and I will add it to our inventory of assets," but added that he would not call for its help "until we have all our outside people lined up."[11]

The White House asked for the AFV's support a few weeks later when heavy fighting erupted in Laos. Although that country ostensibly had been accorded a neutral status by agreements reached in Geneva in 1962, it had actually been a battleground between the communist Pathet Lao, backed by North Vietnamese anxious to protect their infiltration routes to the South, and the Royal Lao Government (RLG), which allowed the Americans to bomb the communist supply lines. When the Pathet Lao staged a major offensive with considerable help from the North Vietnamese in early 1970, the RLG called for American air strikes in an effort to stop the communist drive. Nixon responded with attacks that included raids by B-52 heavy bombers. He announced his decision in a statement released on March 6, 1970, that accused the DRV and the Pathet Lao of violating the Geneva accords.[12]

Colson called the AFV that same day and asked the organization for its endorsement, which it gave. William Ward called Nixon's statement "a clear and appropriate warning to Hanoi that the United States is determined to resist this latest episode of Communist aggression in Southeast Asia."[13] The White House reacted to this gesture of support with delight. On a note attached to a collection of messages that included the AFV's announcement, an aide wrote, "The pay off!"[14] Colson himself expressed his own gratitude in a letter to Henderson. "We appreciated very much your quick response to our telephone request, and the very fine statement which you issued."[15] He also showed his appreciation by meeting with Ward and by making arrangements for briefings to be given to Ward, Henderson, and Trager at the State Department and at Kissinger's office.[16] A dramatic turn of events in Southeast Asia, however, soon demanded the complete attention of Colson and other White House staff members.

On March 18, 1970, a group of right-wing military officers overthrew Prince Norodom Sihanouk, Cambodia's chief of state. The new government, which was violently anti-Vietnamese, soon ordered the withdrawal of NLF and North Vietnamese units from Cambodian base camps built along the RVN border during Sihanouk's rule. This demand only triggered widespread fighting between battle-hardened Vietnamese formations and Cambodia's poorly trained army. The escalating violence presented the Americans with an opportunity to strike at strongholds that had troubled their forces for years. After weeks of heated debate among his advisers, Nixon sent U.S. troops into Cambodia. The decision triggered widespread protests across the country, especially on college campuses. Demonstrations at two universities, Kent State in Ohio and Jackson State in Mississippi, ended with the deaths of students shot down by police and National Guardsmen. As thousands of students protested, Congress took its own stand against the administration's policies. The Senate repealed the Gulf of Tonkin Resolution in June and also passed the Cooper-Church amendment, which threatened to cut off funds for American operations in Cambodia after June 30. These gestures were largely symbolic since Capitol Hill still approved appropriations for U.S. military forces in Indochina, but they signified a growing congressional impatience with the war that Nixon would find increasingly difficult to control in the years ahead.[17]

The AFV made no formal statement about the Cambodian invasion, but its continuing contacts with the White House indicate that it endorsed the administration's policy. The AFV officers tried to attract Washington's assistance by describing their work and plans, including the sponsorship of a journal and a conference concerning Vietnam. They confessed that the AFV had trouble raising "sufficient funds to augment our program," but ruled out the association's dissolution because "such a step might be interpreted as a vote of non-confidence in United States policy, and even in the concept of a free and independent Vietnam; and we are not prepared to admit this."[18] On one occasion, Henderson actually asked the White House to help the AFV carry out its activities, noting that the group "would be most grateful for your advice and assistance in their implementation."[19]

Some officials reacted sympathetically to the AFV's pleas, but they apparently did not secure the kind of help Johnson's aides had provided. After receiving a letter and résumé from Henderson, George T. Bell, one of Colson's assistants, forwarded the correspondence to William J. Baroody, the president of the conservative American Enterprise Institute. Bell called the AFV "a good group" and urged Baroody to get in touch with Henderson and "at least talk to them about their problems."[20] There is, however, no record of a response to this request in the Nixon archives, nor of any correspondence between the White House and the AFV after the summer of 1970.

The Nixon administration may have decided that backing the AFV may not have been a worthwhile endeavor. A set of notes in the White House files indicate that the association received "seed money" from Johnson that it "spent unwisely."[21] Moreover, the administration may have been uneasy about aiding a group that might not give unconditional support to Nixon's policies. In a conversation with Bell on August 17, 1970, Ward reported that "there are indications of some anti-Administration viewpoints" within the AFV, including "super-hawk opinion." He also noted misgivings of those "who feel the Administration is too preoccupied with military aspects" at the expense of such issues as pacification programs and the RVN's economic problems.[22]

The White House also gave far greater attention to the AFV's more prestigious counterpart—the Citizens Committee for Peace with Freedom in Vietnam. By having such well-known and distinguished members as President Truman, General Omar Bradley, and former secretary of state Dean Acheson, the Citizens Committee, unlike the AFV, was able to attract continuing national attention in periodically releasing policy papers supporting the administration.[23] Colson, who regarded the organization as "the most effective outside group to begin to counter the current anti-war campaign," proposed assisting the Citizens Committee by securing financial aid for it and assembling an administrative staff to supervise its activities. H. R. Haldeman, Nixon's chief of staff, approved these suggestions, and the president himself took steps to boost the association's standing. Nixon saw representatives from the Citizens Committee on three occasions in the fall of 1969 and the spring of 1970 and listened to their reports and advice.[24] At the last of these meetings, a week after the announcement of the Cambodian invasion, Nixon thanked the group's members for the support they had given and asked that they continue to help "in the fight to preserve America's role in the world."[25] With such attention being given to the Citizens Committee, the AFV fared poorly by comparison and received little in the way of substantial help from the White House.

Despite the difficulties in attracting government assistance, the AFV operated as effectively as could be expected at a time when popular enthusiasm for the war had vanished. It continued providing speakers for debates and discussions concerning Vietnam and distributing AFV brochures.[26] Its members occasionally disputed the antiwar opinions expressed in the media as well. After *New York Times* columnist Tom Wicker expressed doubts about Nixon's claims that a communist victory would lead to a massacre of Vietnamese anticommunists, William Ward sent a letter to the editor describing Wicker's views as "a futile and pathetic rationalization of the bloodbath potential in Vietnam if the North Vietnamese prevail."[27] Ward also appeared as a guest editorialist on the New York television affiliate of the Columbia Broadcasting System (CBS) to voice his "profound disagreement" with the station's opinion that Nixon's Vietnamization policy threatened "to fall short of thoroughly disengaging the country from the unsound position we have taken up in Vietnam and Southeast Asia."[28] Henderson, who drafted Ward's reply, expressed satisfaction after hearing that it had been "carried on a nationwide hook-up" in early January 1970. He called it a "useful effort" on which he would be willing to work again.[29]

The AFV focused much of its attention on reviving *Vietnam Perspectives*, unpublished since 1968 because of a shortage of funds. Henderson expressed a particularly strong desire to "resuscitate" the journal, and by 1971 he had raised enough money to begin printing another periodical.[30] The new magazine, *Southeast Asian Perspectives*, appeared in the form of brief monographs and ran forty to sixty pages. The articles in *Southeast Asian Perspectives* concentrated on the conflict in Indochina and expressed a strong anticommunist line. They generally backed the Nixon administration's Asian policy, although a few contributors voiced anxiety about Nixon's decision to open diplomatic contacts with the People's Republic of China in the summer of 1971.[31] Nine issues of *Southeast Asian Perspectives* were published before financial troubles brought about its demise.

The AFV's new journal appeared as direct American involvement in the war drew to a rapid close. U.S. troop strength in Vietnam, which had peaked at 543,400 during Nixon's first months in office, dropped to 47,000 by the summer of 1972 as Vietnamese units replaced the departing Americans.[32] The ARVN's ability to fight on its own faced a severe test when the communists launched a major offensive at the end of March 1972, but the attack eventually ground to a halt after Nixon ordered heavy air strikes against North Vietnamese and NLF formations in the South and communist supply lines in North Vietnam. Stalemate on the battlefield forced Washington and Hanoi to settle their differences at the negotiating table. By mid-October, the two sides hammered out a peace agreement that included provisions for a cease-fire, the withdrawal of American forces, and the framework for a settlement between the NLF and the Saigon regime. Plans for signing these accords, however, were abruptly upset by Nguyen Van Thieu, the RVN's president, who complained that he had been misinformed about the progress of the negotiations and that the terms of the agreement undermined the legitimacy of his government. Nixon himself had doubts about the settlement's ability to guarantee the RVN's survival, and he sent Henry Kissinger to Paris to start another round of peace talks with the North Vietnamese.[33]

Thieu denounced the accords in a speech on October 24, and two AFV officers quickly backed the Vietnamese president. In a telegram, Frank Trager and a conservative businessman named James Gerard told Thieu, "Millions of Americans support your brave stand in defense of your country." The two men declared that the "sacrifices of thousands of heroic Vietnamese and American soldiers must not be bartered away at the conference table."[34] The AFV's chairman, William Ward, later said Trager and Gerard had acted on their own and not on behalf of the AFV, but both men had identified themselves as members of the group, and the association consequently received a letter of appreciation from the RVN's Washington embassy. This note stated that Thieu had been "deeply touched by your expression of sympathy and support" and assured the AFV that "President Nguyen Van Thieu and . . . the South Vietnamese people are grateful for your gesture of solidarity in this crucial hour of our history."[35]

This exchange of messages between AFV officers and Saigon took place just before the beginning of a bitter round of peace negotiations in Paris. Kissinger presented several proposals for a revision of the accords, but Hanoi's diplomats, who had received assurances that the earlier settlement was acceptable, angrily accused the Americans of acting in bad faith. Desperate efforts to salvage the agreement failed when the talks came to an abrupt end in mid-December. Nixon decided to force the DRV back to the conference table by ordering a massive bombardment of North Vietnam. The air raids stirred up an international outcry against the United States, but the DRV did agree to a resumption of talks in January 1973. The two sides reached an agreement that differed little from the October agreement, although the document did include references to the separate status of South Vietnam. Thieu acquiesced after receiving letters from Nixon that promised a forceful American response to any communist violations of the armistice while warning that "the gravest consequences will ensue" if Saigon withheld its approval.[36] On January 23, 1973, representatives from the United States, the RVN, the DRV, and the NLF's political arm, the Provisional Revolutionary Government, initialed the Paris accords. Four days later, a cease-fire was declared in Vietnam and America's military participation in the Vietnam War came to an end.[37]

The armistice forced the AFV's leaders to question what role, if any, the organization could still play. The AFV had done little since the summer of 1971 except publish *Southeast Asian Perspectives*. When the Paris agreements were initialed, General Lansdale, who had retired from government service in 1968, proposed the creation of a private support association for the RVN on the assumption that the AFV had become "a defunct group."[38] The AFV had attempted a resumption of contacts with the White House in the autumn of 1972, but met with no success. In a reply to a letter from Ward about a possible AFV role in the postwar rehabilitation of Vietnam, John Holdridge, a White House staff member, wrote that an attempt to involve private organizations in a reconstruction program before the actual signing of a cease-fire would be "premature."[39]

William Henderson made another effort to revive the AFV's fortunes after the armistice. He proposed a new project after discussing the AFV's future with F. P. Serong, a retired Australian officer who provided military advice to Thieu. Serong, whom Henderson had met in Vietnam in early 1973, suggested that the AFV consider helping restore Vietnamese cultural sites near Hue or in assisting Vietnamese orphans, especially those fathered by Americans.⁴⁰ Henderson decided that the adoption project would have a greater appeal and turned to Harold Oram for advice on how to carry it out. Oram, who had not been active in the AFV's affairs since the mid-1960s, agreed to help but warned Henderson that the AFV needed to develop "a hard program that meets human needs" and that would receive the cooperation of the Saigon government.⁴¹

Henderson satisfied many of Oram's requirements by the autumn of 1973, but he failed to persuade the AFV's leadership to back the project. When he asked Serong for information on the situation in Saigon, the Australian replied that the Vietnamese had been considering legislation to facilitate the departure of orphans from Vietnam and that the AFV might be able to work with a relief organization operating in Saigon. Henderson also tried attracting the support of Nguyen Huu Chi, the head of the RVN's UN observer mission. In a memorandum to Chi on March 15, 1973, Henderson declared that the AFV would be able to survive only if it expanded "the basis of its hitherto largely political appeal to include broad humanitarian objectives as well." An adoption program, he told Chi, not only would "add an important humanitarian dimension" to the AFV's work but would strengthen its fund-raising potential, "thus enabling us to continue our activities in support of the Republic of Vietnam and its defense against Communist aggression."⁴² The Vietnamese responded favorably, and Henderson proposed what he considered a feasible project to the AFV's board of directors on October 2, 1973. The AFV's officers, however, turned down the program on the grounds that the organization lacked the resources needed to carry it out. "We took a look at it," Ward recalled, "and we said we don't even have enough money to put out our own magazine."⁴³

The rejection of Henderson's proposal reflected the continuing decline of the AFV's fortunes as the organization's activities ground to a halt and some of its members quit. At the meeting that saw the rejection of his adoption plan, Henderson announced the demise of *Southeast Asian Perspectives* because of inadequate funding.⁴⁴ The end of the publishing effort left the AFV with virtually nothing to do, and some officers, including the chairman, began leaving their posts. William Ward had been proud to be "associated with such an outstanding group of scholars," but preoccupation with business concerns and military duties prevented him from devoting any time to the AFV's affairs. He resigned in September 1974.[45] Despite such resignations, the AFV lingered on because it remained solvent and because the few active members thought the AFV's continued existence would at least signal American concern for the future of the Republic of Vietnam.[46]

Anxiety over the RVN's fate led to a final AFV campaign in late 1974. American forces had left Vietnam by April 1973, but the war raged on as the opposing sides, deeply suspicious of one another after years of bitter struggle, abandoned negotiations and sought military victory. Thieu launched a campaign to retake territory seized by communist troops, but, after a period of initial success, his forces faltered as casualties mounted. Moreover, they displayed little enthusiasm for a regime that failed to remedy deeply rooted economic and social inequalities that worsened as unemployment and inflation ravaged the RVN's economy. Developments in the United States compounded Thieu's difficulties. Nixon, whom Thieu regarded as a reliable protector, became increasingly preoccupied with his own political survival after some of his aides were implicated in a 1972 attempt to burglarize Democratic Party headquarters in Washington's Watergate apartment complex. Judicial and congressional investigations of the Watergate scandal made it evident that the president himself had been involved in efforts to cover up the crime. Nixon eventually resigned on August 9, 1974, when it became clear that he faced an impeachment trial.[47]

Nixon's successor, former Michigan congressman Gerald R. Ford, quickly assured Thieu, "The existing commitments this nation has made in the past are still valid and will be fully honored in my administration." This promise was challenged, however, by a Congress determined to exercise its foreign policy prerogatives.[48] Legislation passed in 1973 made America's reentry into the Vietnam conflict extremely unlikely because it banned military operations in Indochina and restricted the president's power to deploy American combat forces overseas. Moreover, Congress limited the amount of economic and military assistance to the RVN. The news of Nixon's downfall and the congressional aid cuts demoralized Thieu and his supporters, and many Vietnamese began wondering whether the regime's days were numbered.[49]

In a desperate effort to help the RVN, the AFV sponsored a support association called the Emergency Committee for a Free Vietnam. This group first met in New York on December 30, 1974, and drew up a plan of action for the coming months. Henderson and Trager got together with James C. Roberts, an officer of the American Conservative Union, as well as William Schneider from New York senator James Buckley's office, and conservative journalist John Chamberlain. The group also included Earl M. Kulp from AID, Mary

Temple from the Aspen Institute, and Leonard R. Sussman, the executive director of Freedom House. The participants elected Chamberlain and Trager as chairmen and placed the administration of the organization in Henderson's hands. The group's objective, they decided, should be the inauguration of an "educational campaign in behalf of supporting and fulfilling U.S. commitments to the Republic of Vietnam as part of the January 1973 truce negotiations."[50] This effort would feature the distribution of literature backing aid appropriations for the RVN, as well as promoting the Saigon regime in the media. Special attention would be paid to congressional representatives, and the Emergency Committee planned the creation of organizations in "key grass-roots locales" to sway opinion on Capitol Hill in favor of the RVN.[51]

Despite its ambitious character, this campaign, like many AFV projects, accomplished little. The group persuaded a few columnists to write pieces supporting the RVN and enlisted the support of a number of well-known Americans for any statements it released, but it met with little success in raising funds or in establishing a nationwide organization. Its most notable achievement seems to have been the publication of a pamphlet entitled "Perspective on Vietnam," which was distributed to every congressional representative in the winter of 1975. This brochure repeated the AFV's early claims that the plebiscite scheduled for 1956 "would have been a farce," that the RVN had been subjected to aggression from "a country very foreign to South Vietnam," and that America's abandonment of the South would be comparable to the appeasement of the Axis dictators in the 1930s. The pamphlet admitted that the United States had made serious mistakes in Vietnam and that the RVN faced grave political and social problems, but it affirmed, "Vietnam is still a far more healthy, egalitarian, and politically vibrant society than before America's role there." In order to save the RVN, the pamphlet asserted, "There would be no obligation—and no need—to send US troops back to Vietnam." Instead, the payment of $6 billion of American aid over a five-year period would ensure the RVN's survival. By spending this money, the brochure averred, "*America can preserve its record of never losing a war.*"[52]

As the Emergency Committee desperately tried generating support for the RVN, the Saigon government's position quickly deteriorated in the spring of 1975. Encouraged by reports of Thieu's growing difficulties, Hanoi's leaders had met in October 1974 and decided to launch a limited offensive in the South in order to set the stage for a decisive attack in 1976. Military operations in January and March 1975 led to the capture of cities in the RVN's mountain and border regions. Thieu, shaken by these defeats, ordered his army's abrupt withdrawal from the central highlands. This retreat, however, soon became a bloody and disorderly rout as the fleeing soldiers, frequently abandoned by their senior commanders, ran into a series of communist ambushes. The ARVN's disintegration in the central highlands was soon followed by the collapse of the RVN's northern provinces as thousands of panic-stricken soldiers and civilians fled before advancing North Vietnamese units. By the end of March, Thieu had lost control of nearly two-thirds of the RVN's territory and millions of its citizens. Surprised and elated by their stunning victories, the DRV's leadership decided to take Saigon before the rainy season began in May. They named the assault on the southern capital after their revered leader—Ho Chi Minh—who had died in 1969.[53]

Alarmed by the sudden collapse of Saigon's forces, the Emergency Committee for a Free Vietnam made a desperate but feeble attempt to create public pressures for saving the Republic of Vietnam. The group arranged for the publication of a full-page advertisement in the March 21 edition of the *Washington Post*, and printed a smaller piece in the *New York Times* a month later. These ads featured the signatures of such prominent figures as William F. Buckley, Paul Nitze, Edward Teller, Clare Booth Luce, Walter Judd, Eugene Rostow, and Admiral Elmo N. Zumwalt. The names of former or active AFV members also appeared, including Murray Baron, Wesley Fishel, William Henderson, I. Milton Sacks, and Frank Trager.[54]

Pleading for increased assistance to the RVN, the advertisements condemned the communists for "flagrantly" violating the Paris accords. America's failure to help the RVN would encourage aggressive communist policies and "create a world situation so perilous that we would have to increase massively our already heavy defense expenditures."[55] Moreover, the United States had a "moral commitment" to millions of Vietnamese whose lives would be endangered by the North's victory. The newspaper statements praised the assistance given to refugees fleeing from the fighting, but added, "*The ultimate humanitarian act is sufficient U.S. military and economic aid to the South Vietnamese so they can maintain their freedom.*" Referring to the approaching bicentennial celebration of America's independence, one advertisement asked, "As we approach our 200th anniversary, do we want to mark that holiday by denying the South Vietnamese the same freedom—not for a lack of will on their part, but through a lack of adequate support on our part?"[56]

Emergency Committee members were also involved in other activities, which had no influence on a public weary of the war. In a letter to former congressman Walter Judd, Frank Trager referred to two demonstrations staged on behalf of the RVN in Washington, but it is unclear what role, if any, the Emergency Committee played in organizing them. A newspaper account of one of the rallies identified most of its 600 participants as "youthful followers of Korean evangelist Sun Myung Moon" and made no reference to the Emergency Committee.[57] Trager also mentioned efforts to arrange a meeting between the AFV and President Ford in an attempt "to strengthen his very weak hand" in obtaining congressional appropriations for the RVN. The AFV's archives contain the draft of a note from Trager to Ford asking the president to see a delegation from the Emergency Committee, but neither the records of the AFV nor the Ford presidential library indicate that such an interview took place. Although sympathetic to the RVN's plight, Ford, unlike his two predecessors, expressed no strong desire to stake the future of his presidency on the conflict in Vietnam. He may not have wanted to associate himself with a group so fervently committed to Saigon's survival.[58]

The Emergency Committee's pleas on behalf of the RVN attracted sympathetic responses from some American citizens who had seen its advertisements, but little else. One correspondent wrote that he had been "appalled" by America's "lack of concern" for the South Vietnamese. Another lamented, "I do not know that we can go into the year of our bicentennial with our heads held high if we take it upon ourselves to act first as protector, then as policemen, judge, jury and executioner in condemning nations to death by refusing to help them defend themselves."[59] The Emergency Committee also received a reply that reflected the public's general attitude toward the war. The author of the letter, Senator Harrison A. Williams of New Jersey, had been one of the first members of the AFV's national committee in the mid-1950s. As Saigon's position crumbled in 1975, however, he opposed continued military assistance to the RVN. Williams wrote that he had drafted legislation to provide humanitarian aid to the Vietnamese, but added, "We must end the use of American resources to continue the bloodshed." He also denied charges that congressional cutbacks in appropriations had been responsible for the South's troubles and ascribed Saigon's collapse to "poor leadership, the inability to mobilize the population, and a lack of determination."[60]

Williams's letter reflected the nation's determination to end America's involvement in a war that was drawing rapidly to a close. A Gallup poll taken in late April reported that, while 56 percent of the people responding favored economic and humanitarian assistance to the RVN, 78 percent opposed the approval of any military aid.[61] When Ford asked a joint session of Congress on April 10 to provide "swift and adequate" help for the RVN, lawmakers authorized the use of American troops to assist in the evacuation of Americans and Vietnamese from Saigon, but they refused to set aside appropriations for the RVN's armed forces.[62] The war in Vietnam continued with unabated fury as American politicians debated the aid issue. ARVN units briefly rallied and halted the communist advance at Xuan Loc, a town northeast of Saigon, but they could only delay, not avert, the RVN's defeat. On April 21, Nguyen Van Thieu announced his resignation in a rambling and bitter speech denouncing the Americans for their failure to provide the aid they had promised. Thieu's vice president, an honest but sickly and ineffectual figure named Tran Van Huong, succeeded Thieu but remained in office for only a week. In a last-minute effort to negotiate an end to the conflict, Huong turned power over to Duong Van Minh, the senior general in the plot against Diem. By then, however, the communists demanded nothing less than the RVN's surrender.[63]

As Saigon's position crumbled, thousands of Americans and Vietnamese fled the country. In the last two days of the war, American helicopters landed directly in Saigon and flew more than 6,000 Vietnamese and 1,300 Americans out of the city. This final evacuation took place under increasingly chaotic conditions as swarms of Vietnamese, terrified at the prospect of communist reprisals, besieged the U.S. embassy and frantically begged the Americans to evacuate them. Recalling these events a few years later, journalist and former AFV member Robert Shaplen wrote, "The looks of contempt and hatred as well as frenzy on the faces of those Vietnamese that last morning still haunt me."[64] The last American helicopter left Saigon early on the morning of April 30; within a few hours, communist tanks and troops had entered the heart of the city. When the victors arrived at the presidential palace, they found that Minh and his cabinet had gathered to meet them in one of its reception rooms. Minh told them that he had been waiting impatiently to turn power over to them, but a communist officer delivered a retort that effectively served as the epitaph of the Republic of Vietnam. "The former administration has collapsed. All power has passed into the hands of the revolution," he told Minh. "You cannot hand over what you no longer have."[65]

After placing its advertisement in the April 21 edition of the *New York Times*, the Emergency Committee for a Free Vietnam did virtually nothing else in the last days of the war. David Martin, a Senate staff member who had been associated with the AFV since its creation in 1955, mentioned one event, a dinner the Vietnamese embassy hosted for the RVN's American sympathizers. In an April 28 letter to Henderson, Martin called the meal "a sad occasion, but somehow dramatically appropriate before the curtain was rung down." He also expressed pride in the Emergency Committee's attempt to generate support for the RVN. "Historians of the future," he wrote, "will at least find some small record in the Post and the Times, proving that were [there?] were some Americans who cared, and who made an effort."66 With the RVN's surrender on April 30, the work of the Emergency Committee, and the AFV, came to an end. An AFV member wrote to Henderson a week after Saigon's fall and remarked that he understood that the "Amer[ican] Friends of Vietnam is dissolving."67 The American Friends of Vietnam, like the Vietnamese state it so fervently supported, no longer existed.

chapter 11
Conclusion

For nearly two decades, the American Friends of Vietnam pursued the goal of securing American support for an anticommunist state in Vietnam. Describing the AFV's purpose in 1956, Harold Oram declared, "My interest in the American Friends of Vietnam is in the creation of a Committee representing people who will unite on the necessity for the defense of Vietnam against any further Communist aggression."[1] The organization's persistent devotion to this objective could be seen almost twenty years later. As the Saigon regime faced imminent collapse, the AFV's last public statement asserted, "Vietnam is ... calling us to enable her people, not the communists, to decide their future."[2] The association consistently followed its aim by trying to convince politicians, officials, and journalists that the Republic of Vietnam deserved America's backing. The South Vietnamese government, they argued, wanted to build a nation free from communist and colonial rule, and America could, and should, help them in this endeavor.

The United States gradually embarked on a long and costly effort to ensure the RVN's survival, but the AFV played a marginal role, at best, in bringing about this intervention. When it drew a favorable picture of Ngo Dinh Diem's regime in the 1950s, the AFV enjoyed considerable attention from prominent figures in the government and the media. The group nevertheless spent much of its time addressing an audience that already accepted the independence of South Vietnam as a vital American interest. As a result, much of the AFV's work amounted, as one historian has noted, to little more than "preaching to the converted."[3] By the time a revived communist insurgency threatened the Saigon government in the early 1960s, the AFV was divided between supporters and critics of Diem. Their bitter disagreements prevented the organization from exerting any influence at a time when the Kennedy administration was making substantial new commitments to the Republic of Vietnam. Diem's overthrow in 1963 put an end to the AFV's internal disputes, and its officers quickly backed Lyndon Johnson's decisions to use American military power to avert a communist victory in Vietnam. The association's organizational and financial weaknesses, however, prevented it from acting as an effective advocate of administration policy, and the AFV became little more than an occasionally useful, but generally ineffectual, ally of the White House.

Because the AFV so frequently endorsed American actions in Vietnam, there has been speculation that the organization may have been created or manipulated by the executive branch or its security agencies. In his study of the Vietnam War, William Conrad Gibbons writes, "It is reasonable to assume that the U.S. Government was indirectly if not directly involved" in the AFV's formation.[4] Evidence supporting this conjecture appears in a diary entry Joseph Buttinger made in the autumn of 1954. While visiting Saigon, Buttinger spoke to a "Mr. X" who recounted a talk he had with an American officer about the need to swing American public opinion in Diem's favor. During the conversation, a suggestion was made that a "Committee of Friends of Vietnam" be established as a means of helping Diem.[5] Unfortunately, Buttinger's journal provides no clue about the identities of "Mr. X" or the American official with whom he spoke. Moreover, the available written record contains no further reference to a "Friends of Vietnam" association until Buttinger sent a letter to Oram in the spring of 1955 authorizing the creation of the AFV. Neither this note nor any subsequent documentary evidence indicates government involvement in the AFV's foundation, even though the original proposal may have come from a U.S. officer in Saigon.

Written records and oral recollections from the 1950s indicate that, while the AFV collaborated with the Eisenhower administration and occasionally acted on the suggestions of its officials, it did not serve as a front for the government in its early years. The same cannot be said of the AFV in the 1960s. Two former members of the group, Gary MacEoin and Supreme Court Justice William O. Douglas, claimed that the CIA began influencing the group during this period. MacEoin, a Catholic journalist and a member of the AFV's executive committee for nearly a decade, said that when the AFV won its tax-exempt status in 1960, "the whole atmosphere changed and money began to pour out of the ceiling."[6] He believed that this development signaled an effort by the CIA to manipulate the AFV in an attempt to advance the CIA's "information-gathering and opinion influencing strategy" throughout the world.[7] In MacEoin's opinion, this CIA campaign succeeded, and the AFV "was no longer a group of concerned citizens but a tool of U.S. policy."[8]

Douglas also made allegations about CIA infiltration of the American Friends of Vietnam. In the spring of 1968, the justice received a letter from a lawyer named Frazier T. Woolard, who asked about possible government or CIA involvement in the establishment of the AFV. Douglas replied that, while he doubted that the CIA played any role in creating the AFV, the agency "later appeared to be having a lot to do with it which led me to resign from the committee."[9] Woolard repeated Douglas's statement in correspondence with the AFV. When the association asked Douglas if he had actually made this assertion, the justice replied, "I resigned after being convinced that the CIA had fastened itself onto our vitals."[10]

Other incidents or threads of circumstantial evidence point to government involvement in the AFV's affairs. The CIA had covertly aided several organizations in the 1950s and 1960s, and some of the groups with which the AFV worked, including the Asia Foundation, the National Student Association, and the United States Youth Council, received agency funds. The CIA also had assisted the firm of Frederick A. Praeger, a publishing house that printed the works of AFV members, including Buttinger, Frank Trager, and George Tanham, in putting out studies concerning communist regimes and Third World trouble spots.[11] Some of the AFV's officers had close ties with Washington as government consultants and advisers, especially Fishel, Trager, and Tanham. Finally, there were occasions when the AFV itself sought and received assistance from the White House in obtaining needed funds. The Johnson administration in 1965 secured donations from the president's campaign contributors, and although the Nixon White House apparently didn't give the AFV any money, some of Nixon's advisers did show an interest in aiding the group.

Despite such indications of government involvement with the AFV's work, it is extremely difficult to prove that efforts were made to control the AFV. As MacEoin claimed, the AFV did receive a number of large donations after it won tax-exempt status in 1960, but these gifts took the form of medical and educational supplies, which Oram said could be easily obtained from companies trying to dispose of old or excess stock.[12] Although the AFV received numerous contributions of this sort, its cash income steadily declined until the organization suspended its operations for several months in 1964. Moreover, the early 1960s marked a low point in the AFV's political activity, since the association's leadership bitterly disagreed about supporting Diem and the group could work effectively only in obtaining humanitarian assistance for the RVN.

There are also problems with Douglas's allegations, since he made them three years after leaving the AFV and not when he quit the group. Correspondence at the time of his departure in the spring of 1965 indicates that he withdrew because of his unhappiness over the AFV's endorsement of Johnson's bombing of North Vietnam; it makes no reference to the CIA. The justice's secretary noted that an AFV statement "doesn't seem to be what you believe in as far as Viet Nam policy goes," and Douglas instructed her to draft his letter of resignation.[13] Writing to an opponent of the war a few weeks later, Douglas declared that he asked the AFV to remove his name from its letterhead "inasmuch as I disagree with their present policies."[14] None of this material discusses CIA activity and it is not clear why Douglas later claimed that the agency had penetrated the AFV. It is possible that he found out about the financial help that the White House had given the AFV and concluded that this was a CIA operation, especially since some of the officials involved, such as Chester Cooper, had served in the agency.

Two other difficulties arise in trying to determine whether the executive branch made attempts to use the AFV. One is that officers far more active in the AFV than either Douglas or MacEoin asserted that the association had no government ties at all.[15] These individuals, of course, may be trying to deny that such connections ever existed, but they nevertheless had a far better knowledge about the AFV's work than either Douglas or MacEoin. The second problem is that the CIA itself claims that it has no files on the American Friends of Vietnam.[16] The most that can be said at this point is that, although the government was interested in the AFV's activities, there is no solid evidence that it penetrated or controlled the organization.

Questions also can be raised about the extent to which the Saigon regime may have shaped the AFV's policies. The association's objective of winning U.S. support for the Republic of Vietnam would have made it receptive to Vietnamese suggestions, and some AFV projects, such as the business investment and educational assistance programs, were inspired, in part, by requests from Vietnam. Saigon also was able to exert its influence through its public relations representatives, Harold Oram and Gilbert Jonas, who served as AFV officers. The Oram firm encouraged the AFV to try to attract American businesses to Vietnam and to highlight South Vietnam's economic and social progress. It also asked the editors of newspapers and magazines to publish articles or letters by AFV members, and, in the case of General O'Daniel, Oram and Jonas wrote the articles themselves. Finally, the company, if it wished to, could block activities that might offend the Vietnamese. In a memorandum discussing a potentially controversial symposium in the early 1960s, Jonas told Oram that "without the full-scale cooperation and participation of our firm, it would be virtually impossible" for the AFV to hold the meeting.[17]

Some of the AFV's critics have implied that the presence of Jonas and Oram in the AFV compromised the organization's independence, but while the influence of the two men cannot be denied, it was limited by various factors.[18] Neither Jonas nor Oram concealed his ties to the Vietnamese government, and the AFV's board members, some of whom had helped Oram secure his contract with Diem, were well aware that the two men represented the RVN. The AFV's executive committee certainly accepted proposals by Oram and Jonas, but it also approved the suggestions of other officers. Furthermore, an examination of records from 1955 until 1961, the years that Oram's firm worked for the RVN, indicates that few AFV members objected to decisions reached by the group's leadership. If they did so, they made no charges of manipulation by the Vietnamese government. In assessing the influence that Oram or Jonas exercised over the AFV's affairs, it should be remembered that all of the AFV's leaders were committed to the survival of the South Vietnamese state and that they would have been receptive to any suggestion, no matter its source, that promised to further this goal.

Even a determined effort by Saigon to control the AFV would have been greatly complicated by the behavior of the RVN's own diplomats. Jonas once referred to the Vietnamese embassy as the "controlling agent" of the Oram firm's work, but he complained that its instructions often "have never arrived or they have come too late to be of use." He noted that this problem had grown worse as Ambassador Tran Van Chuong gave verbal, and subsequently untraceable, orders that actually prevented the company from responding to reports describing the Diem regime's troubles.[19] These difficulties were compounded by limited funds, a small and undertrained embassy staff, and an absence of up-to-date information about developments in Vietnam. In early 1961, Jonas told Wolf Ladejinsky, "I am working from a crystal ball and an ouiji [sic] board to ascertain what has been going on in Viet Nam for the past year."[20] Moreover, other embassy officers, particularly an official named Nguyen Phu Duc, seemed to be operating at cross-purposes with Chuong. Jonas later speculated that Duc "worked for some other power source, probably Nhu."[21] Instead of enabling their government to influence the activities of its U.S. supporters, South Vietnam's representatives undermined its position by undercutting the efforts of the Americans.

The AFV's relationship with the Vietnamese became much less convoluted after the Diem regime's collapse in 1963, but there is little evidence that suggests the RVN's representatives made a serious effort to shape the policies of the AFV. The ambassadors with whom the AFV worked most frequently after 1963, Vu Van Thai and Bui Diem, had extensive contacts with Americans before coming to Washington, and their experiences may have convinced them that any attempt to control the AFV could very well backfire. They seem to have confined themselves to expressions of approval of the group's programs and requests that AFV members present the South's case to officials and congressional representatives in Washington. The one apparent occasion when some of the RVN's diplomats tried to exploit the group, the effort to buy large quantities of materials from William Brownell, stands out as an isolated episode in which a few Vietnamese apparently hoped they could manipulate an inexperienced AFV officer.

The AFV's willingness to collaborate with Vietnamese diplomats and to promote the RVN's interests occasionally has invited comparison with another group that championed an anticommunist regime in Asia—the China Lobby. The AFV certainly had common bonds with Nationalist China's advocates, and a few of its members, including Murray Baron, Christopher Emmet, and Harold Oram, worked with some of the committees or publishing ventures that constituted the China Lobby. Its promotion of the accomplishments of Diem echoed a tactic the Republic of China's supporters had employed years before by praising Chiang Kai-shek. The AFV and the China Lobby encountered similar problems as well. There were times when Chinese in the Kuomintang's embassy in Washington, like Chuong and Duc in the late 1950s and early 1960s, worked at cross-purposes with one another or the government they represented.[22]

Significant differences, however, also can be found between the AFV and the China Lobby. The attitudes they adopted toward the regimes they supported is one important contrast. Although it shared the China Lobby's commitment to the survival of an anticommunist state, the AFV did not identify that government's future with the man who led it. Many of the AFV's officers held more liberal views than the China Lobby's membership; they actually expected Diem to pursue enlightened social and economic policies. When he failed to do this, they concluded that his behavior only strengthened the communists by antagonizing the RVN's populace, and they firmly, if reluctantly, turned against him. The AFV's members continued to act as advocates for the RVN after Diem's downfall, but they never again placed excessive hopes on the South's leaders after their disillusioning experiences with Diem.

The AFV differed with the China Lobby not only in its stance toward the regime it backed, but also in its ability to shape American policy in Asia. The association was not as well organized or financed as some of the groups with ties to the China Lobby. It therefore faced greater difficulty in exercising a strong voice in public discussion concerning Vietnam. AFV views did receive a sympathetic hearing in Washington, but this was because U.S. officials already shared the AFV's conviction that South Vietnam's independence represented a vital American interest. Since the AFV had little trouble in pleading the RVN's case, it felt no need to resort to the strident rhetoric and pressure tactics that so often characterized the China Lobby. Unlike a pressure group that harshly condemned "traitors in . . . the government" for Washington's reluctance to assist an Asian ally and which eventually intimidated numerous figures in American public life, the AFV usually collaborated with the government and supported and defended its policies.[23]

Despite such major differences, both the AFV and the China Lobby subscribed to a set of assumptions that governed the thinking of many Americans concerned with Asian affairs. They saw Marxism as an "alien Communist creed" promoted by aggressive powers like the Soviet Union and rejected by the peoples of Asia.[24] America could help the Asians resist communism by backing anticommunist nationalists with the "force of American diplomacy and political intervention."[25] This assistance, the AFV believed, not only would safeguard Asia from communist domination but would contribute to political and economic development and transform countries like Vietnam into "a showcase for democracy in Southeast Asia."[26] Finally, America's involvement in Asia would benefit not only the societies of the region but the United States itself by presenting the nation with a challenge that would renew its spirit and its sense of purpose, a sentiment Leo Cherne expressed when he voiced the hope that the "healthy aspiration of the freedom-loving American liberal and conservative for liberty, independence and a bright economic future may yet be born in Vietnam."[27]

The experience in Vietnam made it painfully clear, however, that the premises guiding American actions in that country were fundamentally, and tragically, flawed. Despite its European origins, communism was not seen as an "alien" creed by many Vietnamese; Ho Chi Minh and his followers adapted it to suit their needs. Marxist doctrine provided the Vietnamese with the strength and cohesion needed to resist foreign rule. It also served as a compelling political and moral alternative to a Confucian worldview shattered by the colonial experience. For a number of Vietnamese, Frances Fitzgerald writes, communism "showed them the way back to many of the traditional values and a way forward to the optimism of the West—to the belief in change as progress and the power of the small people," and it therefore found a receptive audience in Vietnam.[28]

Ho's opponents, on the other hand, never developed an ideology or the unity needed to defeat him. Many Vietnamese fervently opposed communism, but this sentiment did not serve as an adequate basis for cooperation among such diverse sects and factions as the Cao Dai, Catholics, Dai Viet parties, and Buddhist associations. Moreover, Saigon's rulers, whom the Americans regarded as the most suitable candidates for achieving this unity, did virtually nothing to bring these various elements of Vietnamese society together. Diem, despite his verbal commitment to creating a modern and democratic nation, tried to govern the RVN as a traditional Confucian ruler with the help of his family, a policy that turned virtually every group in South Vietnam against his regime. His successors, who tried to confront a rapidly growing insurgency in the South while protecting themselves from the intrigues of nominal friends and colleagues, proved themselves to be no more successful. American attempts to unify the Vietnamese yielded meager results. The Americans often found, to their dismay, that the Vietnamese regarded such actions as heavy-handed foreign interference in Vietnam's affairs.

The Americans discovered not only that their effort to influence Vietnam's future would end in failure, but that its consequences would be exactly the opposite of those for which they had hoped. Instead of creating a "showcase of democracy in Southeast Asia," the United States vainly propped up a series of authoritarian regimes in its struggle against the communists. Vietnam did not become Asia's "single economic and political paradise" under American tutelage, but an impoverished country battered by years of savage fighting.[29] America's entanglement in Vietnam's affairs did not lead to America's spiritual renewal, but to a harrowing ordeal that divided the nation and shattered its confidence. By the time the war reached its ignominious conclusion in 1975, many Americans had concluded that the Vietnam experience not only had shaken America's spirit, but had threatened to destroy its soul.

appendix
Officers of the AFV

1956

General William J. Donovan, Honorary Chairman
General John W. O'Daniel, National Chairman
Joseph Buttinger, Vice Chairman
Dr. M. L. Anson, Treasurer
Angier Biddle Duke, Chairman, Executive Committee

Executive Committee Members:
Admiral Richard E. Byrd	Elliott H. Newcomb
Leo Cherne	Harold L. Oram
Christopher Emmet	I. Milton Sacks
Wesley R. Fishel	Richard R. Salzmann
Alfred Katz	Sol Sanders
Gary MacEoin	William vanden Heuvel
Norbert Muhlen	

Eighty national committee members.

Source: Letter, Angier Biddle Duke to John F. Kennedy, April 25, 1956, Box 12, Theodore Sorenson Papers, John F. Kennedy Presidential Library, Dorchester, Mass.

1961

General John W. O'Daniel, Chairman
Joseph Buttinger, Chairman, Executive Committee
Elliott H. Newcomb, Treasurer
Louis Andreatta, Executive Secretary

Executive Committee Members:
Angier Biddle Duke	Gilbert Jonas
Christopher Emmet	Franklin J. Leerburger
Wesley R. Fishel	Diana N. Lockard
Monsignor Joseph J. Harnett	Gary MacEoin
William Henderson	Frank Trager
James A. Jacobson	William vanden Heuvel

Ninety-four national committee members (a partial listing).

Source: Form letter signed by John W. O'Daniel, June 16, 1961, Wesley R. Fishel Papers, University Archives and Historical Collections, Michigan State University, East Lansing, Mich.

1966

Henry Cabot Lodge, Honorary Chairman
General Maxwell D. Taylor, Honorary Chairman
Wesley R. Fishel, Chairman
Edmund A. Gullion, Vice Chairman
William Henderson, Vice Chairman
George K. Tanham, Vice Chairman
George E. Taylor, Vice Chairman
Robert A. Scalapino, Vice Chairman
Frank N. Trager, Treasurer
Marjorie Normand, Secretary

Board of Directors:
Charles T. R. Bohannon
Leo Cherne
Christopher Emmet
Arthur Z. Gardiner
Monsignor Joseph J. Harnett
Roger Hilsman
Amrom H. Katz
Wolf Ladejinsky
Harold L. Oram
Rufus C. Phillips
I. Milton Sacks
Robert Shaplen
Gerald Steibel
Kenneth T. Young

Fifty-one national committee members.

Source: Memorandum, Anne Henehan to Gilbert Jonas, May 6, 1966, Gilbert A. Jonas Papers, University Archives and Historical Collections, Michigan State University, East Lansing, Mich.

1971

Henry Cabot Lodge, Honorary Chairman
General Maxwell D. Taylor, Honorary Chairman
William F. Ward, National Chairman
Edmund A. Gullion, Vice Chairman
Robert A. Scalapino, Vice Chairman
George E. Taylor, Vice Chairman
Frank N. Trager, Treasurer
Gerald Steibel, Secretary

Board of Directors:
Joseph D. Ardleigh
Murray Baron
Leo Cherne
Hugh B. O'Neill
Rufus C. Phillips
I. Milton Sacks

Christopher Emmet Robert Shaplen
Monsignor Joseph J. Harnett George K. Tanham
Amrom H. Katz

Thirty-four national committee members (a partial listing).

Source: Memorandum, William F. Ward to board of directors, January 20, 1971, Records of the American Friends of Vietnam, Archive of the Vietnam Conflict, Texas Tech University, Lubbock, Tex.

notes

Abbreviations

The following abbreviations are used in the notes.

AFV—American Friends of Vietnam
CEC—Christopher Emmet Collection, Hoover Institution Archives, Stanford, Calif.
DDE—Dwight D. Eisenhower Presidential Library, Abilene, Kans.
ELC—Edward G. Lansdale Collection, Hoover Institution Archives, Stanford, Calif.
FO—Foreign Office, Great Britain, London, England
FRUS—Foreign Relations of the United States, U.S. Department of State, Washington, D.C.
GJP—Gilbert Jonas Papers, University Archives and Historical Collections, Michigan State University, East Lansing, Mich.
GRF—Gerald Ford Presidential Library, Ann Arbor, Mich.
HOP—Harold Oram Papers, Special Collections and Archives, Indiana University/Purdue University at Indianapolis, Indianapolis, Ind.
JBP—Joseph Buttinger Papers, Harvard-Yenching Library, Harvard University, Cambridge, Mass.
JFDOHP—John Foster Dulles Oral History Project, Seeley Mudd Manuscript Library, Princeton, N.J.
JFDP—John Foster Dulles Papers, Seeley Mudd Manuscript Library, Princeton, N.J.
JFK—John F. Kennedy Presidential Library, Dorchester, Mass.
JFKOHP—John F. Kennedy Oral History Program, John F. Kennedy Presidential Library, Dorchester, Mass.
JHP—Monsignor Joseph Harnett Papers, University of Notre Dame Archives, South Bend, Ind.
JODP—John O'Daniel Papers, United States Army Military History Institute, Carlisle Barracks, Carlisle, Pa.
JTP—James C. Thompson Papers, John F. Kennedy Presidential Library, Dorchester, Mass.
LBJ—Lyndon B. Johnson Presidential Library, Austin, Tex.
LC—Library of Congress
MSUVP—Michigan State University Vietnam Project, University Archives and Historical Collections, Michigan State University, East Lansing, Mich.
NA—National Archives
NP—Nixon Materials Project, National Archives, Alexandria, Va.
NSA—National Security Archives, Washington, D.C.

NTP—Norman Thomas Papers, Rare Books and Manuscripts Division, New York Public Library, Astor, Lenox and Tilden Foundations, New York, N.Y.
PRO—Public Record Office, London, England
RAFV—American Friends of Vietnam, Records, Archive of the Vietnam Conflict, Texas Tech University, Lubbock, Tex.
RG—Record Group
SWC—Samuel T. Williams Collection, Hoover Institution Archives. A separate collection at the United States Army Military History Institute is cited as SWP, USAMHI.
USAMHI—United States Army Military History Institute, Carlisle Barracks, Carlisle, Pa.
WFP—Wesley Fishel Papers, University Archives and Historical Collections, Michigan State University, East Lansing, Mich.
WJDP—William J. Donovan Papers, United States Army Military History Institute, Carlisle Barracks, Carlisle, Pa.
WODP—William O. Douglas Papers, Library of Congress, Washington, D.C.

Preface

1. Scheer and Hinckle, "Vietnam Lobby," 32.
2. Scheer, "Leo Cherne," 16.
3. Scheer, *United States Involved in Vietnam*, 43. Similar attacks appeared in Thong, "'Greatest Little Man,'" 142; Z [pseud.], "War in Vietnam," 22; and du Berrier, *Background to Betrayal*, 146–47, 198–200, and 211–12.
4. Discussions of the AFV which virtually repeat the early claims about its influence can be found in Boettcher, *Vietnam*, 107–9; Aronson, *Press and the Cold War*, 182–91; and Freeman, "American Friends of Vietnam," 18–19.
5. See, for example, Herring, *America's Longest War*, 49–50, and Gibbons, *U.S. Government and the Vietnam War*, 1:261–62.
6. Gibbons, *U.S. Government and the Vietnam War*, 1:303; 3:265–66; Kahin, *Intervention*, 80; and Small, *Johnson, Nixon, and the Doves*, 45–48.
7. Cooper, *Lost Crusade*, 120–21. See also Karnow, *Vietnam*, 218, and Buttinger, *Dragon Embattled*, 2:847–50.
8. Buttinger, *Dragon Embattled*, 2:1129, n. 16, and Buttinger, *Vietnam: Tragedy*, 50.
9. Herring, *America's Longest War*, 57.
10. Joseph Buttinger to Hanne Benzione, December 4, 1961, JBP. Disagreement with the term "Vietnam lobby" can also be found in "Notes on Scheer's *Ramparts* Article," July 1965, RAFV.
11. Memorandum, Buttinger to the Executive Committee of the American Friends of Vietnam, November 3, 1958, WFP.
12. Some of the characteristics of lobbying groups are outlined in Cohen, *Political Process and Foreign Policy*, 94–104; Turner, "How Pressure Groups Operate," 63–72; and Schlozman and Tierney, *Organized Interests and American Democracy*.
13. Buttinger, *Dragon Embattled*, 2:927.
14. Letter, Paul Kattenburg to the author, February 18, 1992.

Chapter 1

1. Warner, *Last Confucian*, 90.

2. Biographical information on Diem can be found in ibid., 84–90; Buttinger, *Dragon Embattled*, 2:1252–57; Shaplen, *Lost Revolution*, 104–13; and Fall, *Two Vietnams*, 234–53. So far, the only book-length biography of Diem is Bouscaren's adulatory *Last of the Mandarins*.

3. Karnow, *Vietnam*, 217; Buttinger, *Dragon Embattled*, 1:289–90 and 2:1255; and Fall, *Two Vietnams*, 239–40. The American legation in Saigon referred to a French police report that cited Viet Minh orders to kill Diem "at any cost" in a cable sent to the State Department. See telegram, Donald Heath to Dean Acheson, July 28, 1950, Box 3667, RG 59, NA. There were times when Diem expressed his fears of assassination to American officials. See memorandum of conversation with Mr. Ngo Dinh Diem, July 26, 1951, Box 3670; and letter, William Gibson to Heath, September 23, 1952, Southeast Asian Affairs, Subject File, 1950–1956, Box 5, RG 59, NA.

4. Accounts and analyses of early American involvement in Vietnam can be found in Herring, *America's Longest War*, 3–15; Cooper, *Lost Crusade*, 18–52; Gibbons, *U.S. Government and the Vietnam War*, 1:1–86; Gardner, *Approaching Vietnam*, 21–87; and *Pentagon Papers*, 1:1–32.

5. Telegram, Donald Heath to Dean Acheson, July 28, 1950, Box 3667, RG 59, NA; and telegram, Edmund A. Gullion to Acheson, June 23, 1950, *FRUS, 1950*, 6:829.

6. Telegrams, Charles N. Spinks to State Department, September 2, 1950, and August 24, 1950, Box 3667, RG 59, NA.

7. Letter, Dallas M. Coors to F. M. Berg, September 22, 1950, and memorandum, Rusk to Simmons, September 8, 1950, Box 10, Records of Philippine and Southeast Asian Affairs, Lot 54D190, RG 59, NA.

8. Telegram, James R. Webb to Donald Heath, September 28, 1950, *FRUS, 1950*, 6:886. The record of another meeting with Diem and Thuc can be found in a memorandum, C. J. Little to Shannon McCune, September 13, 1950, Box 10, Lot 54D190, RG 59, NA.

9. Buttinger, *Dragon Embattled*, 1:847, and memoranda of conversation with Diem, January 15, 1951, Box 3669, RG 59, NA.

10. Telegram, Dean Acheson to Donald Heath, January 16, 1951, *FRUS, 1951*, 6:348.

11. Memorandum of conversation with Diem, July 26, 1951, Box 3670, RG 59, NA.

12. Letter, Peter White to the author, May 9, 1989.

13. Obituary, *New York Times*, February 13, 1974, and "Christopher Emmet, R.I.P.," *National Review* 26 (March 1, 1974): 249.

14. Letter, Emmet to Herter, July 10, 1951, Box 78, CEC. It is not clear whether Herter actually met Diem, but he did mention Diem to Walter Judd. See Letter, Emmet to Herter, July 24, 1951, Box 78, CEC.

15. Memorandum of conversation, Livingston Merchant with Kelly, August 18, 1951, *FRUS, 1951*, 6:480. Emmet referred to his assistance to Diem in drafting a memorandum for Kelly in a letter written to Diem on August 2, 1951, Box 69, CEC. Although Emmet drafted the memorandum to Kelly, the introduction of Diem to Kelly was probably made by Joseph Calderon, a conservative Catholic who was a friend of Peter White. Letter, White to author, June 24, 1989.

16. Memorandum of conversation with Thuc, June 18, 1950, *FRUS, 1950*, 6:831.

17. These views may be found in Buttinger, *Dragon Embattled*, 2:846–47; Larsen, "Third Force," 20–26; Cooney, *American Pope*, 240–42; and Scheer and Hinckle, "'Vietnam Lobby,'" 32. The author would like to thank William Brownell for bringing the Larsen manuscript to his attention.

Some have also expressed their doubts about Spellman's influence. See Cooper, *Lost Crusade*, 125. Justice William O. Douglas, whose association with Diem will be described in subsequent pages, also doubted that Spellman was close to Diem in the early 1950s. See letter, Douglas to Frazier T. Woolard, May 14, 1968, Box 293, WODP.

18. Spellman's assistance in finding a residence for Diem is mentioned in a letter Peter White wrote to the author on May 9, 1989. Accounts of Spellman's meetings with Diem after the latter's accession to power can be found in Collins, *Lightning Joe*, 389, and telegram, American Embassy in Saigon to Department of State, January 12, 1956, Box 4593, RG 59, NA.

19. Memorandum of conversation with Diem, June 21, 1951, Box 8a(1), WJDP.

20. Letter, James H. Duff to Dulles, January 6, 1953, Box 69, JFDP.

21. Memorandum, Bonsal to John Allison, January 16, 1953, RG 59, NA, and letter, Dulles to Duff, January 28, 1953, Box 69, JFDP.

22. De Jaegher and Kuhn, *Enemy Within*, 38, 261.

23. Biographical information about de Jaegher can be found in an obituary in the *New York Times*, February 8, 1980. De Jaegher's role in introducing Diem to Donovan is mentioned in a letter from de Jaegher to Donovan, August 29, 1951, Box 11B, WJDP.

24. Letter, Peter White to the author, June 24, 1989.

25. "Little Mr. Diem," *The Reporter* 11, 10 (December 2, 1954): 4. A brief sketch of Paulding can be found in Doudna, *Concerned about the Planet*, 72–73.

26. Telephone interview of Gary MacEoin, March 18, 1989, and letter, MacEoin to the author, April 11, 1989.

27. Interview of Sol Sanders, September 19, 1991; Sanders, *Sense of Asia*, 149–52; and Evoy, *Contemporary Authors*. Sanders outlined his views on the possibility of forming a nationalist "Third Force" in "Viet Nam *Has* a Third Force," 14–15, and "One Way to Save Indo-China," 8–9.

28. Chester L. Cooper believed Sacks may have introduced Diem to politicians and former State Department colleagues in Washington, but Paul M. Kattenburg, who dealt with Vietnamese affairs for the department in the early and mid-1950s, could not recall this and expressed doubts that Sacks promoted Diem's cause. Cooper, *Lost Crusade*, 125; and letter, Paul M. Kattenburg to the author, June 8, 1992.

29. The attack on Fishel's scholarship can be found in Hinckle, Scheer, and Stern, "University on the Make," 55. Wright was asked to comment on this charge and made his reply in a letter written to Frank Trager on October 8, 1966, GJP. In this same letter, however, Wright wrote, "I think his [Fishel's] close association with Diem has biased his views on Far Eastern affairs."

30. Buttinger diary, December 14, 1954, JBP.

31. Interview of Chester L. Cooper, April 20, 1989. Biographical information concerning Fishel can be found in an obituary in the *New York Times*, April 15, 1977, and in Lochner, *Contemporary Authors*, 73–76:205.

32. Assertions that Fishel encouraged Diem to go to the United States can be found in Scheer and Hinckle, "'Vietnam Lobby,'" 32, and Scheer, *United States Involved in Vietnam*, 14. Fishel wrote a letter to *Ramparts* objecting to some of the claims made by Scheer and Hinckle. See letter, Fishel to the editors of *Ramparts*, July 6, 1965, Box 11, CEC. Fishel's letter was not published, but a later article said Fishel was teaching at University of California in Los Angeles at the time he met Diem. See Hinckle, Scheer, and Stern, "University on the Make," 55.

33. Interview of Ralph Smuckler, September 16, 1988, and letter, Ralph Smuckler to the author, October 19, 1990.

34. The arrangements made for this meeting can be seen in letters Douglas sent to Diem on October 11 and 24, 1952, and in a letter Diem sent to Douglas on October 14, 1952, Box 1716, WODP.

35. Letter, Douglas to Gregory, November 10, 1952, Box 1716, WODP.

36. Douglas, *North From Malaya*, 180–81. Correspondence between Douglas and Diem about the book can be found in Box 1716, WODP.

37. William O. Douglas Oral History Interview, JFKOHP. The day before he met Diem, Kennedy sent a lengthy set of questions to the State Department on the situation in Indochina. See letter, Kennedy to Dulles, May 7, 1953, Box 3371, RG 59, NA.

38. Mansfield, "Reprieve in Viet Nam," 47.

39. Memorandum of conversation with Diem, May 8, 1953, *FRUS, 1952–1954*, 13: 553–54. This meeting is also mentioned in letters Douglas wrote to Diem on May 2 and 8, 1953, Box 1716, WODP. Diem's early contacts with Douglas, Kennedy, and Mansfield are recounted in Larsen, "Third Force," 26–34.

40. Herring, *America's Longest War*, 19–37; Gardner, *Approaching Vietnam*, 179–211; *Pentagon Papers*, 1:75–107; Gibbons, *U.S. Government and the Vietnam War*, 1:121–227; Anderson, *Trapped By Success*, 19–39; Herring and Immerman, "Eisenhower, Dulles, and Dienbienphu," 343–63; and Billings-Yun, *Decision against War*.

41. Anderson, *Trapped By Success*, 54. See also Bao Dai, *Le Dragon D'Annam*, 328–29. See also Fall, *Two Vietnams*, 244, and Larsen, "Third Force," 56–61.

42. See telegrams, Walter Bedell Smith to Douglas Dillon, September 14, 1953; Dillon to John Foster Dulles, September 15, 1953; Dulles to Dillon, September 25, 1953; and Dillon to Dulles, September 26, 1953, Box 3675, RG 59, NA; telegrams, Donald Heath to Dulles, March 22, 1954; Dillon to Dulles, March 22, 1954, Box 3676, RG 59, NA; and memorandum, Richard K. Stuart to Robert E. Hoey, May 10, 1954, Box 3677, RG 59, NA.

43. Memorandum of conversation with Luyen, May 18, 1954, *FRUS, 1952–1954*, 16:843–46.

44. Telegram, Dillon to John Foster Dulles, May 24, 1954, *FRUS, 1952–1954*, 13:1609, and telegram, Dillon to Dulles, June 15, 1954, Box 3679, RG 59, NA.

45. Telegram, U.S. Army Liaison Office, Singapore, to Department of the Army, June 1, 1954, Box 3679, RG 59, NA.

46. Parmet, "Making and Unmaking of Ngo Dinh Diem," 45.

47. Bao Dai, *L'Dragon Annam*, 328, and Cooper, *Lost Crusade*, 125–28. Although Cooper mentions this meeting, he believes that the American role in Diem's appointment has been exaggerated. Other arguments that American influence has been overemphasized include Anderson, *Trapped By Success*, 51–58; Buttinger, *Dragon Embattled*, 2:847–

50; and Karnow, *Vietnam*, 217–18. Accounts that give a greater weight to the American role in Diem's accession to power include Kahin, *Intervention*, 78; Parmet, "Making and Unmaking of Ngo Dinh Diem," 45; Gibbons, *U.S. Government and the Vietnam War*, 1:261–62; and Larsen, "Third Force," 61–64.

48. Parmet, "Making and Unmaking of Ngo Dinh Diem," 45.

49. Gibbons, *U.S. Government and the Vietnam War*, 1:262, and Devillers and Lacouture, *End of a War*, 223–24.

50. Buttinger briefly discusses these claims in *Dragon Embattled*, 1:848 and 1096–97, n. 8.

51. Letter, Douglas to Frazier T. Woolard, May 14, 1968, Box 293, WODP.

52. Gibbons, *U.S. Government and the Vietnam War*, 1:90 and telegrams, Charles N. Spinks to Department of State, August 24, 1950, and September 25, 1950, Box 3667, RG 59, NA.

53. Anderson, *Trapped By Success*, 75.

54. Letter, Christopher Emmet to Christian Herter, July 10, 1951, Box 78, CEC; and letter, Peter White to the author, May 9, 1989.

55. Fall, *Two Vietnams*, 239.

56. Letter, White to author, May 10, 1989.

57. Letter, Emmet to Herter, July 10, 1951, Box 78, CEC.

58. Letter, White to the author, May 10, 1989. The article to which White referred is Wertenbaker, "China Lobby," 4–24.

59. Letter, Diem to Emmet, July 25, 1951, Box 69, CEC.

60. Letter, Emmet to Herter, July 10, 1951, Box 78, CEC; and letter, Douglas to John Fisher, June 12, 1953, Box 1716, WODP.

Discussions of anticommunism in postwar America can be found in Caute, *The Great Fear*; Griffith and Theoharis, *The Specter*; Heale, *American Anticommunism*; McAuliffe, *Crisis on the Left*; Nash, *Conservative Intellectual Movement in America*; and Pells, *Liberal Mind in a Conservative Age*.

61. Thomson, Stanley, and Perry, *Sentimental Imperialists*, 310.

62. The notion of an American mission to Asia is outlined in ibid., 16–18, 81; and Iriye, *Across the Pacific*, 5–7, 17–18. The belief in America's mission to Vietnam itself is examined in Roper, "Western Idea," 17–31.

63. Packenham, *Liberal America*, 132.

64. Schlesinger, *Vital Center*, 234. Packenham gives an overall view and analysis of liberal perceptions of the Third World. Other discussions of modernization theories and hopes for a "Third Force" may be found in Larsen, "Third Force," 9–13; Black, *Development in Theory and Practice*, 24–25, 47–52; Hamby, *Beyond the New Deal*, 366–70, 429–33; So, *Social Change and Development*, 17–37; Tomes, "American Intellectuals," 6–23.

65. Telegram, Charles N. Spinks to Department of State, September 2, 1950, Box 3667, and memoranda of conversation, January 31, 1951, Box 3669, and July 26, 1951, Box 3670, RG 59, NA.

66. Personal note on Ngo Dinh Diem, Box 82 (1), WJDP, and memorandum, C. J. Little to Shannon McCune, September 13, 1950, Box 10, Records of Philippine and Southeast Asian Affairs, Lot 54D190, RG 59, NA.

67. Telegram, Charles N. Spinks to Department of State, September 2, 1950, Box 3667, RG 59, NA; and undated memorandum by Ngo Dinh Diem, Box 11B, WJDP.

Chapter 2

1. Kahin, *Intervention*, 52–64; *Pentagon Papers*, 1:108–78. A lengthy description and analysis of the Geneva Conference may be found in Randle, *Geneva 1954*.
2. The flight of the northern refugees is discussed in Kahin, *Intervention*, 75–77; Department of Defense, *US-VN Relations*, 2, IVA5: 8–12; and Currey, *Edward Lansdale*, 156–59.
3. Dooley, *Deliver Us from Evil*, photograph caption.
4. *US-VN Relations*, 2, IVA5: 9. A recent analysis of Dooley's work in Vietnam can be found in Fisher, *Catholic Counterculture*, 144–65.
5. Obituary, *New York Times*, August 28, 1987, and *New Catholic Encyclopedia*, s.v. "Catholic Relief Services-NCWC" by E. E. Swanstrom.
6. Levenstein's *Escape to Freedom* outlines the history of the IRC.
7. Persico, *Casey*, 43.
8. Biographical information about Cherne can be found in Levenstein, *Escape to Freedom*, 51–52; Persico, *Casey*, 40–43; and *American Jewish Biographies*, 60–61.
9. Interview of Leo Cherne, March 15, 1989; Levenstein, *Escape to Freedom*, 204–5.
10. Interview of Leo Cherne, March 15, 1989; and undated memorandum, Cherne to Donovan, Box 9A, WJDP.
11. Interview of Leo Cherne, March 15, 1989.
12. Undated memorandum, Leo Cherne to William Donovan, Box 9A, WJDP.
13. Cooper, *Lost Crusade*, 132.
14. Reference to this decision can be found in a letter from Joseph Buttinger to Mrs. Kermit Roosevelt, October 8, 1954, and in an undated memorandum, JBP. Christopher Emmet, one of the Americans who befriended Diem in the early 1950s, was also on the IRC board. He supported Cherne's recommendations, although he did not claim a decisive role in persuading the board to send help to Vietnam. See letter, Emmet to Diem, April 1, 1957, Box 69, CEC.
15. Buttinger gives an autobiographical sketch in his *Twilight of Socialism*, 398–411. He refers to himself as Gustav Richter, one of his code names from the underground. His wife, who many believe was the figure for Lillian Hellman's "Julia," recounts her experiences in Gardiner, *Code Name "Mary."*
16. Buttinger, *Twilight of Socialism*, 386, 384–92, 531–46.
17. Interview of Leo Cherne, March 15, 1989. Cherne also thought that Buttinger's fluency in French would be an asset.
18. Undated letter, Eisenhower to Diem, *FRUS, 1952-1954*, 13:2167.
19. Anderson, *Trapped By Success*, 65–88; Herring, *America's Longest War*, 44–45; Kahin, *Intervention*, 70–75; Gardner, *Approaching Vietnam*, 270–75; and Gibbons, *U.S. Government and the Vietnam War*, 1:271–81.
20. Buttinger, *Smaller Dragon*, 4.
21. Levenstein, *Escape to Freedom*, 205–6, and Buttinger, *Vietnam: Tragedy*, 44–45.

Buttinger kept a diary of his experiences in Vietnam and wrote letters to Cherne about the political situation. Unfortunately, he named few of the Vietnamese who discussed political matters with him. The diary and letters may be found in his papers. The views of the Dai Viet members are outlined in a letter Buttinger wrote to Cherne on December 4, 1954, JBP. The Dai Viet initially became split over the issue of seeking Japanese and Chinese assistance in winning Vietnamese independence in the early 1940s. New splits occurred later in the decade when party members debated the issue of collaboration with the French-sponsored Bao Dai regime. See Buttinger, *Dragon Embattled*, 1:262 and 2:731–33, and Diem, *Jaws of History*, 59–60.

22. Letter, Buttinger to Cherne, November 21, 1954, JBP.

23. Buttinger, *Smaller Dragon*, 5.

24. "Job for Joe," *Time*, November 15, 1954, 45; and Buttinger diary, November 20, 1954, JBP.

25. "U.S. Inherits Another Headache," *U.S News and World Report*, December 10, 1954, 24–26.

26. Durdin, "Shadow of Doom," 7.

27. Ibid., 40.

28. Joseph Alsop, "An Asian Munich," *Washington Post*, December 31, 1954, 11.

29. Joseph Alsop, "Real 'Government' in South Vietnam Is Red Underground," *Washington Post*, December 13, 1954, 19.

30. Joseph Alsop, "Recurring Nightmare," *Washington Post*, December 15, 1954, 19.

31. Joseph Alsop, "With the Viet Minh," *Washington Post*, December 20, 1954, 13.

32. Buttinger's reaction to the Alsop articles can be found in diary entries made on December 13 and 18, 1954, and in a letter written to Cherne, December 11, 1954, JBP.

33. Interview of Ralph Smuckler, September 16, 1988.

34. Telegrams, Heath to John Foster Dulles, July 23, 1954, and Dulles to Douglas Dillon, July 19, 1954, RG 59, NA.

35. Letter, Paul Kattenburg to the author, February 18, 1992.

36. Telegram, Heath to John Foster Dulles, August 23, 1954, RG 59, NA.

37. Telegram, Collins to John Foster Dulles, November 18, 1954, RG 59, NA. For some of Fishel's activities as an intermediary, see telegrams from Heath to Dulles, September 5, 1954, *FRUS, 1952-1954*, 13:2006; Heath to Dulles, September 14, 1954, ibid., 2014–15; Heath to Dulles, September 27, 1954, ibid., 2075–76; Dulles to Heath, October 30, 1954, ibid., 2196; and Collins to Dulles, December 13, 1954, ibid., 2363.

38. Buttinger diary, December 14, 1954, JBP. Buttinger recorded meetings with Fishel on December 8, 9, 10, 14, 15, and 17, 1954. He also met Colonel Edward Lansdale. Much was made of this meeting by Scheer and Hinckle, who claimed that the two men worked closely together in an effort to save Diem. See Scheer and Hinckle, "Vietnam Lobby," 33–34, and Scheer, "Leo Cherne," 16. Buttinger, however, denied that he was close to Lansdale and said he did not know of Lansdale's ties to the CIA. See draft of letter, Buttinger to editors of *New Times*, undated, JBP. Buttinger's diary notes one meeting with Lansdale, and Lansdale is identified as being involved in "psychological warfare with Gen. Collins." Diary entry, December 2, 1954, JBP.

39. Telegram, Collins to Dulles, December 16, 1954, *FRUS, 1952-1954*, 13:2379, and Anderson, *Trapped By Success*, 95–97.

40. Telegram, Dulles to Collins, December 24, 1954, *FRUS, 1952–1954*, 13:2419.

41. Interview of Harold Oram, April 5, 1989; Levenstein, *Escape to Freedom*, 9; Memorandum, David Martin to Diem, undated, JBP; letter, Fishel to Diem, April 30[?], 1960, *FRUS, 1958–1960*, 1:430–31; and Oram obituary, *New York Times*, August 23, 1990.

42. Interview of Harold Oram, April 5, 1989, and memorandum, Kenneth Young to Bureau of Far Eastern Affairs, January 6, 1955, Box 3332, RG 59, NA. Some accounts claim that Spellman secured Joseph Kennedy's assistance in lobbying for Diem. See Scheer, *United States Involved in Vietnam*, 21–25, and Scheer and Hinckle, "Vietnam Lobby," 33. Oram did not believe that Kennedy was involved in this matter at all; interview of Harold Oram, April 5, 1989. Cherne also voiced doubts about Kennedy's involvement and added that he had never met with Joseph Kennedy himself; interview of Leo Cherne, March 15, 1989, and letter, Cherne to author, July 20, 1989.

43. Buttinger, memorandum on Indochina (Vietnam), Box 3332, RG 59, NA, and Buttinger, "Eyewitness Report," 19.

44. Buttinger, memorandum on Indochina (Vietnam), Box 3332, RG 59, NA, and Buttinger "Eyewitness Report," 19–20.

45. Buttinger, memorandum on Indochina (Vietnam), Box 3332, RG 59, NA. See also Buttinger, "Eyewitness Report," 20, and letter, Buttinger to the editor, *New York Times*, January 30, 1955, 8B.

46. Buttinger, "Saigon—Intrigue," 10.

47. Interview of Leo Cherne, March 15, 1989. Cherne said the highest official he spoke to was Dorothy Houghton, a woman involved in foreign aid programs. Cherne's contact with Houghton is referred to in a letter written by Buttinger to Cherne on November 21, 1954, JBP.

48. Letter, Cherne to editors, *New York Times Magazine*, December 12, 1954, 4.

49. Undated memorandum by Leo Cherne, WFP. It is not certain to whom this memorandum is addressed. After being shown a copy of the memorandum by the author, Cherne said he had written it, but he could not recall when he had done it. He agreed with the author's suggestion that it was probably written in early 1955; see letter, Cherne to the author, July 20, 1989. It is possible that the memorandum had been sent to Henry Luce because Cherne told Fishel that he had addressed a memorandum to Luce; letter, Cherne to Fishel, April 17, 1955, WFP.

50. Telegram, Collins to John Foster Dulles, March 31, 1955, *FRUS, 1955–1957*, 1:169. Anderson, *Trapped By Success*, 97–101; Collins, *Lightning Joe*, 396–402; Buttinger, *Dragon Embattled*, 2:865–72; and Lansdale, *Midst of Wars*, 244–67.

51. Memorandum of telephone conversation between the president and the secretary of state, April 1, 1955, *FRUS, 1955–1957*, 1:176.

52. Senate Committee on Foreign Relations, *Report on Indochina*, 83rd Cong., 2nd sess., 1954, SFo-2, 11.

53. Memorandum for the record by Mansfield, April 1, 1955, *FRUS, 1955–1957*, 1:177. Although he frequently gave advice on Vietnam in 1954 and 1955, Mansfield later said that he felt uncomfortable about his relationship with the State Department on this matter "because it was outside the ken of my responsibility and entirely within the purview of the Executive branch under the Constitution"; interview of Mike Mansfield, JFDOHP.

54. Memorandum, Young to Walter S. Robertson, April 30, 1955, *FRUS, 1955-1957*, 1:337-39.

55. Memorandum of discussion, 246th meeting of the National Security Council, April 28, 1955, *FRUS, 1955-1957*, 1:311.

56. Buttinger, *Dragon Embattled*, 2:878-85; Anderson, *Trapped By Success*, 108-10, 113-19; Collins, *Lightning Joe*, 402-4; *Pentagon Papers*, 1:233-39; Lansdale, *Midst of Wars*, 282-311; and Shaplen, *Lost Revolution*, 122-26.

57. Buttinger diary, November 20, 1954, JBP. The suggestion for creating such a group may have been made by an American military or Foreign Service officer, but the passage is not clear on this matter. The full passage reads, "Spoke to American officer. You must get American public opinion on our side. Create a Committee of Friends of Vietnam." Unfortunately, Buttinger did not name the Vietnamese to whom he spoke and simply called him "X."

58. Joseph Alsop, "The Major Casualty," *Washington Post*, April 4, 1955, 19.

59. Letter, Buttinger to Oram, April 22, 1955, JBP.

60. Minutes, executive committee meeting, December 8, 1955, RAFV; and Levenstein, *Escape to Freedom*, 36, 55.

61. Letter, Angier Biddle Duke to the author, May 9, 1989, and interview of Duke, April 3, 1989.

62. Interview of Sol Sanders, September 19, 1991.

63. Letter, Norman Thomas to John W. O'Daniel, December 17, 1957, JBP; and letter, Norman Thomas to Sol Stein, May 2, 1955, Reel 29, NTP.

64. Letters, Thomas to Duke, November 30, 1955, and Duke to Thomas, November 25, 1955, Reel 29, NTP.

65. Minutes, executive committee meeting, December 8, 1955, RAFV; interviews of Angier Biddle Duke and Harold Oram, April 3 and 5, 1989.

66. Memorandum, Robert G. Barnes to Colonel A. J. Goodpaster, November 17, 1955; and letter, Florence Kirlin to Robert L. King, November 16, 1955, Box.3336, RG 59, NA.

67. Minutes, executive committee meeting, December 8, 1955, RAFV.

68. Letter, Peter White to the author, May 9, 1989; letter, Fishel to Diem, April 30[?], 1960, *FRUS, 1958-1960*, 1:430; and interview of Harold Oram, April 5, 1989. Correspondence concerning public relations activities on behalf of the Diem regime can be found in letters from David Martin to Diem, undated; David Martin to Buttinger, February 24, 1955; Cao Thai Bao to Buttinger, March 10, 1955; and Oram to Buttinger, May 25, 1955, JBP.

69. Memorandum, Oram to Chuong, September 2, 1955, JBP.

70. Ibid.

71. Ibid.

72. Telegram, G. Frederick Reinhardt to John Foster Dulles, October 25, 1955, *FRUS, 1955-1957*, 1:565.

73. Buttinger, *Dragon Embattled*, 2:885-93, and Fall, *Two Vietnams*, 254-58.

74. Scheer and Hinckle, "Vietnam Lobby," 33.

75. Letter, David Martin to Buttinger, February 24, 1955, JBP. Buttinger also expressed satisfaction with the changed tone of the press coverage in a letter written to Emmet. Letter, Buttinger to Emmet, February 8, 1955, Box 65, CEC.

76. Letter, Cherne to Fishel, WFP.
77. Editorial, *New York Times*, January 29, 1955, 14.
78. Ibid.
79. Memorandum, Kenneth Young to Walter Robertson, April 30, 1955, *FRUS, 1955–1957*, 1:338.
80. Letter, Paul Kattenburg to the author, February 18, 1992. The emphasis in the quotation is in the original.
81. Interview of Mike Mansfield, JFDOHP.
82. Memorandum of conversation, Kenneth Young with Wesley Fishel, May 3, 1955, Box 3333, RG 59, NA.
83. Anderson, *Trapped By Success*, 111–13.
84. Interview of Leo Cherne, March 15, 1989.
85. Shaplen, *Lost Revolution*, 104. See also memorandum, Cherne to Donovan, undated, Box 9A, WJDP, and undated memorandum from Leo Cherne, WFP.
86. Telegram, Randolph A. Kidder to State Department, December 3, 1954, RG 59, NA. See also memorandum, Cherne to Donovan, undated, Box 9A, WJDP, and letter, Buttinger to Cherne, December 4, 1954, JBP.
87. Scheer and Hinckle, "Vietnam Lobby," 33, and Scheer, "Tom Dooley," 15–19.
88. Statement of Purpose of the American Friends of Vietnam, RAFV.
89. Interview of Cherne, March 15, 1989. In the same interview, Cherne said public anger over this exodus was insufficient and "the fact that that did not create more of a sense of concern, outrage, I can't get out of my craw."
90. Statement of Purpose of the American Friends of Vietnam, RAFV.
91. Letter, Buttinger to Cherne, November 21, 1954, JBP; and undated memorandum by Leo Cherne, WFP.
92. Undated memorandum by Cherne, WFP. Commenting on the tone of the memorandum from which this passage comes, Cherne later wrote, "There is an air of nearly euphoric expectation which subsequent events, had I known them, would have compelled me to modify." Letter, Cherne to the author, July 20, 1989.

Chapter 3

1. Clippings of these news reports can be found in RAFV.
2. A copy of the message was sent in a telegram from Ambassador G. Frederick Reinhardt to Dulles, January 3, 1956, Box 3337, RG 59, NA. This document, however, was a translation of a version that had been published in the Vietnamese press. The author has been unable to find an original copy of the telegram.
3. Statement of Purpose of the American Friends of Vietnam, RAFV.
4. This message was included in an undated telegram from Tran Van Chuong to Angier Biddle Duke, RAFV.
5. Telegram, Reinhardt to John Foster Dulles, January 3, 1956, Box 3337, RG 59, NA.
6. Vietnam News Agency, "Americans Form Aid Group," December 5, 1955, RAFV.
7. Scheer, *United States Involved in Vietnam*, 32; minutes, executive committee meeting, December 8, 1955, RAFV; Levenstein, *Escape to Freedom*, 36, 55; and Sacks obituary, *New York Times*, August 18, 1981.

The structure and offices of the AFV are outlined in "By-Laws of the American Friends of Vietnam," WFP. Minutes of both executive committee and board meetings were kept and may be found in the AFV's records and the Fishel papers.

8. Minutes, executive committee meetings, March 14, 1956, WFP; and May 8, 1956, RAFV. A list of associate members can be found in the AFV's records. The category of associate membership may have been discontinued in the early 1960s; the last associate member was accepted in 1961.

9. Interview of Leo Cherne, March 15, 1989. The last quote is from the AFV's letterhead.

10. Minutes, executive committee meetings, February 14, 1956, RAFV; and September 28, 1956, and May 14, 1957, WFP.

11. Biographical information on O'Daniel can be found in an obituary in the *New York Times*, March 29, 1975.

12. Letters, Heath to Philip Bonsal, February 2, 1954, Box 3676, RG 59, NA; Heath to Walter Robertson, September 16, 1954, *US-VN Relations*, 10:753, 755.

13. Telegram, O'Daniel to Admiral Robert Carney, April 29, 1955, *FRUS, 1955-1957*, 1:325.

14. Lansdale, *Midst of Wars*, 288.

15. John W. O'Daniel, "A Brief Concerning the Situation in Vietnam," Kahin-Indochina/Vietnam Documents, NSA.

16. Interview of Harold Oram, April 5, 1989, and letter, Harold Oram to the author, May 7, 1989. Oram sent a letter to O'Daniel on December 7, 1955, asking the general to attend the reception and referring to a telephone conversation the two men had earlier in the day. No mention, however, was made of the position of chairman. This document may be found in the RAFV.

17. Letter, Duke to O'Daniel, December 14, 1955, RAFV.

18. Letter, O'Daniel to W. B. Persons, May 20, 1956, Box 784, White House Central Files, President's Personal File, DDE.

19. Transcript, press conference by American Friends of Vietnam, A92-19, Box 1, HOP.

20. Letter, O'Daniel to Williams, December 26, 1955, Box 2, SWP, USAMHI.

21. Memorandum, Cherne to Donovan, September 29, 1954, Box 9A, WJDP.

22. Buttinger, "Are We Saving South Vietnam?," Box 3334, RG 59, NA. This was the title of a memorandum Oram forwarded to Secretary of State Dulles on June 3, 1955.

23. Statement of Purpose of the American Friends of Vietnam, RAFV.

24. Undated memorandum, Martin to Emmet, Box 89, CEC. The only evidence the author has seen of this campaign is a letter sent by O'Daniel to the *Times of London*. This note, which was printed in the April 3, 1956, edition of the *Times*, denounced the elections and communist calls for a new Geneva Conference.

25. Letter, Donovan to Eisenhower, February 5, 1956, Box 8, Ann Whitman File, Names Series, DDE. The text of Chou's request for the reconvocation of the Geneva Conference can be found in Cameron, *Viet-Nam Crisis*, 1:417–18.

26. Letter, Eisenhower to Donovan, February 7, 1956, Box 8, Ann Whitman File, Names Series, DDE. Donovan's work in Thailand is described in Brown, *Last Hero*, 821–29, and Dunlop, *Donovan*, 500–505.

27. Memorandum, Dulles to Eisenhower, February 10, 1956, *FRUS, 1955-1957*, 1:641–42. A record of the Anglo-American discussions to which Dulles referred can be found in a minute of the Bilateral Foreign Ministers Meeting with the United Kingdom, January 31, 1956, *FRUS, 1955-1957*, 1:628–30.

28. Eisenhower, *Mandate for Change*, 372. American predictions of Viet Minh success can be found in a National Intelligence Estimate, August 3, 1954, and memorandum by Richard Bissell, December 20, 1954, in *FRUS, 1952-1954*, 13:1905–14 and 2407–9.

29. Summary minute of a meeting in the office of the secretary of state, October 8, 1954, *FRUS, 1952-1954*, 13:2123. Dulles also used this argument against elections in press conferences. See news conference statement by Dulles, July 11, 1955, in Porter, *Vietnam: Definitive Documentation*, 1:704–5, and press statement by Dulles, August 30, 1955, in *FRUS, 1955-1957*, 1:533–34, n. 5.

30. Telegram, Dulles to Ambassador Collins, April 6, 1955, *FRUS, 1955-1957*, 1:209. See also telegram, Dulles to Reinhardt, May 17, 1955, *FRUS, 1955-1957*, 1:421–22.

31. Broadcast declaration by President Diem, July 16, 1955, in Porter, *Vietnam: Definitive Documentation*, 1:707.

32. Discussions of Diem's refusal to discuss elections can be found in Shaplen, *Lost Revolution*, 128–39; Buttinger, *Dragon Embattled*, 2:853, 888–93, 972–73; *Pentagon Papers*, 1:295–96, 305–6; and Duncanson, *Government and Revolution in Vietnam*, 223–25.

33. Program of Activities for *The American Friends of Vietnam* for the Six-Month Period Commencing March 1, 1956, JBP. Hereafter cited as Program of Activities.

34. Program of Activities, JBP. Discussion of this project can be found in the minutes of executive committee meetings on January 26, 1956, and February 14, 1956, RAFV.

35. Interview of Gilbert Jonas, May 8, 1989.

36. Biographical information about Jonas comes from an interview the author conducted on May 8, 1989, and from *Who's Who in the East, 1989-1990*.

37. Press release, March 2, 1956, WFP; and letter, Jonas to Colonel J. J. Sustar, March 9, 1956, RAFV.

38. Minutes of executive committee meeting, March 14, 1956, WFP. The initial proposal for the conference can be found in minutes of the executive committee meeting, February 14, 1956, RAFV.

39. Letter, Jonas to Angier Biddle Duke, April 25, 1956, RAFV.

40. Anderson, *Trapped By Success*, 83.

41. Letter, Robertson to Duke, May 17, 1956, RAFV. Information on Robertson's background and views can be found in Hoopes, *Devil and John Foster Dulles*, 146–47, and in Graebner, "Eisenhower and Communism," 69.

42. Telegram, Reinhardt to Dulles, May 6, 1956, Box 3338, RG 59, NA.

43. Memorandum of conversation, May 7, 1956, and telegram, Dulles to Reinhardt, May 10, 1956, Box 3338, RG 59, NA.

44. Letter, O'Daniel to Jonas, May 10, 1956, RAFV.

45. The author has no precise figure for the number of conference participants. In a letter written shortly after the meeting, O'Daniel claimed that 180 people attended, but an AFV statement written several months later refers to 250 conferees. A preliminary list

of the participants gives an idea of the groups represented at the meeting. See Conference Participants, May 29, 1956; form letter by O'Daniel, June 13, 1956; and Statement of Activities Conducted by the American Friends of Vietnam, RAFV.

46. Buttinger, "Vietnam's Capabilities," UA 2.9.5.5: Box 609, MSUVP. The emphasis is in the original text.

47. John F. Kennedy, "America's Stake in Vietnam," Box 895, Pre-Presidential Papers, Senate Files, Speech File, JFK. The AFV's invitation to Kennedy was sent by Duke on April 25, 1956, and Kennedy's reply to the AFV was sent on April 27, 1956. The above correspondence may be found in Box 12, Sorenson Papers, JFK.

48. American Friends of Vietnam, *America's Stake in Vietnam*, 47, 55.

49. Address by Walter S. Robertson, June 1, 1956, RAFV.

50. American Friends of Vietnam, *America's Stake in Vietnam*, 9.

51. Ibid., 11–18.

52. Ibid., 42–50.

53. American Friends of Vietnam, *America's Stake in Vietnam*, 41. This work was an edited version of the June 1 conference that was published by the AFV for distribution purposes. Hereafter cited as *America's Stake in Vietnam*, edited version.

54. Message of President Ngo Dinh Diem to the American Friends of Viet Nam Meeting in Washington, D.C., June 1, 1956, RAFV.

55. Telegram, Dulles to General O'Daniel, May 25, 1956, Box 2510, RG 59, NA.

56. Memorandum, Fisher Howe to Colonel A. J. Goodpaster, May 28, 1956, Box 784, White House Central Files, President's Personal File, DDE.

57. Letter, Eisenhower to O'Daniel, June 1, 1956, Box 784, White House Central Files, President's Personal File, DDE.

58. Letter, O'Daniel to Persons, June 11, 1956. O'Daniel's request was sent to the White House in a letter to Persons on May 20, 1956. A memorandum was later sent to Persons asking whether a letter should be sent in the light of the State Department's objections. See memorandum, Kevin McCann to Persons, May 29, 1956. The above correspondence may be found in Box 784, White House Central Files, President's Personal File, DDE. A brief description of Person's activities in the White House may be found in Greenstein, *Hidden-Hand Presidency*, 147.

59. American Friends of Vietnam, *America's Stake in Vietnam*, edited version, 106–7.

60. Letter, Graves to F. S. Tomlinson, May 29, 1956, PRO, FO 371/123429, DFo 10345/1.

61. Letter, A. J. de la Mare to F. S. Tomlinson, June 18, 1956, PRO, FO 371/123429, DFo 10345/3.

62. Letter, Graves to F. S. Tomlinson, June 4, 1956, PRO, FO 371/123429, DFo 10345/2.

63. Letter, Sir Hugh Stephenson to F. S. Tomlinson, June 15, 1956, PRO, FO 371/123429, DFo 10345/4, and letter, A. J. de la Mare to F. S. Tomlinson, June 18, 1956, PRO, FO 371/123429, DFo 10345/3.

64. Minute by Cable, June 25, 1956, PRO, FO 371/123429, DFo 10345/3.

65. Press reports of the meeting appear in the *New York Times*, June 2, 1956; Marguerite Higgins, "U.S. Charges Red 'Plot' Hurts Indochina Truce," *New York Herald-Tribune*, June 2, 1956; and Wellington Long, "Friends of Viet Nam," *Washington News*, June 2, 1956. Clippings of the Higgins and Long articles can be found in GJP. See Ander-

son, *Trapped By Success*, 160, for the importance that the State Department attached to Robertson's statement to the AFV's June 1 conference.

66. Scheer and Hinckle, "Vietnam Lobby," 33.

67. Telephone interview of Paul Kattenburg, August 13, 1991.

Chapter 4

1. Memorandum, Buttinger to executive committee members, November 3, 1958, WFP.

2. Minutes, Annual Meeting of the Members of the Corporation, March 14, 1957, RAFV. Donovan's declining health is discussed in Brown, *Last Hero*, 830.

3. Interview of Harold Oram, April 3, 1989. There were also complaints about close ties between the AFV and the International Rescue Committee. Hilaire du Berrier, a right-wing critic of the Diem regime, crudely called the AFV a "bed-partner" of the IRC, and Jonas mentioned criticisms of the AFV-IRC relationship in a letter to Duke. See letter, Hilaire du Berrier to Cherne, January 7, 1957, and letter, Jonas to Duke, February 1957, RAFV. Former AFV members maintained that, although the two groups shared members, their activities and policies were strictly separate. With the exception of joint activities honoring Diem during his visit to the United States in May 1957, this claim seems to be true.

4. Minutes, executive committee meeting, September 18, 1958, WFP. Duke later claimed that his decision was also influenced by uneasiness over the emphasis that O'Daniel, the national chairman, placed on security matters and a sense that the AFV "was moving away from its 'liberal' roots." This may be true, but it is not reflected in the contemporary documentary record. Letter, Duke to the author, May 8, 1989, and interview of Duke, April 3, 1989.

5. Some accounts allege that Harnett acted as Francis Cardinal Spellman's representative on the AFV. See Scheer and Hinckle, "Vietnam Lobby," 34, and Cooney, *American Pope*, 242. Both Cherne and Oram disputed this claim, and Oram pointed out that if Spellman wanted to affect issues concerning Vietnam, he could directly contact key political figures. Interviews of Leo Cherne, March 15, 1989, and Harold Oram, April 5, 1989.

6. Minutes, Annual Meeting of the Members of the Corporation, March 14, 1957; executive committee meetings, January 25 and May 5, 1958, RAFV; and minutes, executive committee meetings, June 18 and November 6, 1958, WFP.

7. Letter, O'Daniel to Edward G. Lansdale, September 26, 1956, Box 391, ELC. See also special memorandum, Diem to O'Daniel, *FRUS, 1955-1957*, 1:743-45.

8. Memorandum, Oram to Tran Van Chuong, October 11, 1956, Box 1, HOP; and minutes, executive committee meeting, September 28, 1956, RAFV. The author has not found a copy of Oram's memorandum, but its contents are discussed in the above documents.

9. Memorandum, Oram to Tran Van Chuong, October 11, 1956, Box 1, HOP.

10. Undated report on the meeting with Carter Goodrich and Frank W. Schiff, and letter, Angier Biddle Duke to General O'Daniel, December 20, 1956, RAFV.

11. Memorandum, Harold Oram to Tran Van Chuong, October 30, 1956, Box 1, HOP; minutes, executive committee meeting, November 12, 1956, WFP; and letters, Jonas to

Kattenburg, November 2, 1956, and Hoyt Price to Jonas, November 19, 1956, RAFV. The booklet that was discussed was apparently one the Commerce Department published on an annual basis. See, for example, Department of Commerce, *Economic Developments in Viet-Nam, 1956*.

12. Summary report of the Conference on "The Economic Needs of Vietnam, March 15, 1957." There are three records of the March 15 conference: the previously cited summary report, a report on the economic needs of Vietnam, and the verbatim transcript. All three records may be found in the RAFV.

13. Letter, O'Daniel to members, November 21, 1957, RAFV; and minutes, executive committee meetings, June 13, 1957, and September 11, 1957, WFP. Both Harold Oram and Gilbert Jonas later said they had drafted almost all of the letters sent out under O'Daniel's signature. Interviews of Harold Oram, April 5, 1989, and Gilbert Jonas, May 8, 1989.

O'Daniel's letter led to Norman Thomas's decision to quit the AFV because its contents convinced Thomas that the association had become "too much a committee in support of capitalism rather than the right of Vietnam to freedom from communist control." Letter, Thomas to O'Daniel, December 17, 1957, JBP.

14. "12 Projects to Aid Vietnam's Industry Gain Her Approval," *New York Times*, March 1, 1958, and Montgomery, *Politics of Foreign Aid*, 94.

15. "12 Projects to Aid Vietnam's Industry Gain Her Approval," *New York Times*, March 1, 1958.

16. American Friends of Vietnam, *Investment Conditions in Vietnam*, 6–7, 9–11.

17. Ibid., 13–60.

18. The proceedings for this conference are recorded in American Friends of Vietnam, *Aid to Vietnam*.

19. American Friends of Vietnam, *Conference of Land Tenure*, 17.

20. Ibid., 70. The texts of the addresses given during this meeting can be found in the previously cited work, as well as in American Friends of Vietnam, *Conference of Education, Health, and Administration*, and Fishel, *Problems of Freedom*.

21. Form letter by O'Daniel, April 2, 1957, RAFV.

22. Minutes, executive committee meeting, April 12, 1957, RAFV. Files that deal with a number of receptions hosted by the AFV may be found in RAFV.

23. Robert Alden, "Maryknoll Stay Relived by Diem," *New York Times*, May 13, 1957, 7; and "City Crowds Accord Diem a Warm Welcome," *New York Times*, May 14, 1957, 22.

24. Address of the President of the Republic of Vietnam at Michigan State University, May 15, 1957, UA 2.9.5.5: Box 672, MSUVP.

25. Buttinger diary, November 30 and December 13, 1954, JBP; memorandum, Kenneth Young to General Collins, January 26, 1955, and letter, Kenneth Young to G. Frederick Reinhardt, November 3, 1955, Boxes 2 and 5, Lot 58D207, Records of Southeast Asia Affairs, RG 59, NA; letter, Oram to Ladejinsky, December 20, 1956, Box 35, HOP; and memorandum, Walter Robertson to John Foster Dulles, February 11, 1957, *FRUS, 1955–1957*, 1:762–63. Other references to an American trip can be found in an undated memorandum from David Martin to Diem (JBP), and a letter from Leo Cherne to Wesley Fishel, April 17, 1955, WFP.

26. Interview of Sol Sanders, September 19, 1991; Anderson, *Trapped By Success*, 160–61; Scheer and Hinckle, "Vietnam Lobby," 35; Buttinger, *Vietnam: Tragedy*, 48; itinerary,

United Airlines to Oram, May 1, 1957, Box 59, HOP; and memorandum, Wesley Fishel to Stanley Sheinbaum, May 6, 1957, UA 2.9.5.5: Box 672, MSUVP.

27. Minutes, executive committee meeting, April 12, 1957, RAFV; and dinner program, May 13, 1957, JODP. The admiral also held a position on the AFV's executive committee, but the records indicate that he never attended a meeting.

28. Press release, May 13, 1957, RAFV; and dinner program, May 13, 1957, JODP.

29. Night letter, Eisenhower to Luce, May 13, 1957, Box 649, White House Central Files, Official File, DDE. Correspondence requesting a White House message can be found in the the same box and file and consists of telegrams sent by Angier Biddle Duke to Eisenhower, February 25 and May 7, 1957; and a letter from Frederic Fox to Duke, February 27, 1957.

30. Dinner program, May 13, 1957, JODP.

31. Address of His Excellency Ngo Dinh Diem, May 13, 1957, JODP.

32. Letter, O'Daniel to Joan Clark, July 9, 1958, RAFV; and letter, Williams to Lansdale, July 31, 1958, Box 43, ELC.

33. "Ngo Gets Freedom Award," *New York Times*, May 7, 1959, and editorial, *New York Times*, May 19, 1959. See also letter, O'Daniel to Harlan Hartness, July 24, 1958, RAFV; and minutes, executive committee meetings, September 18 and November 6, 1958, WFP.

34. Letter, Jonas to Dorothy Marks, September 20, 1957, RAFV; and letter, Lansdale to Mankiewicz, March 17, 1956, Box 35, ELC. After previewing the movie, Lansdale himself commended the film's changes in letters that he sent to O'Daniel and Diem on October 28, 1957. Both letters may be found in Box 39, ELC.

35. Minutes, executive committee meeting, January 25, 1958, RAFV; and Marie McNair, "Dragon Visits 'Quiet American,'" *Washington Post*, January 23, 1958. Correspondence regarding preparations for the premiere can be found in RAFV.

36. Clipping of a letter from Greene to *Le Monde*, February 7, 1958, JBP.

37. Minutes, executive committee meetings, September 28, 1956; May 14 and September 11, 1957; and October 22, 1959, WFP. Also, January 25 and February 27, 1958, and April 13, 1960, RAFV. Files for a number of the AFV's educational projects can be found in RAFV.

38. Fishel, "One-Man Rule," 12, and letter, O'Daniel to the editor of the *Denver Post*, January 7, 1959, GJP.

39. O'Daniel, "Free Vietnam," 149; Ladejinsky, "First Five Years," 20; and Fishel, "One-Man Rule," 13.

40. Telephone interview of Paul Kattenburg, August 13, 1991.

41. Night letter, Eisenhower to O'Daniel, April 14, 1959, Box 784, White House Central Files, President's Personal File, DDE. Correspondence between the AFV and the White House about this message is also in this file.

42. Letter, J. Graham Parsons to O'Daniel, July 6, 1959, RAFV.

43. The AFV membership cited in this paragraph appears on a letter sent by Angier Biddle Duke to Kennedy on May 11, 1956, Box 12, Sorenson Papers, JFK.

44. *Congressional Record*, 84th Cong., 2nd sess. (June 21, 1956), 102, pt. 8:10793.

45. *Congressional Record*, 85th Cong., 1st sess. (May 13, 1957), 103, pt. 5:6759.

46. *Congressional Record*, 85th Cong., 2nd sess. (February 19, 1958), 103 (Appendix), A3117; *Congressional Record*, 84th Cong., 2nd sess. (March 1, 1956), 102 (Appen-

dix), A2611; and *Congressional Record*, 85th Cong., 2nd sess. (February 27, 1958), 104, pt. 3:3046.

47. Fitzgerald, *Fire in the Lake*, 94.

48. Shaplen, *Lost Revolution*, 106.

49. Diem's family dictatorship and its repressive policies are described in Anderson, *Trapped By Success*, 127–33; Buttinger, *Dragon Embattled*, 2:952–69; Fitzgerald, *Fire in the Lake*, 94–98; Scigliano, *South Vietnam*, 55–62, 167–78; and Fishel, "Vietnam Reconsidered," 26–38, Box 46, ELC.

50. "She Asks for an Answer," *Washington Post*, February 25, 1958; and letter, Nguyen Ton Hoan to the *Christian Science Monitor*, March 31, 1958, GJP.

51. Du Berrier, "Report from Saigon," 44. In the winter of 1956–57, du Berrier and an associate named Doris Parks made an unsuccessful attempt to convince Leo Cherne, Angier Biddle Duke, and John O'Daniel that Diem no longer deserved American support. Their correspondence with Cherne may be found in JBP. A reference to this episode may also be found in a memorandum Gilbert Jonas sent to Nguyen Phu Duc on April 24, 1958, Box 49, HOP.

Du Berrier later wrote his version of events in Vietnam in *Background to Betrayal*, a book that makes some valid criticisms of Diem and the willingness of his American supporters to overlook his flaws, but which must be treated with considerable caution since one of its major premises is that the AFV's backing of Diem represented a left-wing plot to deliver Vietnam into communist hands.

52. Hotham, "Trouble in North," 36. See also Hotham, "U.S. Aid to Vietnam," 30–33, and Hotham, "South Vietnam," 13–16.

53. Fall, *Viet-Nam Witness*, 160.

54. Telegram, Buttinger, Duke, and Cherne to Diem, September 12, 1957, RAFV; and telegram, Sanders to Diem, September 12, 1957, Reel 33, NTP.

55. The possibility of aid cutbacks was mentioned in the telegram that Buttinger, Cherne, and Duke sent to Diem. Tuong himself returned to Saigon after Diem's overthrow in 1963, but was arrested again after the communist victory in 1975. He died shortly after being released from prison in 1980. Harrison, *Endless War*, 306, and Khanh, *Vietnamese Communism*, 197, n. 19.

56. Letter, O'Daniel to Thomas, June 26, 1957, JBP. See also letters, Thomas to O'Daniel, May 13, 1957, WFP; Buttinger to Thomas, May 27, 1957, Reel 32, NTP; and Thomas to O'Daniel, June 27, 1957, JBP.

Thomas expressed his dissatisfaction with this response in a letter to John Foster Dulles by writing, "I have written to various people in the American Friends of Vietnam who tend to mitigate the seriousness of the charges rather than to deny them." Letter, Thomas to Dulles, July 26, 1957, Box 3340, RG 59, NA.

57. Ladejinsky, "First Five Years," 21. Diem apparently found any admission of repressive behavior objectionable; Ladejinsky later told Harold Oram that "our friend did not like my saying that he is compelled to ration democracy." Letter, Ladejinsky to Oram, February 11, 1960, Box 35, HOP.

58. Fishel, "One-Man Rule," 12. See also Fishel, "Free Vietnam," 79.

59. Letter, Buttinger to Thomas, April 22, 1958, JBP.

60. Cherne delivered the address at the AFV's investment conference of February 28,

1958, and sent a copy to the White House on March 19. Maxwell Rabb, Eisenhower's cabinet secretary, was the official who praised the speech in a reply sent to Cherne. The texts of the letters and the address may be found in Box 33, White House Central Files, General File, DDE.

The "Little Vietnamese Girl's" letter appeared on the front page of the *Washington Post* on February 25, 1958. The British ambassador to Saigon identified this woman as "a young Vietnamese film star, Mlle. Trang Thien Kim." Letter, R. W. Parks to Selwyn Lloyd, June 23, 1958, PRO, FO 371/136125/DV 10345/1.

61. O'Daniel, "Free Vietnam," 146–52. See also letters, Buttinger to the editor of *The Reporter*, March 4, 1957, RAFV; and O'Daniel to the editor, *The Reporter* 16 (October 31, 1957): 6. The article that appeared in *American Mercury* was actually written by Gilbert Jonas. Unsigned memorandum to Ladejinsky, February 17, 1959, Box 35, HOP.

62. Albert M. Colegrove, "Fiasco in Vietnam, Our Hidden Aid Scandal," *Washington Daily News*, July 20, 1959; and "We Aren't Building Much Democracy in Viet Nam," *Washington Daily News*, July 25, 1959.

63. Letter, O'Daniel to Walker Stone, August 21, 1959, Box 69, Senate Foreign Relations Committee, Vietnam Correspondence, RG 46, NA.

64. Reprint, Raymond de Jaegher, "Myopic Muckraking Beclouds Aid Report," *Free Front* 2 (July, 1959), UA 2.9.5.5: Box 657, MSUVP; and letter, Fishel to Mike Mansfield, July 25, 1959, WFP. De Jaegher's article was reprinted and distributed by the AFV.

65. Memorandum, Gilbert Jonas to Louis Andreatta, July 27, 1959, RAFV; and letters, Andreatta to Mike Mansfield, July 28, 1959; Carl Marcy to Andreatta, August 10, 1959; O'Daniel to Senator J. William Fulbright, August 21, 1959; and Fulbright to O'Daniel, August 25, 1959, Box 69, Senate Foreign Relations Committee, Vietnam Correspondence, RG 46, NA.

Mike Mansfield chaired the Senate subcommittee investigating Colegrove's charges. Although he admired Diem and applauded the AFV's work, he had misgivings about the character of the U.S. aid program to Vietnam, especially its heavy emphasis on military assistance. Interview of Harold Oram, April 5, 1989; undated memorandum, Gilbert Jonas to Wolf Ladejinsky, Box 35, HOP; and Montgomery, *Politics of Foreign Aid*, 223–24.

66. House Committee on Foreign Affairs, *Current Situation in the Far East*, and Moritz, *Current Biography Yearbook, 1983*, 455–58. Zablocki and Judd eventually joined the AFV's national committee in the 1960s.

67. Minutes, executive committee meeting, October 22, 1959, WFP.

68. Letters, Ladejinsky to Jonas, August 18 and 7, 1959, Box 35, HOP.

69. Letter, Jonas to Ladejinsky, September 11, 1959, Box 35, HOP.

70. Memorandum, Jonas to Nguyen Phu Duc, April 24, 1958, Box 49, HOP.

71. Letters, Buttinger to Thomas, April 22, 1958, and Thomas to Buttinger, April 23, 1958, Reel 34, NTP.

72. Interview of Gilbert Jonas, May 8, 1989.

73. Senate Committee on Foreign Relations, *Situation in Vietnam*, 68.

74. Letters, Curt Schaefer to General O'Daniel, January 10, 1958, and Stanley Sheinbaum to Wolf Ladejinsky, January 24, 1958, and Leo Cherne, February 12, 1958, UA 2.9.5.5: Box 631, MSUVP; letter, Thomas McKay to Leo Cherne, February 20, 1958, RAFV; and letter, O'Daniel to Walter Robertson, October 31, 1956, Box 3338, RG 59, NA.

75. Undated memorandum, Oram to Gilbert Jonas, RAFV.

76. Undated memorandum by O'Daniel, RAFV.

77. Letter, Vu Van Thai to the author, January 23, 1990.

78. The Diem regime's investment policies and its dependence on the Commercial Import Program are discussed in Anderson, *Trapped By Success*, 155–57; Buttinger, *Dragon Embattled*, 2:966–70; Kahin, *Intervention*, 85–88; Montgomery, *Politics of Foreign Aid*, 85–93; and Scigliano, *South Vietnam*, 118–20. There were also discussions of the failure of the AFV's investment campaign in interviews of Angier Biddle Duke, April 3, 1989; Gilbert Jonas, May 8, 1989; and Sol Sanders, September 19, 1991; as well as in a letter that Vu Van Thai sent to the author on January 23, 1990.

79. Letter, Roy Howard to O'Daniel, September 3, 1959, RAFV; and Montgomery, *Politics of Foreign Aid*, 313. In another incident, *The New Republic* did not accede to requests by Harold Oram and Wesley Fishel that the magazine print articles to counterbalance a pessimistic essay written by David Hotham. Letter, Fishel to Helen Fuller, January 14, 1958, UA 2.9.5.5: Box 632, MSUVP; and letter, Oram to Wolf Ladejinsky, December 27, 1957, Box 35, HOP.

For a discussion of critical press coverage of the Diem regime, see Bindas, "Strains of Commitment." The author would like to thank Professor Bindas for providing him with a copy of the paper.

80. Minutes, executive committee meetings, May 14, 1957, and May 5, 1958, RAFV; and minutes, meeting of the board of directors, May 21, 1959, WFP.

81. Minutes, executive committee meeting, November 6, 1958, WFP.

82. Minutes, executive committee meeting, May 5, 1958, RAFV. Some AFV officers made a similar observation nearly eighteen months later. Minutes, executive committee meeting, October 22, 1959, WFP.

83. Letter, James L. Kunen to Louis Andreatta, July 31, 1959, RAFV. Kunen was the lawyer who represented the AFV in the last year of its effort to obtain tax-exempt status.

84. Minutes, executive committee meetings, December 14, 1957, and May 5, 1958; and meeting of the board of directors, February 27, 1958, RAFV; and minutes, executive committee meeting, October 22, 1959, WFP.

85. Certification of Incorporation of American Friends of Vietnam, RAFV. Correspondence concerning the AFV's prolonged effort to get tax-exempt status may be found in RAFV.

The AFV's difficulties in getting tax-exemption may also explain why the group's members did not testify before congressional committees in the 1950s. O'Daniel made an informal appearance before the House Foreign Affairs Committee a few days before he became the AFV's chairman, and a Foreign Service officer who accompanied him thought that the general "could be a highly useful witness," but there is no record of O'Daniel or any other AFV member giving any formal testimony on Vietnam in the 1950s. Memorandum, Robert Hoey to Eric Kocher, March 2, 1956, Box 3337, RG 59, NA.

Chapter 5

1. Spector, *Advice and Support*, 303–16; Kahin, *Intervention*, 98–110; *Pentagon Papers*, 1:306–14; Scigliano, 104–5, 120–24; Buttinger, *Dragon Embattled*, 2:930–35, 950–53; Duiker, *Communist Road to Power*, 172–93.
2. Undated letter or memorandum, Gregory to Joseph Buttinger, JBP. Gregory overcame his misgivings after becoming a close friend of the Nhus, and Gregory and his wife, Ann, eventually became the editors of *Times of Vietnam*, the English-language mouthpiece of the Diem regime. Kahin, *Intervention*, 155.
3. Henderson, "South Vietnam Finds Itself," 285.
4. The texts of these letters can be found in Buttinger, *Vietnam: Tragedy*, 53–71.
5. Buttinger, *Vietnam: Tragedy*, 49, and *Dragon Embattled*, 2:1156, n. 110.
6. Letter, Thai to the author, January 23, 1990.
7. Buttinger, *Dragon Embattled*, 2:1133, n. 27.
8. Undated memorandum, Gilbert Jonas to Wolf Ladejinsky, Box 35, HOP.
9. Minutes, executive committee meeting, September 18, 1958, WFP. Accounts of Buttinger's 1958 trip can be found in Cooper, *Lost Crusade*, 154–55, and Buttinger, *Vietnam: Tragedy*, 49–50. Buttinger later gave two contradictory accounts of his support for Diem after this trip. In 1967, he wrote that he continued backing Diem until the end of 1960, but a decade later he stated that he refused to support Diem publicly after his 1958 trip to Vietnam. The documentary record bears out his earlier recollection, which is found in *Dragon Embattled*, 2:1133, n. 37.
10. Interview of Gilbert Jonas, May 8, 1989; Gibbons, *U.S. Government and the Vietnam War*, 1:310–11; Ladejinsky obituary, *New York Times*, July 4, 1975; and Walinsky, *Agrarian Reform*, 4–16, 215.
11. Letters, Ladejinsky to Harold Oram, July 16 and August 28, 1957, Box 35, HOP.
12. Jonas, undated notes, GJP. These notes are unsigned, but Jonas identified them as his in an interview by the author on May 8, 1989.
13. Letter, Ladejinsky to Oram, April 16, 1959, Box 35, HOP. The emphasis is in the original.
14. Interview of Gilbert Jonas, May 8, 1989.
15. Letter, Jonas to the author, December 18, 1991. The idea that Cherne should see Diem first appeared in notes that Jonas took at the time of his trip to Vietnam. Writing of the need to convince Diem that more authority should be given to "able creative men," Jonas wrote, "Leo can sell him on it." Undated notes, GJP.
16. Letter, Jonas to Fishel, June 24, 1959, WFP.
17. Letter, Ladejinsky to Oram, February 11, 1960, Box 35, HOP.
18. Interview of Leo Cherne, March 15, 1989.
19. Ibid.
20. Letter, Jonas to Ladejinsky, March 15, 1960, Box 35, HOP.
21. Letter, Ladejinsky to Jonas, March 23, 1960, Box 35, HOP.
22. Letter, Ladejinsky to Jonas, March 26, 1960, Box 35, HOP. The emphasis is in the original.
23. Letter, Cherne to Arthur G. McDowell, October 25, 1963, GJP.
24. Letter, Fishel to Diem, April 30[?], 1960, *FRUS, 1958–1960*, 1:428.

25. Ibid., 426–29.

26. Postscript, Fishel to Diem, May 2, 1960, *FRUS, 1958-1960*, 1:433.

27. "The Political Petition to President Ngo Dinh Diem of April 30, 1960: A Background Paper," and letter, Gilbert Jonas to Fishel, June 15, 1960, WFP. Accounts of the Caravelle Group can be found in *Pentagon Papers*, 1:316–21; Buttinger, *Dragon Embattled*, 2:962–3; and Gibbons, *U.S. Government and the Vietnam War*, 1:339–41.

28. Letter, Andreatta to O'Daniel, August 15, 1960, and note, O'Daniel to Andreatta, August 17, 1960, RAFV; and minutes, executive committee meeting, October 6, 1960, WFP.

29. Jonas, progress report attached to a letter from Harold Oram to Tran Van Chuong, August 22, 1960, RAFV. Most of the reservations about the conference were voiced by the Oram firm, which sought guidance from the Vietnamese embassy about the meeting. Jonas, who held positions in both the company and the AFV, favored the symposium because he thought it could "provide a platform in a more highly controlled situation" for voicing criticisms of Diem's policies, but he did his best to make sure that this framework was established before plans for the conference went forward. Jonas's efforts are recounted in the above progress report, as well as in a memorandum he sent to Oram on August 5, 1960, RAFV.

30. Duiker, *Communist Road to Power*, 193–99; Kahin, *Intervention*, 111–25; and Spector, *Advice and Support*, 369–70.

31. *New York Times*, November 17, 1960, and February 7, 1961.

32. Spector, *Advice and Support*, 370–71, and Kahin, *Intervention*, 125–26.

33. Telegram, American Friends of Vietnam to Diem, November 14, 1960, RAFV.

34. Memorandum, Andreatta to Franklin Leerburger, December 30, 1960, RAFV.

35. Thong, "'Greatest Little Man in Asia,'" 143.

36. Telegram, Chuong to the American Friends of Vietnam, December 15, 1960, WFP.

37. Unsigned and undated note, RAFV.

38. Letters, Jonas to Ladejinsky, December 5, 1960, and Ladejinsky to Jonas, December 14, 1960, Box 35, HOP. The emphasis is in the original.

39. Transcript, *Foreign Affairs Round Table*, WEVD, New York, November 18, 1960, GJP. The AFV's records do not indicate when Young joined the organization, but the minutes of an executive committee meeting held on May 24, 1961, noted that Young left the AFV after being appointed as the Kennedy administration's ambassador to Thailand. Minutes, executive committee meeting, May 24, 1961, JBP.

40. Transcript, *Foreign Affairs Round Table*, WEVD, New York, November 18, 1960, GJP; and letter, Buttinger to "Herb," December 15, 1960, JBP. See also letter, Buttinger to Hanne Benzione, November 18, 1960, JBP.

"Herb" may not be a real person but the name used in the draft of a lengthy letter Buttinger wrote in order to justify continued support of Diem. The letter to "Herb" is over thirty pages long and Buttinger mentions such a letter in a note sent to Fishel on January 10, 1961, JBP.

41. Letter, Buttinger to "Herb," December 15, 1960, JBP.

42. Revised Draft of Statement to N.D.D., RAFV.

43. Memoranda, Louis Andreatta to Wesley Fishel, January 3 and 17, 1961, RAFV.

44. Thong, "'Greatest Little Man in Asia,'" 140–42.

45. Letters, Buttinger to Jonas, March 9, 1961, and Jonas to Buttinger, March 3, 1961, RAFV.
46. Letter, Jonas to Buttinger, March 23, 1961, RAFV.
47. Ibid.
48. Scigliano, *South Vietnam*, 92–93; Buttinger, *Dragon Embattled*, 2:1140, n. 51; and Robert Trumbull, "Ngo Sweeps Vote in South Vietnam," *New York Times*, April 10, 1961.
49. Letter, O'Daniel to *New York Times*, April 8, 1961.
50. Irene Corbally Kuhn, "Vietnam Is Also in Danger," *Long Island Press*, March 28, 1961, GJP.
51. Cherne, "Deepening Red Shadow," 11, 115. Cherne later said, "I was more concerned with opposition to North Vietnam than, after 1960, with questions essentially involving South Vietnam." Interview of Leo Cherne, March 15, 1989.
52. Telegram, O'Daniel, Buttinger, Cherne, Fishel, Ladejinsky, and Henderson to Diem, April 10, 1961, RAFV. The *Times of Vietnam*, the Diem regime's English-language mouthpiece, claimed that the telegram had been sent by the AFV. Louis Andreatta later wrote a note asking the paper to print a correction stating that the cable had been sent by individuals, not the entire organization. Letter, Andreatta to *Times of Vietnam*, June 16, 1961, RAFV.
53. Buttinger, *Dragon Embattled*, 2:1158, n. 119.
54. Letters, Buttinger to "Herb," December 15, 1960, and Buttinger to Hanne Benzione, November 18, 1960, JBP.
55. Interview of Gilbert Jonas, May 8, 1989.
56. Fishel, "Vietnam Reconsidered," Box 46, ELC; and memorandum of conversation, July 11, 1960, *FRUS, 1958–1960*, 1:516. Cherne shared similar views of Nhu's influence. Interview of Leo Cherne, March 15, 1989.
57. Buttinger, *Dragon Embattled*, 2:959.
58. Ibid., 1158, n. 119.
59. Letter, Buttinger to S. M. Levitas, October 17, 1960, JBP.
60. Letter from O'Daniel to the *Christian Science Monitor*, April 6, 1961, GJP.
61. Fishel, "One-Man Rule," 12.
62. Letter, Buttinger to "Herb," December 15, 1960, JBP. See also Fishel, "One-Man Rule," 12.
63. Letter, Thai to the author, January 23, 1990.
64. Letter, Gilbert Jonas to the author, December 18, 1991, and interview of Gilbert Jonas, May 8, 1989. Although recognizing Chuong's ambition, Jonas expressed a high regard for the ambassador and remembered him as "a very gentle and tolerant man." Sol Sanders, however, saw Chuong as "an opportunist" who "wanted to be on the winning side," a view that can also be found in Hammer, *Death in November*, 150–51.
65. Telegram, Elbridge Durbrow to John Foster Dulles, October 3, 1958, *FRUS, 1958–1960*, 1:87.
66. Buttinger, *Dragon Embattled*, 2:954.
67. Memorandum Re: Wolf's Letter on Ambassador Chuong, Box 35, HOP, and letter, Fishel to Diem, April 30, 1960, *FRUS, 1958–1960*, 1:430.
68. Memorandum Re: Wolf's Letter on Ambassador Chuong, Box 35, HOP.
69. Letter, Fishel to Diem, April 30, 1960, *FRUS, 1958–1960*, 1:428.

70. Fitzgerald, *Fire in the Lake*, 119.

71. McAlister and Mus, *Vietnamese and Their Revolution*, 116.

Chapter 6

1. Letter, Buttinger to Dean Rusk, April 14, 1961, Box 2, White House Staff Files, General Correspondence, JFK.

2. Letter, Henderson to Walt W. Rostow, April 14, 1961, Box 2, White House Staff Files, General Correspondence, JFK.

3. Memorandum, Louis Andreatta to Fishel, May 17, 1961, RAFV.

4. Interview of Gilbert Jonas, May 8, 1989.

5. William P. Bundy, in Gibbons, *U.S. Government and the Vietnam War*, 2:41.

6. Letter, Kennedy to Diem, May 8, 1961, *US-VN Relations*, 11:132; Kahin, *Intervention*, 126-33; Gibbons, *U.S. Government and the Vietnam War*, 2:1-16, 33-44; and *Pentagon Papers*, 2:25-59.

7. Letter, Buttinger to O'Daniel, August 27, 1961, JBP.

8. Minutes, executive committee meeting, September 27, 1961, JBP.

9. Letter, O'Daniel to Buttinger, October 3, 1961, JBP.

10. Letter, Leerburger to Buttinger, September 29, 1961, JBP.

11. Minutes, executive committee meeting, October 12, 1961, and letter, Buttinger to O'Daniel, October 17, 1961, JBP. In the event, Buttinger sent no message to Diem. At an executive committee meeting in early 1962, he told his fellow officers that the recent report of General Taylor's mission expressed most of his views and that he thought a letter from the AFV would only "irritate the government even further." He also thought that a personal note to Diem would be ineffective. The question of writing to Diem was therefore deferred, and the record indicates that it was never pursued again. Minutes, executive committee meeting, January 10, 1962, JBP.

12. Letters, O'Daniel to Buttinger, October 21 and December 26, 1961; and minutes, executive committee meeting, October 12, 1961, JBP.

13. Interviews of Harold Oram, April 5, 1989, and Gilbert Jonas, May 8, 1989.

14. Telegram, Durbrow to Christian Herter, December 15, 1960, *FRUS, 1958-1960*, 1:734.

15. Interview of Gilbert Jonas, May 8, 1989, and letter, Jonas to Wolf Ladejinsky, December 5, 1960, Box 35, HOP. In the letter to Ladejinsky, Jonas also said the memorandum recommended that Diem help the Oram firm expand the scope of its activities and invite Jonas to Vietnam for an up-to-date assessment of the situation.

16. Scheer claimed that the Diem regime paid Kastor, Hilton an annual fee of $200,000, but a contemporary news account set the figure at $100,000. See Scheer, *United States Involved in Vietnam*, 32-33, 62; and Underhill, "Foreign Lobbyists," 22.

17. Letter, Chuong to Oram, May 12, 1961, Box 49, HOP; and interviews of Harold Oram and Gilbert Jonas, April 5 and May 8, 1989.

18. Cooper, *Lost Crusade*, 175, and Rust, *Kennedy in Vietnam*, 53.

19. Notes on Scheer's *Ramparts* article, July 1965, RAFV. The authorship of this document is not entirely clear, but Jonas probably wrote it. When shown a copy of the paper, Jonas said he thought that he wrote it. Interview of Gilbert Jonas, May 8, 1989.

20. Telegram, Durbrow to Christian Herter, December 15, 1960, *FRUS, 1958-1960*, 1:734.

21. Letter, Lansdale to Diem, September 12, 1960, Box 39, ELC.

22. Letter, Williams to de Jaegher, June 14, 1961, Box 9, SWC. The emphasis is in the original.

23. Memorandum, Louis Andreatta to Buttinger, Oram, and Jonas, September 11, 1961, Box 8, RAFV.

24. Letter, Ladejinsky to Oram, June 16, 1960, Box 35, HOP.

25. Letter, Jonas to Ladejinsky, June 21, 1960, Box 35, HOP.

26. Oram told Ladejinsky of an improved relationship with the embassy in a letter written on August 31, 1960, Box 35, HOP.

27. The text of Taylor's report, as well as a covering letter written by Taylor on November 3, 1961, can be found in *FRUS, 1961-1963*, 1:479-532. Kennedy's decisions in the autumn of 1961 are described in Rust, *Kennedy in Vietnam*, 42-59; Gibbons, *U.S. Government and the Vietnam War*, 2:48-87; Herring, *America's Longest War*, 80-87; and *Pentagon Papers*, 2:84-120.

28. Letter, Jonas to Thai, September 15, 1961, JBP.

29. Letter, Thai to the author, January 23, 1990; interview of Gilbert Jonas, May 8, 1989; and Buttinger, *Dragon Embattled*, 2:1153-54, n. 99.

30. Letters, Jonas to Wolf Ladejinsky, November 10, 1961, Box 35, HOP; and Buttinger to Thomas, December 4, 1961, and Buttinger to AFV Members, October 27, 1961, Reel 41, NTP.

31. Letter, Jonas to Frank Valeo, GJP.

32. Letter, Thai to the author, January 23, 1990. Not all AFV members, however, agreed with Thai's views. General O'Daniel bitterly objected to the distribution of a *Washington Post* article about Thai to executive committee officers. He regarded an individual who acted like Thai "as disloyal and verging on being a traitor." Jonas defended the circulation of the piece on the grounds that the executive committee needed to know all important points of view about Vietnam and that he saw Thai as being "as patriotic as the President of Vietnam and as courageous." See letters, O'Daniel to Jonas, December 2, 1961, and Jonas to O'Daniel, December 5, 1961, JBP.

33. Telegram, Rusk to Nolting, November 24, 1961, *FRUS, 1961-1963*, 1:665. The article in question (the same one that the AFV's executive committee members received) is Warren Unna, "U.S. Is Advised to Restrain Vietnamese Leader," *Washington Post*, November 24, 1961.

34. Memorandum of conversation, January 16, 1962, *FRUS, 1961-1963*, 2:45.

35. Letter, Fishel to Hannah, February 17, 1962. Hannah sent a copy of this note in a letter to Kennedy on February 26, 1962. Both documents may be found in Box 74, White House Central Files, CO-312-Vietnam, JFK.

36. Letter, Fishel to Hannah, February 17, 1962, Box 74, White House Central Files, CO-312-Viet-Nam, JFK.

37. Memorandum of conversation, January 16, 1962, *FRUS, 1961-1963*, 2:46.

38. Letter, Fishel to Oram, March 28, 1962, WFP.

39. Letter, Fishel to John Hannah, February 17, 1962, White House Central Files, CO-312-Viet-Nam, JFK. Diem's anger over the articles is also mentioned in a memorandum

written by the head of the Michigan State University advisory group in February 1962. See memorandum, Guy H. Fox to James B. Hendry, February 19, 1962, *FRUS, 1961–1963*, 2:152–55. However, a brief study of MSU's work in Vietnam suggests that the Diem regime may have also been influenced by MSU's cutbacks in the number of personnel sent to Vietnam, especially in the withdrawal of its staff members from a police training program. See Scigliano and Fox, *Technical Assistance in Vietnam*, 11–12, 52–53.

40. Letter, Fishel to Oram, March 28, 1962, WFP.

41. Karnow, *Vietnam*, 263–65.

42. Letter, de Jaegher to Andreatta, March 7, 1962, RAFV. According to Sol Sanders, de Jaegher served as an intermediary between the regime and the RVN's overseas Chinese population, a wealthy minority that many Vietnamese, including Diem, disliked and distrusted. De Jaegher's press agency acted as a news service for the Chinese, but it also tried to prevent them from being exposed to what it regarded as communist propaganda. Interview of Sol Sanders, September 19, 1991.

43. Letter, Andreatta to de Jaegher, March 12, 1962, RAFV.

44. Summaries of activities, April 1, 1960–March 31, 1961, and April 1, 1962–March 31, 1963, WFP; and minutes, board of directors meeting, May 24, 1961, JBP. Files on these various programs can be found in RAFV.

45. Letter, Buttinger to O'Daniel, March 15, 1962, WFP.

46. Letters, Emmet to Oram, July 3, 1962, and Emmet to O'Daniel, July 5, 1962, Box 92, CEC. Oram later recalled that Emmet tended to side with O'Daniel at most executive committee meetings. Interview of Harold Oram, April 5, 1989.

47. Minutes, executive committee meeting, June 21, 1962, WFP.

48. Letter, Leerburger to William Henderson, June 29, 1962, RAFV.

O'Daniel also expressed anger over the course the dispute had taken, but he remained in the AFV. Calling the debate "quite a battle," he wrote, "I came away from the meeting with the feeling that several of our executive committee members know damn little about what is going on. They are inclined to condemn Diem on general principles without being specific." Letter, O'Daniel to Edward Lansdale, Box 39, ELC.

49. Letter, Lockard to Henderson, July 3, 1962, RAFV. Buttinger later wrote that Lockard and Leerburger resigned from the AFV because of their objections to the Diem regime. This may be true, but neither specifically mentioned this issue in his or her letter of resignation. Leerburger's criticisms of Diem are mentioned in other letters that he and other AFV members wrote, but there is little written evidence revealing Lockard's attitude toward Diem. See Buttinger, *Dragon Embattled*, 2:1187, n. 244.

50. Letters, Emmet to O'Daniel, July 5, 1962, and O'Daniel to Emmet, July 15, 1962, Box 92, CEC.

51. Minutes, executive committee meeting, October 4, 1962, WFP.

52. Jonas, "The Genesis of U.S. Policy in Southeast Asia," February 3, 1962, Box 1390, White House Central Name File, JFK; and letter, Buttinger to O'Daniel, October 6, 1961, JBP.

53. Letter, Harnett to O'Daniel, June 10, 1962, Monsignor Joseph Harnett Papers. See also letter, Trager to O'Daniel, May 11, 1962, JBP.

54. Appeal letters signed by O'Daniel, October 18, 1961, and April 3, 1962, RAFV.

55. Statement of cash receipts and disbursements, May 1, 1961, and minutes, board

of directors meeting, May 24, 1961, JBP; statements of cash receipts and disbursements, April 18, 1962, and May 6, 1963; and minutes, board of directors meeting, April 26, 1962, WFP; and interview of Harold Oram, April 5, 1989.

56. Summary of activities, April 1, 1960–March 31, 1961, WFP.

57. Minutes, board of directors meeting, April 26, 1962, WFP.

58. Statement of cash receipts and disbursements, May 1, 1961, JBP; and statements of cash receipts and disbursements, April 18, 1962, and May 6, 1963, WFP.

59. Minutes, board of directors meeting, April 26, 1962, and executive committee meeting, October 4, 1962, WFP.

60. Minutes, board of directors meeting, May 9, 1963, WFP.

61. Taylor Report, *FRUS, 1961-1963*, 1:493, 489.

62. Letter, Bundy to Hannah, March 26, 1962, Box 74, White House Central Files, CO-312-Viet-Nam, JFK. A notation to this letter states that copies of the notes from Fishel and Hannah were sent to General Taylor and Lucius Battle, the executive secretary for the State Department.

63. Letter, Cherne to Arthur G. McDowell, October 25, 1963, WFP; notes on Scheer's *Ramparts* article, July 1965, RAFV; interview of Gilbert Jonas, May 8, 1989; and Scheer, *United States Involved in Vietnam*, 61.

Chapter 7

1. Letter, Buttinger to Norman Thomas, April 22, 1958, Reel 34, NTP. Buttinger still had a low opinion of Hoan's abilities five years later, but he did not object to efforts to introduce him to people in the United States as long as it did not appear that "the American Friends are promoting him." Letter, Buttinger to Fishel, March 27, 1963, JBP.

2. Letters, Jonas to Frank Valeo, February 18, 1963; Jonas to Hoan, February 21, 1963; and Jonas to Thomas Hughes, February 18 and March 29, 1963, GJP.

3. Fishel, "Vietnam Reconsidered," 43, Box 46, ELC.

4. Note by Lansdale, April 22, 1963, Box 46, ELC.

5. Currey, *Edward Lansdale*, 283. Currey also outlines Lansdale's views on Diem and the consequences of his overthrow. Ibid., 180–85, 237–38, 254–55.

6. Letter, Lansdale to Fishel, March 27, 1963. Lansdale may also have thought that Fishel's criticisms stemmed from personal motives; he wrote in a note to a State Department official that Fishel "is in a peeve at Diem." See memorandum, Lansdale to William Jorden, March 27, 1963. Both documents may be found in Box 46, ELC.

7. Hammer, *Death in November*, 103–19, 134–52; Kahin, *Intervention*, 138–50; and *Pentagon Papers*, 2:225–28. Diem's treatment of the Buddhists is discussed in Scigliano, *South Vietnam*, 2–3, 51–55; Fitzgerald, *Fire in the Lake*, 130–34; and Geddo, *The Cross and the Bo-Tree*.

8. Karnow, *Vietnam*, 281.

9. Editorial, *New York Times*, June 17, 1963, and advertisement, "We, Too, Protest," *New York Times*, June 27, 1963. Early antiwar activities are described in Gibbons, *U.S. Government and the Vietnam War*, 2:144–45, and DeBenedetti and Chatfield, *American Ordeal*, 86–87.

10. Memorandum of conversation, July 4, 1963, *US-VN Relations*, 12:527. See also

Pentagon Papers, 2:228–32; Gibbons, *U.S. Government and the Vietnam War*, 2:145–47; and Rust, *Kennedy in Vietnam*, 96–103.

11. Letter, Buttinger to Gilbert Jonas, June 3, 1963, GJP; and Buttinger, *Vietnam: Tragedy*, 50–51.

12. Memorandum by Fishel, June 6 and 7, 1963, Box 37, ELC. This document, which was declassified under a Freedom of Information Act request made by the author, does not designate the individual who originally received it. The name of the Vietnamese who spoke to Fishel also has been deleted.

13. Letter, Norbert Muhlen to Christopher Emmet, July 17, 1963, Box 91, CEC.

14. Letter, Muhlen to the executive committee, July 17, 1963, WFP.

15. Undated letter, William Henderson to Muhlen, WFP.

16. Letter, Lansdale to O'Daniel, August 5, 1963, Box 39, ELC.

17. Letter, O'Daniel to Lansdale, August 11, 1963, Box 39, ELC.

18. Karnow, *Vietnam*, 285–86; Hammer, *Death in November*, 163–68, 172–77; and Rust, *Kennedy in Vietnam*, 104–11.

19. Telegram, State Department to Lodge, August 24, 1963, *US-VN Relations*, 12:536.

20. The administration's August decisions are recounted in Kahin, *Intervention*, 158–65; Rust, *Kennedy in Vietnam*, 108–27; Hammer, *Death in Vietnam*, 177–98; and *Pentagon Papers*, 2:234–40.

21. Louis Andreatta, undated notes on comments by Jonas, and memorandum, Andreatta to William Henderson, August 23, 1963, RAFV.

22. Memorandum, Louis Andreatta to William Henderson, September 10, 1963, and telegram, Joseph Buttinger to the American Friends of Vietnam, August 28, 1963, RAFV.

23. Letter, Louis Andreatta to General O'Daniel, September 5, 1963, RAFV.

24. Letter, O'Daniel to the executive committee, September 7, 1963; and Louis Andreatta, notes of a telephone conversation, August 27, 1963, RAFV.

25. Letter, Louis Andreatta to O'Daniel, September 12, 1963, RAFV.

26. Letters, Henderson to Andreatta, September 10, 1963, and Andreatta to O'Daniel, September 12, 1963, RAFV.

27. Press release, September 14, 1963. The AFV's announcement of the suspension of assistance programs to the University of Hue is found in a press release issued on September 15, 1963. Copies of both releases can be found in WFP.

28. *New York Times*, October 9, 1963.

29. Letter, Au Ngoc Ho to Le Thanh Chau, September 9, 1963, RAFV. Ho and Chau served as administrators for the University of Hue. Mme. Chuong distributed copies of Ho's letter to reporters at the Overseas Press Club, an act that upset Andreatta, who feared that the safety of the writer might be jeopardized if the letter received the attention of the Diem regime. See memorandum, Andreatta to Wesley Fishel, October 18, 1963, RAFV.

30. Correspondence concerning AFV assistance to Chuong can be found in letter, Andreatta to Le Thanh Chau, October 4, 1963, RAFV; letter, American Friends of Vietnam to Norman Thomas, October 1, 1963, Reel 45, NTP; and letter, Joseph Newman to Chuong, October 4, 1963, GJP.

31. Minutes, executive committee meeting, October 9, 1963, WFP.

32. Executive committee newsletter, October 21, 1963, JHP.

33. Letter, Kattenburg to the author, June 8, 1992.

34. Interview of Jonas, May 8, 1989. The author asked Paul Kattenburg if he remembered this episode and Kattenburg said that he did not. Kattenburg added that "hundreds of interested or quasi-interested people" probably "drafted so-called contingency plans, but they played no role worth mentioning." Letter, Kattenburg to the author, June 8, 1992. The contents of a memorandum Roger Hilsman sent to Dean Rusk on August 30, 1963, seem to correspond to that of the paper that Jonas mentioned, but there is no indication that Jonas or Fishel had a hand in drafting it. The text of the document may be found in *FRUS, 1961-1963*, 4:49-52.

35. Telegram, CIA to Lodge, October 6, 1963, *Pentagon Papers*, 2:769.

36. Gibbons, *U.S. Government and the Vietnam War*, 2:187-99; Hammer, *Death in November*, 232-79; Rust, *Kennedy in Vietnam*, 146-60; and *Pentagon Papers*, 2:252-62.

37. AFV appeal letter, June 10, 1957, RAFV. Accounts of Diem's overthrow and death can be found in Gibbons, *U.S. Government and the Vietnam War*, 2:200-208; Hammer, *Death in November*, 280-307; *Pentagon Papers*, 2:264-70; Rust, *Kennedy in Vietnam*, 161-76; and Halberstam, *Making of a Quagmire*, 287-99.

38. Gibbons, *U.S. Government and the Vietnam War*, 2:202, and Hammer, *Death in November*, 305-7. Louis Andreatta raised the issue of Can's sentence in a memorandum to Joseph Buttinger in April 1964. Andreatta asked Buttinger to give "serious consideration" to making an appeal to commute the sentence because some AFV officers had expressed dismay over the murders of Diem and Nhu. Moreover, he argued that the AFV had set the precedent for such an action by requesting clemency for a group of dissidents in the late 1950s. Buttinger, however, apparently disregarded Andreatta's advice; there is no record of an appeal being made. Memorandum, Andreatta to Buttinger, April 22, 1964, RAFV.

39. Interview of Leo Cherne, March 15, 1989.

40. Buttinger, *Vietnam: Tragedy*, 51.

41. Letter, Buttinger to Catherine E. Purcell, November 15, 1963, RAFV.

42. Telegram, American Friends of Vietnam, Buttinger, Cherne, and Gilbert Jonas to Nguyen Ngoc Tho, November 3, 1963, in Executive Committee Newsletter, November 4, 1963, JBP.

43. Appeal letter signed by Buttinger, November 19, 1963, WFP.

44. This was first reported in Scheer and Hinckle, "Vietnam Lobby," 35. Sanders confirmed the story in an interview by the author on September 19, 1991. Sanders's name, however, remained on AFV letterheads until December 1964, so he may have actually made the request at a later date.

45. Letter, O'Daniel to Samuel Williams, November 3, 1963, Box 10, SWC.

46. O'Daniel, "When I Think of Ngo Dinh Diem," JODP.

47. Letter, O'Daniel to the chairman of the executive committee of the American Friends of Vietnam, November 19, 1963, RAFV.

48. Letter, Buttinger to Louis Andreatta, November 11, 1963, RAFV.

49. Letter, Buttinger to O'Daniel, January 15, 1964, RAFV.

50. Letter, Mme. Nhu to General and Mrs. O'Daniel, April 27, 1964, JODP.

51. Taylor, *Swords and Plowshares*, 301.

52. Schlesinger, *Thousand Days*, 909.

53. Collier and Horowitz, *The Kennedys*, 309.

54. Memorandum, Louis Andreatta for the files, and letter, Andreatta to O'Daniel, September 26, 1963, RAFV. See also Department of State, American Opinion Summary, September 25, 1963, Box 20, Office of Public Opinion Studies, RG 59, NA.
55. Letter, Andreatta to O'Daniel, September 5, 1963, RAFV.
56. Appeal letter signed by Joseph Buttinger, November 19, 1963, WFP.
57. Notes on a proposed statement of policy, October 9, 1963, RAFV.

Chapter 8

1. Minutes, executive committee meetings, October 9, 1963, and December 17, 1963, and minutes, board of directors meeting, May 19, 1964, WFP.
2. Telegram, Lodge to Dean Rusk, February 1, 1964, *FRUS, 1964-1968*, 1:55.
3. Accounts and analyses of the South's political troubles can be found in Fitzgerald, *Fire in the Lake*, 236–63; Kahin, *Intervention*, 182–217, 227–33, 254–59; and Shaplen, *Lost Revolution*, 213–48, 266–92.
4. Minutes, executive committee meeting, February 6, 1964, WFP.
5. Minutes, executive committee meeting, March 23, 1964; statement of cash receipts and disbursements, May 15, 1964; and annual report of the executive secretary, May 19, 1964, WFP.
6. Letter, Andreatta to Joseph Buttinger, May 11, 1964, RAFV.
7. Kearns, *Lyndon Johnson and the American Dream*, 252.
8. Herring, *America's Longest War*, 113–19; Gibbons, *U.S. Government and the Vietnam War*, 2:209–79; Kahin, *Intervention*, 205–19; Kearns, *Lyndon Johnson and the American Dream*, 251–60; *Pentagon Papers*, 3:149–83; Bornet, *Presidency of Lyndon Johnson*, 63–74; and DeBenedetti, "Lyndon Johnson and the Antiwar Opposition," 30–33.
9. Gulf of Tonkin Resolution, August 7, 1964, in Porter, *Vietnam: Documentation*, 2:307.
10. Gibbons, *U.S. Government and the Vietnam War*, 2:280–393; *Pentagon Papers*, 3:182–251; R. B. Smith, *International History of the Vietnam War*, 2:277–303, 321–43. Lengthier accounts and analyses of the Gulf of Tonkin incidents and legislation may be found in Austin, *President's War*; Windchy, *Tonkin Gulf*; and Galloway, *Gulf of Tonkin Resolution*.
11. Minutes, executive committee meeting, December 17, 1964, RAFV. In some handwritten notes of this meeting, Washington's attitude is described as follows: "They like 'Friends'—only available group." Undated notes, Box 56, CEC.
12. Minutes, executive committee meeting, December 2, 1964, WFP.
13. Memorandum, James C. Thomson to Michael Forrestal, December 9, 1964, Box 13, JTP; and minutes, executive committee meeting, December 2, 1964, WFP.
14. Executive Committee, American Friends of Vietnam, "Outline for New Policies in Vietnam," November 15, 1964, Box 214, White House Central Files, National Security-Defense File, LBJ. Young's proposals appear in two essays: "New U.S. Policies for Vietnam and Southeast Asia" and "A Mekong Strategy for Southeast Asia," GJP.
15. Minutes, executive committee meeting, December 17, 1964, RAFV.
16. Memorandum, Thomson to Michael Forrestal, December 9, 1964, Box 13, JTP, and

memorandum, Chester L. Cooper and Thomson to Lyndon B. Johnson, January 22, 1965, Box 79, EX CO312, LBJ.

17. Letter, Fishel to Johnson, December 5, 1964, Box 214, White House Central Files, National Defense File, LBJ.

18. Memorandum, Thomson to Forrestal, December 9, 1964, Box 13, JTP.

19. Memorandum, Thomson and Chester Cooper to Johnson, January 22, 1965, Box 79, EX CO312, LBJ. Johnson's refusal is recorded on this document and on a note that McGeorge Bundy wrote to Cooper that reads, "Can you keep 'em happy for a while?"

20. Gibbons, *U.S. Government and the Vietnam War*, 3:47.

21. Ibid., 47–53, and Kahin, *Intervention*, 271–76.

22. Gibbons, *U.S. Government and the Vietnam War*, 3:31–97, 148–205; *Pentagon Papers*, 3:417–52; Berman, *Planning a Tragedy*, 34–58; and Westmoreland, *A Soldier Reports*, 115–31.

23. Discussions of the policy statement can be found in minutes of the executive committee meetings of December 2 and 17, 1964, WFP, and minutes of the executive committee meeting of February 1, 1965, GJP.

24. Department of State, INR morning briefing, February 11, 1965, *Declassified Documents Retrospective*, 871D, microfiche.

25. This paper, "A New Policy for Vietnam," was enclosed in an undated letter that Fishel sent to AFV members, Box 521, WODP.

26. Ibid.

27. Gibbons, *U.S. Government and the Vietnam War*, 3:217, n. 2, and memorandum, Douglass Cater to Johnson, June 23, 1964, *FRUS, 1964-1968*, 1:524–25.

28. The development of the Mekong valley is outlined in Kenneth Young, "New U.S. Policies for Vietnam and Southeast Asia" and "A Mekong Strategy for Southeast Asia," GJP.

29. Letter, Jonas to Buttinger, March 9, 1965, GJP.

30. Letter, John V. Lindsay to Jonas, April 21, 1965, RAFV.

31. Undated letter, Clement Zablocki to Wesley Fishel, RAFV.

32. Letter, James Scheuer to Jonas, April 12, 1965, RAFV.

33. The antiwar movement's origins and early development are dealt with in DeBenedetti, "Lyndon Johnson and the Antiwar Opposition," 24–27; DeBenedetti and Chatfield, *American Ordeal*, 9–112; Gibbons, *U.S. Government and the Vietnam War*, 3:141–48, 221–25; and Zaroulis and Sullivan, *Who Spoke Up?*, 7–42. Two AFV members, Leo Cherne and Wesley Fishel, participated in the Washington teach-in as defenders of Johnson's policy. See "Principal Participants in the Debate," *New York Times*, May 16, 1965.

34. Address at Johns Hopkins University, April 7, 1965, Johnson, *Public Papers*, 1:394–99.

35. Interview of Chester Cooper, April 20, 1989; Small, *Johnson, Nixon, and the Doves*, 33–45; and Gibbons, *U.S. Government and the Vietnam War*, 3:265–70.

36. Interview of Chester Cooper, April 20, 1989, and Gibbons, *U.S. Government and the Vietnam War*, 3:xiii.

37. Memorandum, Cooper to Valenti, April 24, 1965, Box 16, White House National Security Country Files, Vietnam, LBJ.

38. Obituary, *New York Times*, July 24, 1969.

39. Undated memorandum, Anne Henehan to Fishel, William Henderson, Frank Trager, and Leo Cherne, RAFV, and memorandum, Cooper to Valenti, May 5, 1965, Box 17, White House National Security Country Files, Vietnam, LBJ. The names of the donors and the amount they paid to the AFV are as follows: Ford Motor Company Fund, $10,000; Procter and Gamble Fund, $5,000; Charles D. Dickey, $500; Sidney J. Weinberg, $2,500; Thomas S. Lamont Charitable Fund, $500; Cabot-Saltonstall Charitable Trust, $1,000; Beinecke Foundation, $5,000; Federated Department Stores, Inc., $2,500.

40. Letter, Fishel to Weinberg, June 4, 1965, RAFV.

41. Letter, Valenti to Weinberg, Box 83, White House Central Files, Gen CO312, LBJ. The administration's financial assistance to the AFV is recounted in DeBenedetti and Chatfield, *American Ordeal*, 109; Gibbons, *U.S. Government and the Vietnam War*, 3:265–67; and Small, *Johnson, Nixon, and the Doves*, 45–47.

42. Memorandum, Cooper to Jack Valenti, May 17, 1965, Boxes 18–19, National Security Files, Bundy Files, LBJ.

43. Memorandum, Cooper to Jack Valenti, June 7, 1965, Box 218, White House National Security Country Files, Vietnam, LBJ.

44. Memorandum, Cooper to Valenti, May 5, 1965, Box 14, White House National Security Country Files, Vietnam, LBJ. HERO had been considering this project since early April. See a HERO document entitled "A Monthly Report on Vietnam," WFP.

45. Letter, Dupuy to Fishel, May 3, 1965, WFP. The author is grateful to George McT. Kahin for providing the copy of a letter sent by Dupuy on May 6, 1965, which invited Kahin to serve on the bulletin's editorial board, as well as the copy of a letter he wrote to Morris B. Schnapper, a journalist concerned about government influence on private groups, on May 6, 1980. See also Kahin, *Intervention*, 80, 457, n. 27.

46. Memorandum by Dupuy, May 7, 1965, WFP.

47. Memorandum by Dupuy, May 11, 1965, WFP.

48. Minutes, board of directors meeting, June 3, 1965, WFP.

49. Memorandum, Cooper to Jack Valenti, June 7, 1965, Box 218, White House National Security Country Files, Vietnam, LBJ.

50. Minutes, executive committee meetings, December 17, 1964, RAFV; and February 1, 1965, GJP.

51. Letter, Buttinger to Fishel, March 1, 1965, GJP.

52. Notes, "Leo Cherne's Report," Box 12, CEC, and minutes, executive committee meeting, July 8, 1965, WFP.

53. In 1964, Bohannon, as did his close friend Edward Lansdale, voiced skepticism about the efficacy of a major U.S. military commitment to Vietnam. He doubted the ability of air strikes to prevent northern infiltration into the South and accurately predicted that if American combat forces were introduced, approximately 500,000 troops would be required. The imminence of the RVN's collapse, however, apparently led to a change of heart. See minutes of executive committee meeting, December 17, 1964, RAFV, and handwritten notes of this meeting in Box 56, CEC.

54. Minutes, executive committee meeting, July 8, 1965, WFP, and notes, "Leo Cherne's Report," Box 12, CEC.

55. Letters, Buttinger to Fishel, July 20, 1965, and Fishel to Buttinger, July 23, 1965, RAFV.

56. Telegram, Westmoreland to U. S. G. Sharp, June 7, 1965, Porter, *Vietnam: Documentation*, 2:374.

57. Kearns, *Lyndon Johnson and the American Dream*, 251.

58. Johnson's summer decisions are discussed and analyzed in Berman, *Planning A Tragedy*, 60–153; Gibbons, *U.S. Government and the Vietnam War*, 3:277–462; Herring, *America's Longest War*, 138–45; Kahin, *Intervention*, 347–401; *Pentagon Papers*, 3:433–85; and Johnson, *Vantage Point*, 143–53.

59. Statement by Robert Shaplen, August 12, 1965, GJP.

60. Statement by Kenneth T. Young, August 13, 1965, GJP.

61. Letter, Jonas to Don Ropa, August 13, 1965, GJP. Buttinger also appeared before the subcommittee, but as an opponent of the war. His testimony, as well as additional correspondence and material concerning these hearings, including testimony given by the witnesses, can be found in GJP.

62. Memoranda, Seymour Reisin to staff and officers, American Friends of Vietnam, July 26 and August 11, 1965, GJP. See also Report of Publicity Activities for American Friends of Vietnam, September 23, 1965, and resume of Gregory Gallo, RAFV.

63. Letter, Fishel to Cooper, August 13, 1965, RAFV.

64. Memorandum by Cooper, September 10, 1965, Box 2, White House National Security Country Files, Vietnam, LBJ. This paper was not addressed to anyone, but Bundy saw it; he mentioned the possibility of approaching David Rockefeller in a note he wrote and initialed on the memorandum.

65. Interview of Murray Baron, June 20, 1990, and Weisl obituary, *New York Times*, January 14, 1972.

66. Bornet, *Presidency of Lyndon B. Johnson*, 39–42.

67. Letter, Trager to Cooper, October 1, 1965, RAFV. The money given to the AFV is recorded in an undated memorandum written by Anne Henehan to Wesley Fishel, William Henderson, Frank Trager, and Leo Cherne, RAFV. The amounts given are as follows: John L. Loeb, $10,000; Robert Benjamin and Arthur Krim, $5,000; Robert Lehman, $5,000.

An archivist at the Lyndon B. Johnson Library informed the author that Johnson met with Weisl, Krim, and Robert Lehman on September 16 and 17, 1965, but that neither Johnson's daily diary nor his diary backup file provides information as to what took place at these meetings. Letter, Regina Greenwell to the author, April 25, 1991.

68. Letter, Trager to Bill Moyers, September 2, 1965, Box 217, National Defense Files, CO 312, LBJ.

69. Memorandum by Cooper, September 10, 1965, Box 22, White House National Security Country Files, Vietnam, LBJ; letter, Gilbert Jonas to Cooper, November 19, 1965, WFP; and Gibbons, *U.S. Government and the Vietnam War*, 3:397, n. 56.

70. Memorandum, James Thomson, Chester Cooper, and Don Ropa to McGeorge Bundy, November 23, 1965, Kahin-Indochina/Vietnam Documents, NSA; minutes, board of directors meeting, November 11, 1965, Box 10, and letter, Gilbert Jonas to Nicholas Kissberg, October 22, 1965, RAFV.

71. Undated memorandum, Anne Henehan and Gregory Gallo to Wesley Fishel, WFP.

72. Undated petition, WFP.

73. Correspondence concerning Rothman's petition and its circulation to a wider group may be found in RAFV.

74. Letter, Jonas to Chester Cooper, November 19, 1965, WFP. Press clippings of the visit and a press release concerning the Vietnamese students may be found in GJP.

75. American Friends of Vietnam, Inc., report for the fiscal year ended March 31, 1966, GJP; and undated memorandum, Anne Henehan to Wesley Fishel, William Henderson, Frank Trager, and Leo Cherne, RAFV.

76. "Two Views of Vietnam," *Time*, November 26, 1965, 52–53.

77. "Educators Back Vietnam Policy," *New York Times*, December 10, 1965.

78. Small, *Johnson, Nixon, and the Doves*, 47–48.

79. Memorandum, Cooper to McGeorge Bundy, Jack Valenti, Bill Moyers, and Douglass Cater, December 14, 1965, Box 71, White House Central Files, Confidential File, LBJ.

80. Interview of Chester Cooper, April 20, 1989.

81. Memorandum, Jonas to Wesley Fishel, January 11, 1966, WFP.

82. Letter, Anne Henehan to Chase Kimball, May 30, 1966, RAFV. As the AFV was seeking funds for an ad, the author of the statement, Stanley Rothman, withdrew his own signature from the petition because conditions had changed so much since the statement had first been written. Letter, Rothman to Gallo, February 11, 1966, RAFV.

83. Letter, Gallo to Wesley Fishel, March 24, 1966, RAFV.

84. Memorandum, Jonas to Fishel, January 11, 1966, WFP.

85. Letter, Gallo to Fishel, March 24, 1966, RAFV. See also letter, Fishel to George Tanham, August 17, 1966, and minutes, executive committee meeting, September 25, 1965, WFP.

86. Letters, Cherne to Louis Andreatta, April 3, 1964; Paul Jacobs to Andreatta, March 6, 1964; and Andreatta to Jacobs, March 11, 1964, RAFV.

87. Scheer and Hinckle, "Vietnam Lobby," 32.

88. Scheer, *United States Involved in Vietnam*, 32.

89. Ibid., 43–44.

90. Ibid., 43.

91. Scheer and Hinckle, "Vietnam Lobby," 36.

92. Notes on Scheer's article, July, 1965, RAFV.

93. Minutes, board of directors meetings, March 2, 1967, WFP; and November 11, 1965, RAFV.

94. Interview of Leo Cherne, March 15, 1989; minutes, board of directors meeting, November 11, 1965, RAFV; and minutes, board of directors meeting, March 2, 1967, WFP.

95. Memorandum by Charles Bohannon, February 24, 1966, Box 53, ELC.

Chapter 9

1. *The Gallup Poll*, 3:2074. Herring, *America's Longest War*, 144–75; DeBenedetti and Chatfield, *American Ordeal*, 128–91; *Pentagon Papers*, 4:18–197, 290–538; Zaroulis and

Sullivan, *Who Spoke Up?*, 54–121; Davidson, *Vietnam at War*, 386–472; and Lewy, *America in Vietnam*, 176–207, 223–30.

2. Letters, Fishel to Vu Van Thai, June 4, 1966, and George K. Tanham to Fishel, November 24, 1967; and minutes, executive committee meeting, May 26, 1966, WFP.

3. Letter, Jonas to Fishel, January 25, 1966, WFP, and interview of Gilbert Jonas, May 8, 1989.

4. Evoy, *Contemporary Authors*, 1:651; *Who's Who in America, 1990–1991*, 2:3392; Thies and Henshaw, *Who's Who in American Politics, 1967–1968*, 36; and interviews of William Ward, March 6, 1989, and Murray Baron, June 20, 1990.

5. Minutes, board of directors meeting, September 8, 1966, WFP.

6. Letter, Gregory Gallo to Wesley Fishel, March 4, 1966, RAFV. An unsigned note attached to a copy of this letter reads, "The board does not seem to concur in this opinion." Letterheads listing AFV members in the late 1960s and early 1970s may be found in the following correspondence: letter, Anne Henehan to Wesley Fishel, February 11, 1966, WFP, and letters, William Ward to the editor of the *New York Times*, May 14, 1970, and Ward to William Henderson, February 14, 1974, RAFV.

7. Interview of William Ward, March 6, 1989.

8. Interview of Murray Baron, June 20, 1990.

9. Statement from Frank N. Trager, August 1965, GJP, and interview of Murray Baron, June 20, 1990.

10. Evoy, *Contemporary Authors*, 1:651; Levy, *The Annual Obituary, 1984*, 454–56; and Trager obituary, *New York Times*, August 31, 1984.

11. Hodgson, *America in Our Time*, 132–33.

12. Sketches of academics who collaborated with the government, sometimes called "defense intellectuals," can be found in Hodgson, *America in Our Time*, 96–97, 132–33; Coburn, "Asian Scholars and Government," 67–107; Levy, *Debate over Vietnam*, 83–87; and Steel, *Imperialists and Other Heroes*, 350–52.

13. Letter, Fishel to the letters editor, *Newsweek*, February 18, 1966, GJP. Fishel expanded on this argument in "The National Liberation Front," *Vietnam Perspectives*, 1:8–16.

14. Brochure, "South Vietnam's People: Victims of Communist Aggression," GJP.

15. Letter, George Tanham to Mrs. Gray, November 15, 1967, RAFV.

16. See letter, Hugh O'Neill to the editor of the *Lakeville Journal*, January 30, 1967, RAFV; and Frank Trager, "Back to Geneva '54?: An Act of Political Folly!," *Vietnam Perspectives* 1:1–7. Some AFV officers admitted that the election process in the South was flawed but nevertheless regarded it as "more nearly up to democratic standards than anything that took place in the North." See letters, Hugh O'Neill to Mrs. E. Wiedeman, July 25, 1967, and O'Neill to Ernest G. Marquis, April 30, 1968, RAFV.

17. Appeal letter by Fishel, January 30, 1966, and brochure, "South Vietnam's People: Victims of Communist Aggression," GJP.

18. Brochure, "The Innocent Suffer," RAFV.

19. Brochure, "Massacre at Dak Son," RAFV.

20. Brochure, "The Face of Liberation," WFP.

21. "The Innocent Suffer," RAFV.

22. Letter, Hugh O'Neill to William Henderson, September 27, 1967, WFP.

23. Minutes, executive committee meeting, May 26, 1966; letter, Wesley Fishel to George Tanham, August 17, 1966; and minutes, board of directors meeting, September 8, 1966, WFP.

24. Interview of Hugh O'Neill, March 2, 1989.

25. Quarterly report (undated), O'Neill to William Henderson, and memorandum, O'Neill to the board of directors, March 2, 1967, WFP.

26. Interview of Gilbert Jonas, May 8, 1989.

27. Interview of Hugh O'Neill, March 2, 1989, and undated memorandum, Anne Henehan to board of directors, WFP.

28. Interview of Murray Baron, June 20, 1990, and telephone interview of Baron, August 30, 1990.

29. Interview of William Ward, March 6, 1989. Hugh O'Neill and Gilbert Jonas also recalled some unpleasant experiences in interviews on March 2, 1989, and May 8, 1989, respectively.

30. Minutes, board of directors meeting, September 8, 1966, WFP.

31. Letters, Hugh O'Neill to Chief of Information, Department of the Army, April 13, 1967, and O'Neill to Daniel Arzac, October 19, 1967, RAFV. Letter, Harold Kaplan to Edward G. Bernard, October 17, 1967, National Defense File, 19, CO 312, LBJ. Interviews of Hugh O'Neill, March 2, 1989, and William Ward, March 6, 1989, respectively. Telephone interview of Murray Baron, August 30, 1990.

32. Memoranda, Louis Andreatta to William Henderson, July 2 and October 9, 1962, RAFV; and letter, Vu Van Thai to the author, January 23, 1990. Phan Huy Quat, the RVN's premier in the spring of 1965, asked Fishel to bring the refugee problem to the attention of the American public in a letter written on March 29, 1965. The AFV's effort to meet this request is reported in Peter Kihss, "Saigon Sends U.S. Group a Refugee-Aid Appeal," *New York Times*, April 26, 1965. Quat's letter may be found in WFP.

33. Editorial, *Vietnam Perspectives* 1:2–3.

34. Letter, Thai to the author, January 23, 1990. Gilbert Jonas later said that Thai's growing pessimism dampened his own enthusiasm for the RVN. Interview of Gilbert Jonas, May 8, 1989.

35. R. W. Apple Jr., "Ky Will Name Closest Aide As Ambassador to the U.S.," *New York Times*, December 5, 1966; and Diem, *Jaws of History*, 11–176.

36. Interview of Hugh O'Neill, March 2, 1989.

37. Letters, Thai to the author, January 23, 1990, and O'Neill to Do Lenh Tuan, July 28, 1967, RAFV. Interviews of Hugh O'Neill, March 2, 1989; William Ward, March 6, 1989; and Bui Diem, April 26, 1989. The RVN's observer mission to the United Nations also helped the AFV.

38. Interview of Bui Diem, April 26, 1989.

39. Interviews of William Ward, March 6, 1989, and Murray Baron, June 20, 1990.

40. Interview of Bui Diem, April 26, 1989, and letter, Thai to the author, January 23, 1990.

41. Levy, *Debate over Vietnam*, 104; Nash, *Conservative Intellectual Movement*, 305; and letter, O'Neill to David Jones, July 27, 1967, RAFV.

42. Letters, William Ward to Hugh O'Neill, October 9, 1968; O'Neill to David Martin,

November 8 and 19, 1968; O'Neill to Mrs. Daniel Teodoru, December 13 and 23, 1968; Charles J. Stephens to Daniel E. Teodoru, February 20, 1970, RAFV. It is not clear whether the students actually went to Vietnam. Ward claimed the trip took place, but O'Neill had no recollection of anything happening. The author has found no documentary evidence indicating whether the journey took place. Interview of William Ward, March 6, 1989, and letter, O'Neill to the author, May 14, 1989.

43. Letters, O'Neill to David Jones, July 27, 1967, and to Don Feder, September 27, 1967, RAFV.

44. Quarterly report, O'Neill to William Henderson, and memorandum, Yolanda Gallardo to Henderson, August 8, 1966, WFP.

45. Minutes, board of directors meeting, September 8, 1966, WFP, and letter, George Field to Major George F. Eliot, February 2, 1967, RAFV. See also letters, Wesley Fishel to Taylor, February 21, 1966, and Taylor to Fishel, March 1, 1966, WFP, and letter, Henderson to Gilbert Jonas, August 23, 1966, GJP.

46. Letter, Anne Henehan to Wesley Fishel, February 11, 1966, and undated memorandum, Henderson to the board of directors, WFP. See also letters, Hugh O'Neill to Frank Trager, September 13, 1967; Allyn R. Bell to O'Neill, November 30, 1967, and December 2, 1968, RAFV. The Pew Foundation frequently asked its beneficiaries to refrain from publicizing its contributions. See Cunningim, *Private Money and Public Service*, 140-41.

47. Undated list of contributions, RAFV. Support from *Reader's Digest* began after the Wallaces or some of their assistants attended a business luncheon hosted by the AFV on September 27, 1966, that featured Ambassador Thai as the main speaker. See letter, Hugh O'Neill to Frank Trager, December 13, 1966, GJP.

48. Letters, O'Neill to Baron, January 31, 1968, and O'Neill to George Tanham, October 4, 1967, RAFV, and quarterly report (undated), O'Neill to Henderson, WFP. O'Neill's January 31 letter to Baron mentions at least two contributors who were probably influenced by Baron, who was active in labor activities. The International Ladies Garment Workers' Union donated a total of $1,000 in 1966 and 1967, and the International Brotherhood of Teamsters gave the AFV $500 in 1967.

49. Letter, O'Neill to Joseph Ardleigh, December 4, 1967, and letter, O'Neill to Sidney Weinberg, June 4, 1968, RAFV.

50. Letters, O'Neill to William Henderson, September 27 and May 4, 1967, WFP. Widespread resentment against the antiwar movement in 1967 is briefly mentioned in DeBenedetti, "Lyndon Johnson and the Antiwar Opposition," 39.

51. Letter, O'Neill to Thomas Conlon, October 10, 1967, RAFV.

52. DeBenedetti and Chatfield, *American Ordeal*, 176-78, and Small, *Johnson, Nixon, and the Doves*, 99-101.

53. Memorandum, James Rowe to Johnson, Box 73, White House Central Files, Confidential File, LBJ.

54. Invitation to join national committee, November 15, 1965, Box 12, CEC, and Small, *Johnson, Nixon, and the Doves*, 47-48.

55. Memorandum, John P. Roche to Johnson, May 19, 1967, Box 11, Office Files of the President, LBJ.

56. Memoranda, Roche to Johnson, May 19 and June 15, 1967, Box 11, Office Files of the President, LBJ. On the June 15 memo, a note reads, "Doing Good Job."

57. E. W. Kenworthy, "Eisenhower Joins Truman in Group Backing the War," *New York Times*, October 26, 1967; and press releases of Douglas's remarks and the membership roster of the Citizens Committee, October 25, 1967, WFP.

58. Besides the *New York Times*, reports and commentaries about the Citizens Committee appeared in *Time, America, The Nation,* and *National Review*.

59. Remarks of former senator Paul H. Douglas, October 25, 1967, and letter, Douglas to founding members of the committee, November 8, 1967, WFP.

60. Letter, Tanham to board members, October 30, 1967, WFP. Tanham proposed that the board gather in mid-November 1967, but no record of such a meeting has been found.

61. Minutes, meeting of board of directors, March 12, 1968, and attached notes, RAFV.

62. Address to the nation, March 31, 1968, Johnson, *Public Papers*, 1:476.

63. *Pentagon Papers*, 4:538–604; Small, *Johnson, Nixon, and the Doves*, 135–58; Johnson, *Vantage Point*, 380–437; Herring, *America's Longest War*, 200–208; and Schandler, *Unmaking of a President*.

64. Letters, O'Neill to Frank Trager, February 21, 1968, and O'Neill to William Henderson, January 24, 1968, RAFV.

65. Interviews of Hugh O'Neill, March 2, 1989, and William Ward, March 6, 1989.

66. Letters, O'Neill to Weinberg, June 4, 1968, and O'Neill to Frank Trager, February 21, 1968, RAFV.

67. Letter, O'Neill to John Roche, January 31, 1968, RAFV.

68. Letters, O'Neill to William Ward, July 2, 1968, and O'Neill to Valenti, February 19, 1968, RAFV.

69. Letter, O'Neill to William Ward, December 31, 1968, RAFV, and interview of Hugh O'Neill, March 2, 1989.

Chapter 10

1. Memoranda, William Henderson to files, January 16 and February 25, 1969, and minutes, board of directors meeting, March 12, 1968, RAFV; interview of William Ward, March 6, 1989; and letter, Johnson to Tanham, April 5, 1968, White House Central Files, Name File, LBJ.

2. Letter, William Brownell to the author, November 7, 1989, and telephone interview of Brownell, November 30, 1989.

3. Letter, Brownell to the author, November 7, 1989.

4. Undated letter, Brownell to Ward, RAFV.

5. Ibid.

6. Letter, Brownell to the author, November 7, 1989; telephone interview of Brownell, November 30, 1989; and undated letter, Brownell to Ward, RAFV.

7. Interview of Hugh O'Neill, March 2, 1989.

8. Ibid., and letters, Ward to the author, June 8, 1989, and Gilbert Jonas to the author, December 18, 1991. In his letter, Ward stated not only that he could recall no trouble with the Vietnamese, but that the "UN-VN group never tried to influence [the] AFVN while I was around."

9. Minutes, board of directors meeting, July 18, 1969, RAFV.

10. Lewy, *America in Vietnam*, 162–89; Hersh, *Price of Power*, 46–65, 77–82, 118–35; Isaacson, *Kissinger*, 157–79, 234–55; Kissinger, *White House Years*, 239–71, 277–303.

11. Letters, Frank R. Barnett to Charles Colson, January 12, 1970, and Colson to Barnett, January 16, 1970, Box 33, Staff Member and Office Files, White House Special Files, NP. Barnett's letter to Colson may have been prompted by a note he received from Henderson that said any major activity of the AFV needed funding because because the group "is nearly broke." Letter, Henderson to Barnett, December 18, 1969, RAFV.

12. Statement on the Situation in Laos, March 6, 1970, Nixon, *Public Papers*, 244–49. Background information on the conflict in Laos can be found in Adams and McCoy, *War and Revolution*; Dommen, *Politics of Neutralization*; and Gettleman, Gettleman, Kaplan, and Kaplan, *Conflict in Indochina*.

13. Draft statement, March 6, 1970, and letter, Henderson to Colson, March 17, 1970, RAFV.

14. Note, Hugh Sloan to Colson, March 9, 1970, Box 121, Staff Member and Office Files, White House Special Files, NP.

15. Letter, Colson to Henderson, April 3, 1970, Box 33, Staff Member and Office Files, White House Special Files, NP.

16. Interview of William Ward, March 6, 1989; letter, Colson to Henderson, April 3, 1970, and undated memorandum, Box 33, Staff Member and Office Files, White House Special Files, NP.

17. DeBenedetti and Chatfield, *American Ordeal*, 277–87; Herring, *America's Longest War*, 233–39; Isaacson, *Kissinger*, 256–82; Kissinger, *White House Years*, 457–517; Small, *Johnson, Nixon, and the Doves*, 199–208; and Zaroulis and Sullivan, *Who Spoke Up?*, 317–32.

18. Letter, William Henderson to Charles Colson, April 10, 1970, Box 33, Staff Member and Office Files, White House Special Files, NP.

19. Letter, Henderson to George T. Bell, June 28, 1970, Box 33, Staff Member and Office Files, White House Special Files, NP.

20. Letter, Bell to William J. Baroody, July 13, 1970, Box 33, Staff Member and Office Files, White House Special Files, NP.

21. Undated and unsigned notes, Box 33, Staff Member and Office Files, White House Special Files, NP.

22. Memorandum, Bell to Colson, August 17, 1970, Box 33, Staff Member and Office Files, White House Special Files, NP.

23. For example, see reports on a statement released in October 1969, in Felix Belair Jr., "Citizens' Panel Sees Peril in Abrupt Vietnam Pullout," *New York Times*, November 1, 1969, and "New Plan for Ending the War," *U.S. News and World Report*, November 10, 1969, 67.

24. Memorandum, Colson to H. R. Haldeman, February 5, 1970, and undated memorandum, Colson to Nixon, Box 20, Staff Member and Office Files, White House Special Files, NP.

25. Memorandum, Colson to president's file, September 9, 1970, Box 20, Staff Member and Office Files, White House Special Files, NP, and *New York Times*, May 8, 1970.

26. Memorandum of discussion, June 19, 1970, Box 78, CEC, and record of an informal meeting of the board of directors, February 8, 1971, RAFV.

27. Letter, Ward to the editor of the *New York Times*, May 14, 1970, and an undated letter of reply, Tom Wicker to Ward, RAFV. Wicker's article appeared in the May 12, 1970, edition of the *New York Times* under the title "Mr. Nixon's Scary Dreams."

28. Reply to WCBS-TV editorial, and transcript, WCBS-TV editorial, December 16, 1969, RAFV.

29. Letter, Henderson to Frank R. Barnett, January 8, 1970, RAFV.

30. Minutes, board of directors meetings, July 18, 1969, and March 10, 1970, RAFV. At the second meeting, Henderson stated that the AFV raised nearly $24,000 in the 1969-1970 fiscal year.

31. Justus M. van der Kroef, "Peking, Hanoi, and Guerrilla Insurgency in Southeast Asia," *Southeast Asian Perspectives* 3:1-67, and Frank N. Trager, "The Nixon Doctrine and Asian Policy," *Southeast Asian Perspectives* 6:1-34.

32. Schandler, *Unmaking of a President*, 352.

33. Hersh, *Price of Power*, 503-28, 589-604; Isaacson, *Kissinger*, 439-60; Karnow, *Vietnam*, 636-52; Kissinger, *White House Years*, 1302-94; Goodman, *Lost Peace*, 123-38; and Porter, *Peace Denied*, 125-42.

34. Telegram, Trager and James W. Gerard to Nguyen Van Thieu, October 25, 1972, RAFV.

35. Letter, Phung Nhat Minh to the American Friends of Vietnam, November 7, 1972, RAFV; and interview of William Ward, March 6, 1989.

36. Letter, Nixon to Thieu, January 5, 1973, in Hung and Schechter, *Palace File*, 392.

37. The final negotiations for the cease-fire are recounted in Goodman, *Lost Peace*, 143-64; Hersh, *Price of Power*, 604-35; Hung and Schechter, *Palace File*, 130-57; Isaacson, *Kissinger*, 461-77, 480-90; Kissinger, *White House Years*, 1395-473; Porter, *Peace Denied*, 142-73; and Isaacs, *Without Honor*, 54-70.

38. Letter, Lansdale to AFV, January 25, 1973, Box 11, SWC. Nothing came of this idea and two of the replies Lansdale received, letters from Generals O'Daniel and Williams, expressed the greatest pessimism about the RVN's future. Williams accurately predicted the panic of the RVN's senior commanders by writing, "Each will look out for himself and his family first and his country second." Letters, Williams to Lansdale, February 4, 1973, Box 6, and O'Daniel to Lansdale, February 6, 1973, Box 5, ELC.

39. Letter, John H. Holdridge to Ward, November 30, 1972, NP.

40. Letters, F. P. Serong to Henderson, January 11, 1973, and Henderson to Serong, March 2, 1973, RAFV.

41. Letter, Oram to Henderson, March 2, 1973, and memoranda, Eva Bates to Oram, February 7, 1973, and Oram to Henderson, March 2, 1973, RAFV.

42. Memorandum, Henderson to Nguyen Huu Chi, March 15, 1973, and letters, Serong to Henderson, April 9 and 26, 1973, RAFV.

43. Interview of William Ward, March 6, 1989. Minutes, board of directors meeting, October 2, 1973, and letter, Henderson to Harold Oram, October 5, 1973, RAFV.

44. Minutes, board of directors meeting, October 2, 1973, RAFV.

45. Letter, Ward to Henderson, February 14, 1974, and minutes, board of directors meeting, September 12, 1974, RAFV. Interview of William Ward, March 6, 1989.

Two of the AFV's earliest members left at this time as well. Monsignor Joseph Harnett resigned as an AFV officer in September 1973, while Christopher Emmet died on February 12, 1974. See letter, Harnett to Ward, September 25, 1973, RAFV, and Emmet obituary, *New York Times*, February 13, 1974.

46. Minutes, board of directors meeting, September 12, 1974, RAFV; and letters, Henderson to Christopher Emmet, October 11, 1973, and Emmet to Henderson, November 6, 1973, Box 78, CEC.

47. Goodman, *Lost Peace*, 167–76; Isaacs, *Without Honor*, 101–22; Lewy, *America in Vietnam*, 215–22; and Porter, *Peace Denied*, 174–232, 239–70.

48. Letter, Gerald R. Ford to Thieu, August 10, 1974, in Hung and Schechter, *Palace File*, 434.

49. DeBenedetti and Chatfield, *American Ordeal*, 364–68; Isaacs, *Without Honor*, 313–21; Lewy, *America in Vietnam*, 205–10; Zaroulis and Sullivan, *Who Spoke Up?*, 406–14; and Snepp, *Decent Interval*, 91–117.

50. Minutes, December 30, 1974, RAFV.

51. Emergency Committee for Vietnam: Preliminary Concepts and Agenda, RAFV.

52. Pamphlet, "Perspective on Vietnam." The emphasis was in the original document. See also letters, Trager to Dr. William Schneider Jr., January 17, 1975, and Trager to Walter Judd, April 17, 1975. All of the above material is in RAFV.

53. Hung and Schechter, *Palace File*, 263–75; Isaacs, *Without Honor*, 329–92; Snepp, *Decent Interval*, 127–41, 170–264; and Van Tien Dung, *Our Great Spring Victory*, 26–130.

54. Advertisements, "Vietnam Is Calling," *New York Times*, April 21, 1975, and "An Appeal to the American Conscience," *Washington Post*, March 21, 1975. Hereafter cited by the titles of the advertisements.

55. "An Appeal to the American Conscience."

56. "Vietnam Is Calling."

57. Athelia Knight, "Marchers Oppose U.S. Vietnam Stand," *Washington Post*, April 11, 1975, and letter, Trager to Judd, April 17, 1975, RAFV.

58. Letter, Trager to Judd, April 17, 1975, and draft of a letter from Trager to Ford, RAFV.

The Ford Library does have an exchange of messages between Trager and Ford on the issue of aid to the RVN, but in his reply to Trager, Ford said he would work closely with the Congress in forging "one foreign policy"—a remark that hardly could have been encouraging given the strength of congressional opposition to aid appropriations for the RVN. Mailgram, Professor and Mrs. Frank N. Trager to Ford, April 10, 1975, and letter, Ford to Professor and Mrs. Frank N. Trager, April 18, 1975, General Exec, SP 2-3-3, GRF.

59. Letters, Lem L. Funk to the Emergency Committee, March 21, 1975, and Commander Sidney E. Wood to the Emergency Committee, March 24, 1975, RAFV.

60. Letter, Harrison A. Williams Jr. to William G. Applegate III, April 11, 1975, RAFV.

61. *New York Times*, April 24, 1975.

62. Bernard Gwertzman, "Ford Asks $972 Million in Aid for Saigon," *New York Times*, April 11, 1975.

63. Dung, *Our Great Spring Victory*, 130–257; Hung and Schechter, *Palace File*, 302–33; Isaacs, *Without Honor*, 404–46; and Snepp, *Decent Interval*, 342–437.

64. Shaplen, *Turning Wheel*, xi.
65. Isaacs, *Without Honor*, 482. See also Hung and Schechter, *Palace File*, 334–49; Isaacs, *Without Honor*, 447–87; and Snepp, *Decent Interval*, 438–580.
66. Letter, Martin to Henderson, April 28, 1975, RAFV.
67. Letter, William Applegate III to Henderson, May 7, 1975, RAFV.

Chapter 11

1. Letter, Oram to Charles A. Edison, May 4, 1956, RAFV.
2. Advertisement, "Vietnam Is Calling," *New York Times*, April 21, 1975.
3. Anderson, *Trapped By Success*, 159.
4. Gibbons, *U.S. Government and the Vietnam War*, 1:301.
5. Buttinger diary, November 20, 1954, JBP.
6. Telephone interview of Gary MacEoin, March 18, 1989.
7. MacEoin, *Memoirs and Memories*, 120–22.
8. Letter, MacEoin to the author, April 11, 1989.
9. Letter, Douglas to Frazier T. Woolard, May 14, 1968, Box 293, WODP.
10. Letter, Douglas to Hugh O'Neill, July 27, 1968, Box 521, WODP.
11. Wise and Ross, *Espionage Establishment*, 155, and Norman Kempster, "CIA Subsidized Dozens of Books on Policy," *Washington Star*, February 9, 1976. The author would like to thank Mr. Morris B. Schnapper for bringing this material to his attention.
12. Interview of Harold Oram, April 5, 1989.
13. Note, Nan Burgess to Douglas, April 27, 1965, Box 521, WODP.
14. Letter, Douglas to Dr. Bertha B. Faust, May 18, 1965, Box 521, WODP.
15. Interview of William Ward, March 6, 1989. Although not speaking directly about the AFV, Harold Oram wrote that no government funds "were given or used" while his firm did public relations work for the RVN. He did, however, say that he thought that the CIA tapped his company's phones while he had the contract with the Diem regime. Interview of Harold Oram, April 5, 1989, and letter, Oram to the author, May 7, 1989. It should be added that the CIA claims that it has no records concerning Oram or his company. Letter, Eunice M. Evans to the author, November 12, 1991.
16. When the author asked the CIA for access to any material concerning the AFV, he was told that no "record responsive to your request has been found." Letter, John H. Wright to the author, June 20, 1989.
17. Memorandum, Jonas to Oram, August 5, 1960, RAFV.
18. Scheer and Hinckle, "Vietnam Lobby," 34.
19. Memorandum Re: Wolf's Letter on Ambassador Chuong, Box 35, HOP.
20. Letter, Jonas to Ladejinsky, January 11, 1961, Box 35, HOP. See also undated memorandum, Jonas to Ladejinsky, and letters, Jonas to Ladejinsky, August 11, 1959, and May 6, 1960, Box 35, HOP.
21. Letter, Jonas to the author, December 18, 1991. In this note Jonas also remembered that Duc antagonized AFV members by acting as if "he could order them about." Wesley Fishel also complained about Duc's behavior. Letter, Fishel to Diem, April 30[?], 1960, *FRUS, 1958-1960*, 1:428.

Chuong apparently kept Diem in the dark about the AFV's work as well. When Jorge

Ortiz, the representative of the firm that replaced Oram's company in 1961, told Diem about what he knew of the AFV's activities, he claimed that "the President was incredulous" and that he suggested that the embassy in Washington "was not passing on information to Saigon." Memorandum, Louis Andreatta to Joseph Buttinger, January 3, 1962, JBP.

22. The conflicting lines of authority that existed in the Republic of China's embassy are described in Koen, *The China Lobby*, 37, and Tucker, *Patterns in the Dust*, 168–69.

23. Koen, *The China Lobby*, 173.

24. Letter, Leo Cherne to the editor, *New York Times Magazine*, December 12, 1954.

25. "Outline for New Policies in Vietnam," WFP.

26. American Friends of Vietnam, *Investment Conditions in Vietnam*, 7.

27. Undated memorandum from Cherne, WFP.

28. Fitzgerald, *Fire in the Lake*, 227.

29. Undated memorandum from Cherne, WFP.

bibliography

Archives and Manuscript Collections

American Friends of Vietnam. Records. Archive of the Vietnam Conflict. Texas Tech University. Lubbock, Tex.
Buttinger, Joseph. Papers. Harvard-Yenching Library. Harvard University. Cambridge, Mass.
Donovan, William J. Papers. United States Army Military History Institute. Carlisle Barracks. Carlisle, Pa.
Douglas, William O. Papers. Manuscripts Division. Library of Congress. Washington, D.C.
Dulles, John Foster. Papers. Seeley Mudd Manuscript Library. Princeton University. Princeton, N.J.
Emmet, Christopher. Collection. Hoover Institution Archives. Stanford, Calif.
Fishel, Wesley R. Papers. University Archives and Historical Collections. Michigan State University. East Lansing, Mich.
Great Britain. Foreign Office. General Records. Public Record Office. London.
Harnett, Monsignor Joseph. Papers. University of Notre Dame Archives. South Bend, Ind.
Jonas, Gilbert A. Papers. University Archives and Historical Collections. Michigan State University. East Lansing, Mich.
Kahin-Indochina/Vietnam Documents. National Security Archive. Washington, D.C.
Kennedy, John F. Pre-Presidential Papers. John F. Kennedy Presidential Library. Dorchester, Mass.
Lansdale, Edward G. Collection. Hoover Institution Archives. Stanford, Calif.
Michigan State University Vietnam Project. University Archives and Historical Collections. Michigan State University. East Lansing, Mich.
O'Daniel, John W. Papers. United States Army Military History Institute. Carlisle Barracks, Pa.
Oram, Harold L. Papers and the Records of the Oram Group, Inc. Special Collections and Archives. Indiana University/Purdue University at Indianapolis. Indianapolis, Ind.
Sorenson, Theodore. Papers. John F. Kennedy Presidential Library. Dorchester, Mass.
Thomas, Norman. Papers. Rare Books and Manuscripts Division. New York Public Library. Astor, Lenox and Tilden Foundations. New York, N.Y.
Thomson, James C. Papers. John F. Kennedy Presidential Library. Dorchester, Mass.
U.S. Congress. Papers of the Senate Committee on Foreign Relations. Record Group 46. National Archives. Washington, D.C.

U.S. Department of State. General Records. Record Group 59. National Archives. Washington, D.C.

———. Office of Public Opinion Studies. Record Group 59. National Archives. Washington, D.C.

———. Records of Philippine and Southeast Asian Affairs. Lot 54D190. Record Group 59. National Archives. Washington, D.C.

White House Central Files. Dwight D. Eisenhower Presidential Library. Abilene, Kans.

White House Central Files. Gerald Ford Presidential Library. Ann Arbor, Mich.

White House Central Files. Lyndon B. Johnson Presidential Library. Austin, Tex.

White House Central Files. John F. Kennedy Presidential Library. Dorchester, Mass.

White House Central Name File. John F. Kennedy Presidential Library. Dorchester, Mass.

White House National Defense Files. Lyndon B. Johnson Presidential Library. Austin, Tex.

White House National Security Country Files. Lyndon B. Johnson Presidential Library. Austin, Tex.

White House National Security Files. Lyndon B. Johnson Presidential Library. Austin, Tex.

White House Office Files of the President. Lyndon B. Johnson Presidential Library. Austin, Tex.

White House Special Files. Nixon Materials Project. National Archives. Washington, D.C.

White House Staff Files. John F. Kennedy Presidential Library. Dorchester, Mass.

Williams, Samuel T. Collection. Hoover Institution Archives. Stanford, Calif.

———. Papers. United States Army Military History Institute. Carlisle Barracks. Carlisle, Pa.

Published Documents

Cameron, Allan W., ed. *Viet-Nam Crisis: A Documentary History.* Vol. 1, *1940-1956.* Ithaca: Cornell University Press, 1971.

Johnson, Lyndon B. *Public Papers of the Presidents of the United States: Lyndon B. Johnson, 1965.* 2 vols. Washington: Government Printing Office, 1966.

———. *Public Papers of the Presidents of the United States: Lyndon B. Johnson, 1968-1969.* 2 vols. Washington: Government Printing Office, 1970.

Nixon, Richard. *Public Papers of the Presidents of the United States: Richard Nixon, 1970.* Washington: Government Printing Office, 1971.

The Pentagon Papers: The Senator Gravel Edition. 4 vols. Boston: Beacon Press, 1971.

Porter, Gareth, ed. *Vietnam: The Definitive Documentation of Human Decisions.* 2 vols. Stanfordville, N.Y.: Earl M. Coleman Enterprises, 1979.

U.S. Congress. House. Committee on Foreign Affairs. *Current Situation in the Far East, July 27-August 14, 1959.* Washington: Government Printing Office, 1959.

U.S. Congress. Senate. Committee on Foreign Relations. *Report on Indochina: Report of Senator Mike Mansfield on a Study Mission to Vietnam, Cambodia, Laos, October 15, 1954.* 83rd Cong., 2nd sess., S Fo-2. Washington: Government Printing Office, 1954.

———. *Situation in Vietnam, July 30–31.* 86th Cong., 1st sess., S 1359–1. Washington: Government Printing Office, 1959.

U.S. Department of Commerce. *Economic Developments in Viet-Nam, 1956.* Washington: Government Printing Office, 1957.

U.S. Department of Defense. *United States–Vietnam Relations, 1945–1967.* 12 vols. Washington: Government Printing Office, 1971.

U.S. Department of State. *Foreign Relations of the United States, 1950.* Vol. 7, *Asia and the Pacific.* Washington: Government Printing Office, 1976. (*Foreign Relations of the United States* will hereafter be cited and abbreviated as *FRUS.*)

———. *FRUS, 1951.* Vol. 6, *Asia and the Pacific.* Washington: Government Printing Office, 1977.

———. *FRUS, 1952–1954.* Vol. 13, *Indochina.* Washington: Government Printing Office, 1982.

———. *FRUS, 1952–1954.* Vol. 16, *The Geneva Conference.* Washington: Government Printing Office, 1982.

———. *FRUS, 1955–1957.* Vol. 1, *Vietnam.* Washington: Government Printing Office, 1985.

———. *FRUS, 1958–1960.* Vol. 1, *Vietnam.* Washington: Government Printing Office, 1987.

———. *FRUS, 1961–1963.* Vol. 1, *Vietnam, 1961.* Washington: Government Printing Office, 1988.

———. *FRUS, 1961–1963.* Vol. 2, *Vietnam, 1962.* Washington: Government Printing Office, 1990.

———. *FRUS, 1961–1963.* Vol. 3, *Vietnam, January–August, 1963.* Washington: Government Printing Office, 1991.

———. *FRUS, 1961–1963.* Vol. 4, *Vietnam, August–December, 1963.* Washington: Government Printing Office, 1991.

———. *FRUS, 1964–1968.* Vol. 1, *Vietnam, 1964.* Washington: Government Printing Office, 1992.

Wile, Annadel, ed. *Declassified Documents Reference System Retrospective Collection.* 2 vols. Washington, D.C.: Carrollton Press, 1976–77.

Interviews, Oral Histories, and Correspondence

Baron, Murray. Interview by the author, June 20, 1990, and telephone interview by the author, August 30, 1990.

Brownell, William. Letter to the author, November 7, 1989, and telephone interview by the author, November 30, 1989.

Bui Diem. Interview by the author, April 26, 1989.

Cherne, Leo. Interview by the author, March 15, 1989, and letter to the author, July 20, 1989.

Cooper, Chester L. Interview by the author, April 20, 1989.

Douglas, William O. Oral History Interview by John F. Stewart on November 9, 1967. John F. Kennedy Oral History Program. John F. Kennedy Presidential Library. Dorchester, Mass.

Duke, Angier Biddle. Interview by the author, April 3, 1989, and letter to the author, May 8, 1989.

Jonas, Gilbert. Interview by the author, May 8, 1989, and letter to the author, December 18, 1991.

Kattenburg, Paul. Telephone interview by the author, August 13, 1991, and letters to the author, February 18, 1992, and June 8, 1992.

MacEoin, Gary. Telephone interview by the author, March 18, 1989, and letter to the author, April 11, 1989.

Mansfield, Mike. Interview by Richard Challener on May 10, 1966. John Foster Dulles Oral History Project. Seeley Mudd Manuscript Library. Princeton University. Princeton, N.J.

O'Neill, Hugh. Interview by the author, March 2, 1989, and letter to the author, May 14, 1989.

Oram, Harold L. Interview by the author, April 5, 1989, and letter to the author, May 7, 1989.

Sanders, Sol. Interview by the author. September 19, 1991.

Smuckler, Ralph. Interview by the author, September 16, 1988, and letter to the author, October 19, 1990.

Vu Van Thai. Letter to the author, January 23, 1990.

Ward, William. Interview by the author, March 6, 1989, and letter to the author, June 8, 1989.

White, Peter. Letters to the author, May 9–10, 1989, and June 24, 1989, and one undated letter.

Newspapers and Periodicals

Congressional Record, 1956–60.
Life, 1957.
The Nation, 1967.
National Review, 1967, 1974.
New York Times, 1954–75.
The Reporter, 1954, 1957.
Southeast Asian Perspectives, 1971–73.
Time, 1954, 1965, 1967.
Times of London, 1956.
U.S. News and World Report, 1954, 1969.
Vietnam Perspectives, 1965–67.
Washington Daily News, 1959.
Washington Post, 1954–75.
Washington Star, 1976.

Articles and Essays

Buttinger, Joseph. "Eyewitness Report on Vietnam." *The Reporter* 12 (January 27, 1955): 19–20.

———. "Saigon—Intrigue." *The New Republic* 132 (February 28, 1955): 9–10.
Cherne, Leo. "The Deepening Red Shadow over Vietnam." *New York Times Magazine*, April 9, 1961.
Corley, Francis J., S.J. "Vietnam Since Geneva." *Thought* 33 (1958–59): 515–68.
Coburn, Judith. "Asian Scholars and Government: The Chrysanthemum and the Sword." In *America's Asia: Dissenting Essays on American-Asian Relations*, edited by Edward Friedman and Mark Selden, 67–107. New York: Pantheon Books, 1971.
DeBenedetti, Charles. "Lyndon Johnson and the Antiwar Opposition." In *The Johnson Years: Vietnam, the Environment, and Science*, edited by Robert A. Divine, 25–33. Lawrence: University of Kansas Press.
du Berrier, Hilaire. "Report from Saigon." *American Mercury* 87 (September 1958): 43–51.
Durdin, Peggy. "Saigon in the Shadow of Doom." *New York Times Magazine*, November 21, 1954.
Fishel, Wesley R. "Free Vietnam Since Geneva." *Yale Review* 49 (Autumn 1959): 68–79.
———. "Vietnam's Democratic One-Man Rule." *The New Leader* 42 (November 2, 1959): 10–13.
Freeman, Samuel. "American Friends of Vietnam." In *Dictionary of the Vietnam War*, edited by James Olson, 18–19. Westport, Conn.: Greenwood Press, 1988.
Graebner, Norman A. "Eisenhower and Communism: The Public Record of the 1950s." In *Reevaluating Eisenhower: American Foreign Policy in the 1950s*, edited by Richard A. Melanson and David Mayers, 67–87. Urbana: University of Illinois Press, 1987.
Henderson, William. "South Vietnam Finds Itself." *Foreign Affairs* 35 (January 1957): 285–301.
Herring, George C., and Richard Immerman. "Eisenhower, Dulles, and Dienbienphu: 'The Day We Didn't Go to War' Revisited." *Journal of American History* 71 (September 1984): 343–63.
Hinckle, Warren, Robert Scheer, and Sol Stern. "The University on the Make." *Ramparts*, January 25, 1969, 52–60.
Hotham, David. "South Vietnam: Shaky Bastion." *The New Republic* 137 (November 25, 1957): 13–16.
———. "Trouble in North, in South, in Future." *The Reporter* 16 (February 21, 1957): 36–38.
———. "U.S. Aid to Vietnam: A Balance Sheet." *The Reporter* 16 (September 19, 1957): 30–33.
Huynh Sanh Thong. "'Greatest Little Man in Asia. . . .'" *The Nation* 192 (February 18, 1961): 140–42.
Ladejinsky, Wolf. "Vietnam—The First Five Years." *The Reporter* 21 (December 21, 1959): 19–21.
Mansfield, Senator Mike. "Reprieve in Viet Nam." *Harper's Magazine* 212 (January 1956): 46–51.
New Catholic Encyclopedia. 1967 ed., s.v. "Catholic Relief Services–NCWC," by E. E. Swanstrom.

O'Daniel, John W. "Free Vietnam: Modern Miracle." *American Mercury* 88 (March 1959): 146–52.
Osborne, John. "The Tough Miracle Man of Vietnam." *Life*, May 13, 1957, 156–76.
Parmet, Herbert. "The Making and Unmaking of Ngo Dinh Diem." In *Second Indochina War Symposium*, edited by John Schlight, 35–63. Washington: Government Printing Office, 1986.
Roper, Jon. "Vietnam and the Western Idea of Mission." In *America, France, and Vietnam: Cultural History and Ideas of Conflict*, edited by Phil Milling and Jon Roper, 17–31. Aldershot, England: Avebury, 1991.
Sanders, Sol. "One Way to Save Indo-China." *The New Leader*, August 27, 1951, 8–9.
———. "Viet Nam *Has* a Third Force." *The New Republic* 125 (July 30, 1951): 14–15.
Scheer, Robert. "Hang Down Your Head, Tom Dooley." *Ramparts*, January 25, 1969, 15–19.
———. "Leo Cherne, Our Man with the CIA." *New Times* 6 (March 19, 1976): 16.
Scheer, Robert, and Warren Hinckle. "The Vietnam Lobby." *Ramparts*, January 25, 1969, 31–36.
Turner, Henry A. "How Pressure Groups Operate." *The Annals of the American Academy of Political Science* 319 (September 1958): 63–72.
Underhill, James B. "Foreign Lobbyists: The Hidden Pressures to Sway U.S. Policy." *Newsweek*, July 30, 1962, 18–22.
Wertenbaker, Charles. "The China Lobby." *The Reporter* 6 (April 15, 1952): 4–24.
Z [pseud.]. "The War in Vietnam: We Have Not Been Told the Whole Truth." *The New Republic* 139 (March 12, 1962): 21–26.

Books and Theses

Adams, Nina S., and Alfred W. McCoy, eds. *Laos: War and Revolution*. New York: Harper and Row, 1970.
American Friends of Vietnam. *America's Stake in Vietnam*. Washington, D.C.: Business Services, 1956.
———. *America's Stake in Vietnam*. Edited version. New York: American Friends of Vietnam, 1956.
———. *Investment Conditions in the Republic of Vietnam*. New York: American Friends of Vietnam, 1958.
———. *Aid to Vietnam: An American Success Story*. New York: American Friends of Vietnam, 1959.
———. *Conference of Education, Health, and Administration*. New York: Sills Reporting Service, 1959.
———. *Conference of Land Tenure*. New York: Sills Reporting Service, 1959.
American Jewish Biographies. New York: Lakeville Press, 1982.
Anderson, David L. *Trapped By Success: The Eisenhower Administration and Vietnam, 1953–1961*. New York: Columbia University Press, 1991.
Aronson, James. *The Press and the Cold War*. Boston: Beacon Press, 1973.
Austin, Anthony. *The President's War*. New York: J. B. Lippincott and Company, 1971.
Bao Dai. *Le Dragon D'Annam*. Paris: Plon, 1980.

Berman, Larry. *Planning a Tragedy: The Americanization of the War in Vietnam.* New York: W. W. Norton, 1982.
Billings-Yun, Melanie. *Decision against War: Eisenhower and Dien Bien Phu.* New York: Columbia University Press, 1988.
Bindas, Kenneth J. "The Strains of Commitment: American Periodical Press and Vietnam, 1955–1960." Paper prepared for the Charles DeBenedetti Memorial Conference, University of Toledo, Toledo, Ohio, May 4–5, 1990.
Black, Jan Knippers. *Development in Theory and Practice: Bridging the Gap.* Boulder, Colo.: Westview, 1991.
Boettcher, Thomas D. *Vietnam: The Valor and the Sorrow.* Boston: Little, Brown and Company, 1985.
Bornet, Vaughn Davis. *The Presidency of Lyndon B. Johnson.* Lawrence: University of Kansas Press, 1981.
Bouscaren, Anthony T. *The Last of the Mandarins: Diem of Vietnam.* Pittsburgh: Duquesne University Press, 1965.
Brown, Anthony Cave. *The Last Hero: Wild Bill Donovan.* New York: Times Books, 1982.
Bui Diem, with David Chanoff. *In the Jaws of History.* Boston: Houghton Mifflin, 1987.
Buttinger, Joseph. *In the Twilight of Socialism: A History of the Revolutionary Socialists of Austria.* New York: Frederick A. Praeger, 1953.
———. *The Smaller Dragon: A Political History of Vietnam.* New York: Frederick A. Praeger, 1958.
———. *Vietnam: A Dragon Embattled.* 2 vols. New York: Frederick A. Praeger, 1967.
———. *Vietnam: The Unforgettable Tragedy.* New York: Horizon Press, 1977.
Caute, David. *The Great Fear: The Anti-Communist Purge under Truman and Eisenhower.* New York: Simon and Schuster, 1978.
Cohen, Bernard C. *The Political Process and Foreign Policy: The Making of the Japanese Peace Settlement.* Princeton: Princeton University Press, 1957.
Collier, Peter, and David Horowitz. *The Kennedys: An American Drama.* New York: Summit Books, 1984.
Collins, J. Lawton. *Lightning Joe: An Autobiography.* Baton Rouge: Louisiana State University Press, 1979.
Cooney, John. *The American Pope: The Life and Times of Francis Cardinal Spellman.* New York: Times Books, 1984.
Cooper, Chester L. *The Lost Crusade: America in Vietnam.* New York: Dodd, Mead, and Company, 1970.
Cunningim, Merrimon. *Private Money and Public Service: The Role of Foundations in American Society.* New York: McGraw Hill, 1972.
Currey, Cecil B. *Edward Lansdale: The Unquiet American.* Boston: Houghton Mifflin, 1988.
Davidson, Philip B. *Vietnam at War: The History, 1946–1975.* Novato, Calif.: Presidio Press, 1988.
DeBenedetti, Charles, and Charles Chatfield. *An American Ordeal: The Antiwar Movement of the Vietnam Era.* Syracuse: Syracuse University Press, 1990.

de Jaegher, Raymond, and Irene Corbally Kuhn. *The Enemy Within: An Eyewitness Account of the Communist Conquest of China.* Garden City, N.Y.: Doubleday, 1952.

Devillers, Philippe, and Jean Lacouture. *End of a War: Indochina, 1954.* New York: Frederick A. Praeger, 1969.

Dommen, Arthur J. *Laos: The Politics of Neutralization.* New York: Frederick A. Praeger, 1965.

Dooley, Thomas A. *Deliver Us from Evil.* New York: Farrar, Strauss, and Cudahy, 1956.

Doudna, Martin K. *Concerned about the Planet: The Reporter Magazine and American Liberalism, 1949-1968.* Westport, Conn.: Greenwood Press, 1977.

Douglas, William O. *North From Malaya: Adventure on Five Fronts.* Garden City, N.Y.: Doubleday, 1953.

du Berrier, Hilaire. *Background to Betrayal: The Tragedy of Vietnam.* Belmont, Mass.: Western Islands, 1965.

Duiker, William J. *The Communist Road to Power in Vietnam.* Boulder, Colo.: Westview, 1981.

Duncanson, Dennis J. *Government and Revolution in Vietnam.* London: Oxford University Press, 1968.

Dunlop, Richard. *Donovan: America's Master Spy.* Chicago: Rand McNally, 1982.

Eisenhower, Dwight D. *The White House Years: Mandate for Change, 1953-1956.* Garden City, N.Y.: Doubleday, 1963.

Evoy, Ann, ed. *Contemporary Authors.* New Revision Series. Vols. 1-2. Detroit: Gale Research Company, 1981.

Fall, Bernard B. *The Two Vietnams: A Political and Military Analysis.* 2nd rev. ed. New York: Frederick A. Praeger, 1967.

———. *Viet-Nam Witness, 1953-1966.* New York: Frederick A. Praeger, 1966.

Fishel, Wesley R., ed. *Problems of Freedom: South Vietnam Since Independence.* New York: Free Press of Glencoe, 1961.

Fisher, James Terence. *The Catholic Counterculture in America, 1933-1962.* Chapel Hill: University of North Carolina Press, 1989.

Fitzgerald, Frances. *Fire in the Lake: The Vietnamese and the Americans in Vietnam.* Boston: Little, Brown and Company, 1972.

Galloway, John. *The Gulf of Tonkin Resolution.* Rutherford, N.J.: Fairleigh Dickinson University Press, 1970.

The Gallup Poll: Public Opinion, 1935-1971. 3 vols. New York: Random House, 1972.

Gardiner, Muriel. *Code Name "Mary": Memoirs of an American Woman in the Austrian Underground.* New Haven: Yale University Press, 1983.

Gardner, Lloyd C. *Approaching Vietnam: From World War II through Dienbienphu.* New York: W. W. Norton, 1988.

Geddo, Piero. *The Cross and the Bo-Tree: Catholics and Buddhists in Vietnam.* New York: Sheed and Ward, 1970.

Gettleman, Marvin, Susan Gettleman, Lawrence Kaplan, and Carol Kaplan, eds. *Conflict in Indochina: A Reader on the Widening War in Laos and Cambodia.* New York: Random House, 1970.

Gibbons, William Conrad. *The U.S. Government and the Vietnam War: Executive and*

Legislative Roles and Relationships. Pts. 1–3. Princeton: Princeton University Press, 1986–89.

Goodman, Allan E. *The Lost Peace: America's Search for a Negotiated Settlement of the Vietnam War*. Stanford: Hoover Institution Press, 1978.

Greenstein, Fred I. *The Hidden-Hand Presidency: Eisenhower as Leader*. New York: Basic Books, 1982.

Griffith, Robert, and Athan Theoharis. *The Specter: Original Essays on the Cold War and the Origins of McCarthyism*. New York: Franklin Watts, 1974.

Halberstam, David. *The Making of a Quagmire*. New York: Random House, 1964.

Hamby, Alonzo L. *Beyond the New Deal: Harry S. Truman and American Liberalism*. New York: Columbia University Press, 1972.

Hammer, Ellen. *A Death in November: America in Vietnam, 1963*. New York: E. P. Dutton, 1987.

Harrison, James Pinckney. *The Endless War: Fifty Years of Struggle in Vietnam*. New York: The Free Press, 1982.

Heale, M. J. *American Anticommunism: Combating the Enemy Within, 1830-1970*. Baltimore: Johns Hopkins University Press, 1990.

Herring, George. *America's Longest War: The United States and Vietnam, 1950-1975*. 2nd ed. Philadelphia: Temple University Press, 1986.

Hersh, Seymour M. *The Price of Power: Kissinger in the White House*. New York: Summit Books, 1983.

Hodgson, Godfrey. *America in Our Time*. Garden City, N.Y.: Doubleday, 1976.

Hoopes, Townsend. *The Devil and John Foster Dulles*. Boston: Little, Brown and Company, 1974.

Huynh Kim Khanh. *Vietnamese Communism, 1925-1945*. Ithaca, N.Y.: Cornell University Press, 1982.

Iriye, Akira. *Across the Pacific: An Inner History of American-East Asian Relations*. New York: Harcourt Brace Jovanovich, 1967.

Isaacs, Arnold R. *Without Honor: Defeat in Vietnam and Cambodia*. Baltimore: Johns Hopkins University Press, 1983.

Isaacson, Walter. *Kissinger: A Biography*. New York: Simon and Schuster, 1992.

Johnson, Lyndon Baines. *The Vantage Point: Perspectives of the Presidency, 1963-1969*. New York: Holt, Rinehart and Winston, 1971.

Kahin, George McT. *Intervention: How America Became Involved in Vietnam*. New York: Alfred A. Knopf, 1986; Garden City, N.Y.: Doubleday, 1987.

Karnow, Stanley. *Vietnam: A History*. New York: Viking, 1983.

Kaufman, Burton I. *Trade and Aid: Eisenhower's Foreign Economic Policy*. Baltimore: Johns Hopkins University Press, 1982.

Kearns, Doris. *Lyndon Johnson and the American Dream*. New York: Harper and Row, 1976.

Kissinger, Henry A. *White House Years*. New York: W. W. Norton, 1979.

Koen, Ross. *The China Lobby in American Politics*. New York: Harper and Row, 1974.

Lansdale, Edward Geary. *In the Midst of Wars: An American's Mission to Southeast Asia*. New York: Harper and Row, 1972.

Larsen, Dana B. "In Search of a Third Force: The American Lobby for Ngo Dinh Diem." Master's thesis, University of Arizona, 1985.

Levenstein, Aaron. *Escape to Freedom: The Story of the International Rescue Committee*. Westport, Conn.: Greenwood Press, 1983.

Levy, David. *The Debate over Vietnam*. Baltimore: Johns Hopkins University Press, 1991.

Levy, Margot, ed. *The Annual Obituary, 1984*. Chicago: St. James Press, 1985.

Lewy, Guenter. *America in Vietnam*. New York: Oxford University Press, 1978.

Lochner, Frances Carol, ed. *Contemporary Authors*. Vols. 73–76. Detroit: Gale Research Company, 1978.

McAlister, John T., Jr., and Paul Mus. *The Vietnamese and Their Revolution*. New York: Harper and Row, 1970.

McAuliffe, Mary Sperling. *Crisis on the Left: Cold War Politics and American Liberals, 1947-1954*. Amherst: University of Massachusetts Press, 1978.

MacEoin, Gary. *Memoirs and Memories*. Mystic, Conn.: Twenty-Third Publications, 1986.

Marr, David G. *Vietnamese Tradition on Trial, 1920-1945*. Berkeley: University of California Press, 1981.

Montgomery, John D. *The Politics of Foreign Aid: American Experience in Southeast Asia*. New York: Frederick A. Praeger, 1962.

Moritz, Charles, ed. *Current Biography Yearbook, 1983*. New York: H. W. Wilson, 1984.

Nash, George H. *The Conservative Intellectual Movement in America Since 1945*. New York: Basic Books, 1976.

Nguyen Tien Hung and Jerrold L. Schechter. *The Palace File*. New York: Harper and Row, 1986.

Packenham, Robert L. *Liberal America and the Third World: Political Development Ideas in Foreign Aid and Social Science*. Princeton: Princeton University Press, 1973.

Pells, Richard H. *The Liberal Mind in a Conservative Age: American Intellectuals and Their World*. New York: Oxford University Press, 1985.

Persico, Joseph E. *Casey: From the OSS to the CIA*. New York: Viking, 1990.

Porter, Gareth. *A Peace Denied: The United States, Vietnam, and the Paris Agreement*. Bloomington: Indiana University Press, 1975.

Randle, Robert. *Geneva 1954: The Settlement of the Indochinese War*. Princeton: Princeton University Press, 1969.

Rust, William J., et al. *Kennedy in Vietnam*. New York: Charles Scribner's Sons, 1985.

Sanders, Sol. *A Sense of Asia*. New York: Charles Scribner's Sons, 1969.

Schandler, Herbert. *The Unmaking of a President: Lyndon Johnson and Vietnam*. Princeton: Princeton University Press, 1977.

Scheer, Robert. *How the United States Got Involved in Vietnam*. Santa Barbara, Calif.: Center for the Study of Democratic Institutions, 1965.

Schlesinger, Arthur M., Jr. *A Thousand Days: John F. Kennedy in the White House*. Boston: Houghton Mifflin, 1965.

———. *The Vital Center: The Politics of Freedom*. Boston: Houghton Mifflin, 1949.

Schlozman, Kay Lehman, and John T. Tierney. *Organized Interests and American Democracy*. New York: Harper and Row, 1986.

Scigliano, Robert. *South Vietnam: Nation Under Stress.* Boston: Houghton Mifflin, 1963.
Scigliano, Robert, and Guy H. Fox. *Technical Assistance in Vietnam: The Michigan State University Experience.* New York: Frederick A. Praeger, 1965.
Shaplen, Robert. *The Lost Revolution.* New York: Harper and Row, 1965.
———. *A Turning Wheel: Three Decades of the Asian Revolution.* New York: Random House, 1979.
Small, Melvin. *Johnson, Nixon, and the Doves.* New Brunswick, N.J.: Rutgers University Press, 1988.
Smith, Ralph B. *An International History of the Vietnam War.* Vol. 2, *The Struggle for South-East Asia.* London: Macmillan, 1985.
Snepp, Frank. *Decent Interval: An Insider's Account of Saigon's Indecent End.* New York: Random House, 1977.
So, Alvin Y. *Social Change and Development: Modernization, Dependency, and World System Theories.* Newbury Park, Calif.: Sage Publications, 1990.
Spector, Ronald H. *Advice and Support: The Early Years, 1941–1960.* Washington, D.C.: Center of Military History, 1983; New York: Free Press, 1985.
Steel, Ronald. *Imperialists and Other Heroes: A Chronicle of the American Empire.* New York: Random House, 1971.
Taylor, Maxwell. *Swords and Plowshares.* New York: W. W. Norton, 1972.
Thies, Paul A., and Edmund L. Henshaw, eds. *Who's Who in American Politics, 1967–1968.* New York: Bowker, 1967.
Thomson, James C., Peter W. Stanley, and John Curtis Perry. *Sentimental Imperialists: The American Experience in East Asia.* New York: Harper and Row, 1981.
Tomes, Robert R. "American Intellectuals and the Vietnam War, 1954–1973." Ph.D. diss., New York University, 1987.
Tucker, Nancy Bernkopf. *Patterns in the Dust: Chinese-American Relations and the Recognition Controversy, 1949–1950.* New York: Columbia University Press, 1983.
Van Tien Dung. *Our Great Spring Victory.* New York: Monthly Review Press, 1977.
Walinsky, Louis J., ed. *Agrarian Reform as Unfinished Business: The Selected Papers of Wolf Ladejinsky.* New York: Oxford University Press, 1977.
Warner, Denis. *The Last Confucian: Vietnam, South-East Asia, and the West.* London: Penguin Books, 1964.
Westmoreland, William C. *A Soldier Reports.* Garden City, N.Y.: Doubleday, 1976.
Who's Who in America, 1990–1991. 2 vols. Wilmette, Ill.: Macmillan Directory Division, 1990.
Who's Who in the East, 1989–1990. 22nd ed. Wilmette, Ill.: Macmillan Directory Division, 1988.
Windchy, Eugene. *Tonkin Gulf.* Garden City, N.Y.: Doubleday, 1971.
Wise, Thomas, and David Ross. *The Espionage Establishment.* New York: Random House, 1967.
Zaroulis, Nancy, and Gerald Sullivan. *Who Spoke Up?: American Protest against the War in Vietnam, 1963–1975.* Garden City, N.Y.: Doubleday, 1984.

index

Acheson, Dean, 132, 133, 143
Adams, Sherman, 26
Agency for International Development (AID), 111, 125, 147
Alsop, Joseph, 20, 24
American Conservative Union, 147
American Friends of Captive Nations, 4
American Friends of Vietnam (AFV), ix, 103, 159. *See also* Ngo Dinh Diem; Republic of Vietnam; State Department (U.S.); Tran Van Chuong; *individual AFV members, presidential administrations, and U.S. presidents*
—activities (1950s): support for Diem, 31–32, 50–53, 55–59; opposition to 1956 elections, 35–37; conferences, 39–44, 47–50, 177–78 (n. 45); special events and projects, 52–53; aid projects, 53
—activities (1960s): aid projects, 67, 88–89; conference, 67–68; support for Diem, 68–69, 72–74; criticisms of Diem, 97–98, 100; support for U.S. Vietnam policy, 108–10, 114–16, 117–18, 122, 124–28; response to antiwar critics, 119–21
—activities (1970s): support for U.S. Vietnam policy, 140–41, 143; aid projects, 145–46; Emergency Committee for a Free Vietnam, 147–52
—as a lobbying group: characteristics, x–xiii; influence on U.S. policy, 44–45, 89–90, 102–3, 153–54, 158–59; influence on Diem regime, 55–56, 72–74, 76; influence on U.S. public opinion, 58–59, 60, 102, 129–30
—organization of: establishment, 15, 24–27, 174 (n. 57); membership, 33–34, 46–47, 104–5, 123–24, 137–38, 175–76 (n. 7), 176 (n. 8); finances, 60–61, 89, 103, 105, 116, 119, 130–31, 134–35, 139–40, 142, 146–47, 203 (n. 11), 204 (n. 30); policy disputes, 78–80, 85–88, 94–97, 102–3.
American Mercury, 56
American Socialist Party, 6, 25
Amory, Robert, 10, 11
Andreatta, Louis, 47, 67, 69, 85, 102, 103, 105, 187 (n. 52), 192 (n. 29), 193 (n. 38)
Anson, M. L., 33
Anticommunism, 12, 29, 126, 159, 160
Antiwar movement, 93, 110–11, 123, 131–32, 140, 141
Ap Bac: battle, 93
Army of the Republic of Vietnam (ARVN), 82, 93, 95, 108, 144, 149, 151
Asia Foundation, 53, 155
Asia Society, 113
Aspen Institute, 148
Atrocities: communist, 126–27, 128, 143

Bao Dai, 38, 63; relationship with Diem, 1–3, 9–11, 23, 27
Barnett, Frank, 140
Baron, Murray, 127–28, 133, 149, 158, 201 (n. 48); as AFV officer, 123–24, 131, 134
Baroody, William J., 142
Beech, Keyes, 84
Bell, George T., 142
Benton, William, 4
Berlin, 78, 90
Binh Xuyen, 16, 23–24, 27, 35, 55

221

Bissell, Richard, 10
Bohannon, Col. Charles T., 107, 114, 196 (n. 53)
Bonsal, Philip W., 5
Bradley, Omar, 133, 135, 143
Brownell, Herbert, 138
Brownell, William, 138–39, 158
Buckley, William F., 149
Buddhists, 93, 94–95, 160
Bui Diem, 128–29, 158
Bundy, McGeorge, 77, 90, 107, 108, 109, 195 (n. 19)
Bundy, William, 107
Bunting, Frederick H., 42
Buttinger, Joseph, xi–xii, 7, 46, 62, 65, 75, 110, 155, 197 (n. 61)
—AFV and: as officer, x, 33, 36, 40, 41, 48, 77–78, 97, 101, 105, 106; establishment, 24–25, 154; resignation, 114–15
—Diem and: support, 21–22, 27–28, 51, 56, 58, 64, 69, 70, 72, 76; doubts and criticisms, 29, 56, 63–64, 70–71, 79, 83, 85–86, 91, 93, 95, 97–98, 185 (n. 9), 186 (n. 40), 188 (n. 11); reaction to Diem assassination, 99–100
—early involvement in Vietnam: background, 18, 171 (n. 15); 1954 trip to Vietnam, 19–20, 171–72 (n. 21); Lansdale and, 172 (n. 38)
Byrd, Richard E., 25, 33, 51, 181 (n. 27)
Byrnes, James, 133

Cable, John, 44
Calderon, Joseph, 167 (n. 15)
Cambodia, 19, 84, 141, 143
Can Lao Party, 55, 99
Cao Dai, 16, 27, 160
Caravelle Group, 67, 68
Castro, Fidel, 79
Catholic Relief Services (CRS), 16, 52
Celler, Emmanuel, 54
Center for the Study of Democratic Institutions, 119–20
Central Intelligence Agency (CIA), 98, 132; role in Diem's appointment, 10; role in Diem's break with Oram, 80–81; allegations of influence in AFV, 154–56, 206 (nn. 15, 16)
Chamberlain, John, 147
Cherne, Leo, 35, 56, 62, 90, 91, 115, 133, 159, 182 (n. 51), 187 (n. 51); as AFV officer, x, 25, 33, 46, 106, 114, 134; background, 17; 1954 trip to Vietnam, 17–18, 26; support for Diem, 22, 27, 29, 51, 56, 69, 71–72, 76, 175 (n. 92); participation in AFV conferences, 42, 48–49; 1960 trip to Vietnam, 65–66, 73, 185 (n. 15); reaction to Diem assassination, 99; reaction to Scheer articles, 120–21
Chiang Kai-shek, 6, 12, 40, 158
Chicago Daily News, 84
China, 6, 13
China, People's Republic of, 37, 114, 115, 144
China, Republic of, 158
China Lobby, 12, 40, 158–59
Chou En-lai, 37, 39
Citizens Committee for Peace With Freedom in Vietnam, 131–34, 143
Clark, Joan, 47
Clifford, Clark, 132
Coffin, William Sloan, 127
Colegrove, Albert M., 57–60
Collins, Gen. J. Lawton, 19, 20, 21, 22–24, 52
Colson, Charles, 140–41, 143
Columbia Broadcasting System (CBS), 143
Columbia University, 39, 48, 53, 64, 88, 118
Commercial Import Program (CIP), 59–60, 98
Committee of One Million Against the Admission of Communist China to the United Nations, 5, 21
Committee to Aid Refugee Chinese Intellectuals, 4–5, 21
Conant, James B., 132, 133

Congress (U.S.), 50; support for Diem, 23–24, 28, 54; relationship with AFV, 25–26, 54, 57–58, 110; opposition to Vietnam war, 141–42, 147, 150–51
—Committee on Foreign Affairs (House), 5, 24, 54, 57, 184 (n. 85)
—Committee on Foreign Relations (Senate), 57, 59, 83
Congressional Record, 54
Cooper, Chester L., 7; relationship with AFV, 111–14, 116–17, 118–19, 156
Cooper-Church amendment, 142
Cornell University, 53
Council on Foreign Relations, 47
Cuba, 78, 79, 90

Dai Viet Party, 19, 129, 171–72 (n. 23)
Da Nang, 108
Defense Department (U.S.), 92, 111, 125
De Jaegher, Raymond, 6, 34, 57, 81, 84–85, 190 (n. 42)
Democratic Republic of Vietnam (DRV), 108, 122, 134, 145; attacks on AFV, 32–33, 43; support of NLF, 62, 106; offensives in RVN, 144, 148–49, 151
Department of Agriculture (U.S.), 64
Dien Bien Phu: battle, 9, 15
Dillon, C. Douglas, 9–10
Donovan, Maj. Gen. William J., x, 10, 17; contacts with Diem, 6; as AFV's honorary chairman, 25, 31; correspondence with Eisenhower, 37; resignation from AFV, 46
Dooley, Thomas A., 16, 34, 42
Dorn, William Jennings Bryan, 54, 58
Douglas, Paul H., 133–34, 135
Douglas, William O., ix, x, 33, 34, 52, 53; Diem and, 8, 10–11, 12; allegations of CIA influence in AFV, 154–56
Du Berrier, Hilaire, 55, 56, 179 (n. 3), 182 (n. 51)
Dubin, Elinor, 47
Duff, James H., 5
Duke, Angier Biddle, 35, 56, 69, 182 (n. 51); as AFV officer, 25, 31, 33, 46–47, 179 (n. 4); participation in AFV activities, 25–26, 35, 40, 48, 51
Dulles, John Foster, 37–38, 43, 64; and Diem, 5–6, 10, 21, 23; 1956 message to AFV, 42–43
Duong Van Minh, 98, 105, 151
Dupuy, Trevor N., 113
Durbrow, Elbridge, 80–81
Durdin, Peg, 20, 22
Durdin, Tillman, 20, 82, 83

Eisenhower, Dwight D., 9, 19, 23, 43, 50, 133; messages to AFV, 37, 42–43, 51, 53–54
Eisenhower administration, x–xi, 120, 154; Vietnam policy of, 10, 15, 18–19, 23–24, 37–38, 41–42, 44–45; relationship with AFV, 26, 53–54, 179–80 (n. 11)
Emergency Committee for a Free Vietnam, 147–52
Emmet, Christopher, x, 11, 38, 48, 133, 158, 171 (n. 14); background, 4–5; support for Diem, 5, 11–12, 88, 167 (n. 15); as AFV officer, 25, 78, 86–87, 96, 102, 107, 114, 190 (n. 46), 204–5 (n. 45); doubts about Diem, 70

Fall, Bernard B., 55, 67
Federal Bureau of Investigation, 132
Feighan, Michael, 54
Fishel, Wesley R., 62, 65, 71, 75, 85, 127, 133, 149, 155
—AFV and: as officer, x, 47, 78; as chairman, 104, 106–8, 113–16, 121; on organizational problems, 119; resignation, 123
—Diem and: early contacts with, 7–8, 169 (n. 32); support, 49, 53, 56, 57, 67, 69, 72, 74, 76; doubts and criticisms, 66–67, 73, 83–84, 87, 91–92, 191 (n. 6)
—early involvement in Vietnam: background, 7; adviser to Diem regime, 20–21
—U.S. government and: contacts with

State Department, 11, 93–94, 98, 107, 109; collaboration with, 125
Ford, Gerald R., 147, 150, 205 (n. 58)
Foreign Affairs, 63
Foreign Office (Great Britain), 43–44
Foreign Operations Administration, 18
France, 8, 15, 19, 27, 36–37; and Diem, 1–2, 16, 23, 24; and war against Viet Minh, 2–3, 9
Frederick A. Praeger (publisher), 155
Freedom House, 133, 148
Freedoms Foundation, 52
Fyan, 85

Gallo, Gregory, 116, 119
Gallup polls, 123, 150
Gardiner, Muriel, 18, 171 (n. 15)
Geneva Conference and Accords, 9, 15, 31; AFV opposition to election provisions, 35–37, 44–45, 120, 126
Gerard, James, 144
Goldschmidt, Arthur, 110
Goodrich, Carter, 48
Graves, Hubert, 43–44
Great Britain, 9, 36–37, 43–44, 176 (n. 24)
Greene, Graham, 34, 52–53
Gregory, Eugene, 8, 48, 63, 185 (n. 2)
Gulf of Tonkin Resolution, 106, 142

Haldeman, H. R., 143
Hanes, John W., 5, 10
Hannah, John B., 83, 90
Harnett, Joseph, 16, 42, 47, 88, 179 (n. 5), 204–5 (n. 45)
Hearst, William Randolph, Jr., 34
Heath, Donald, 21, 34–35
Henderson, William, 34, 77–78, 121, 149, 151–52; as AFV officer, x, 47, 79–80, 86–87, 94, 96, 103, 106–7, 113, 130, 139–41, 142, 143, 145–46; criticisms of Diem, 63, 70, 91; support for Diem, 69, 72
Herter, Christian A., 5, 12
Hillings, Patrick J., 54

Hilsman, Roger, 113
Historical Evaluation and Research Organization (HERO), 113
Hoa Hao, 16, 27
Ho Chi Minh, 2, 7, 35, 38, 44, 149, 159
Ho Huu Tuong, 55–56, 58, 63, 182 (n. 55)
Holdridge, John, 145
Ho Nhut Tan, 71
Hotham, David, 55
Houghton, Dorothy, 173 (n. 47)
Hovgard, Carl, 65–66
Howard, Roy, 60
Howe, Fisher, 42
Hue, 1, 93, 99, 126
Humphrey, Hubert H., 112, 135
Hutchins, Robert Maynard, 120

Industrial Development Center, 49, 59
Internal Revenue Service (IRS), 60–61
International Control Commission, 36
International Cooperation Administration (ICA), 42, 49, 64
International Rescue Committee (IRC): background, 16–17; relief work in Vietnam, 17–18, 171 (n. 14); relationship with AFV, 25, 33, 51–52, 179 (n. 3)

Jacques, Emmanuel, 4
Japan, 2, 11, 13, 17, 64
Johns Hopkins University, 53, 111
Johnson, Lyndon B., 104, 110, 111, 122, 132–34, 154; relationship with AFV, 107–8, 117, 197 (n. 67)
Johnson, U. Alexis, 78
Johnson administration, 137; Vietnam policy of, 105–6, 108, 111, 115, 122–23, 132, 134; relationship with AFV, 107–8, 111–14, 116–17, 118–19, 128, 155
Jonas, Gilbert A., 48, 58, 60, 62, 66, 69, 75, 127, 187 (n. 64)
—AFV and: as officer, x, 47, 78, 79, 86, 96, 104–5, 106, 110, 114, 116, 118, 186

(n. 29); early career, 39–40, 41; on organizational problems, 119; and reaction to Scheer articles, 120–21; resignation from, 123
—Diem and: 1959 trip to Vietnam, 64–65; support, 71, 72; doubts and criticisms, 82–83, 87–88, 91–92, 95, 98, 189 (n. 32)
—RVN and: public relations work, 156–57, 200 (n. 34)
Judd, Walter H., 5, 21, 40, 57, 64, 149

Kahin, George McT., 113, 196 (n. 45)
Karnow, Stanley, 82
Kastor, Hilton, Chesley, Clifford, and Atherton (public relations firm), 80, 128, 188 (n. 16)
Kattenburg, Paul, 21, 28, 40, 48, 98, 193 (n. 34)
Kelly, Edna F., 5, 24, 54, 167 (n. 15)
Kennedy, John F., ix–x, 31, 43, 67, 78, 82, 89–90; 1953 meeting with Diem, 8, 169 (n. 37); relationship with AFV, 41, 54; reaction to Diem assassination, 101
Kennedy, Joseph P., 173 (n. 42)
Kennedy, Robert F., 131–32
Kennedy administration, xiii, 70, 81, 153; Vietnam policy of, 77, 78, 82, 89–90, 92–93, 95, 98; relationship with AFV, 90
King, Martin Luther, Jr., 131
King and Maheu Associates, 81
Kissberg, Nicholas, 117
Kissinger, Henry A., 140, 144–45
Korean War, 2, 34
Krim, Arthur, 116–17, 118, 197 (n. 67)
Kuhn, Irene Corbally, 71
Kulp, Earl M., 147
Kunen, James L., 184 (n. 83)

Ladejinsky, Wolf, 48, 51, 58, 62, 71, 75, 81, 157, 182 (n. 57); support for Diem, 49, 53, 56, 72, 73, 76; background, 64; doubts and criticisms of Diem, 64–65, 66, 69

La Gazette, 32
Land reform: Vietnamese, 62, 73
Lansdale, Maj. Gen. Edward G., 10, 27, 35, 81, 107, 172 (n. 38); support for Diem, 28, 92; relationship with AFV, 52, 94, 145; *Quiet American* and, 52, 181 (n. 34)
Laos, 19, 78, 90, 140–41
Lee, J. Bracken, 58
Leerburger, Franklin J., 47, 78, 79, 86–87, 190 (n. 49)
Leibman, Morris I., 117, 135
Life, 22
Lindsay, John V., 110
Lockard, Diana N., 47, 69, 86–87, 190 (n. 49)
Lodge, Henry Cabot, 98, 99, 105, 130
Lowenstein, Allard, 127
Luce, Clare Booth, 149
Luce, Henry R., 27, 34, 51, 52, 173 (n. 49)

MacArthur, Douglas, II, 43
McCarthy, Joseph, 12, 17
McCloy, John, 132
MacEoin, Gary, 6; allegations of CIA influence in AFV, 154–56
McNamara, Robert S., 108
Makins, Roger, 43
Mankiewicz, Joseph, 34, 52
Mansfield, Mike, ix–x, 5, 52, 92, 183 (n. 65); 1953 meeting with Diem, 8; support for Diem, 23–24, 28, 54, 173 (n. 53); membership in AFV, 54
Martin, David, 36, 38, 151–52
Maryknoll Mission Society, 3, 5, 50
Meany, George, 132, 133
Mekong Delta, 85
Mekong River: development plan, 107, 109–10
Mesta, Perle, 52
Michener, James, 53
Michigan State University, 8, 50, 53, 112–13; assistance program to Diem regime, 47, 84, 125, 189–90 (n. 39)

Military Assistance and Advisory Group (MAAG), 34, 35
Modernization and development theories, 12–13
Morgenthau, Hans J., 41, 43
Muhlen, Norbert, 33, 94
Murphy, Audie, 34

Nation, 55, 70
National Association for the Advancement of Colored People (NAACP), 21, 39
National Liberation Front (NLF), 68, 82, 92, 104, 144, 145. *See also* Democratic Republic of Vietnam (DRV); Republic of Vietnam (RVN)
National Security Council, (NSC), 107–8, 111
National Student Association (NSA), 116, 155
Nehru, Jawaharlal, 13
Newcomb, Elliot H., 33, 95–96
New Leader, 33
Newman, Edwin, 118
New Republic, 184 (n. 79)
New York, N.Y., 47, 49, 50, 51, 79, 86, 103, 118, 147
New Yorker, 104
New York Herald-Tribune, 22, 31
New York Times, 22, 27, 28, 52, 71, 93, 117, 119, 149, 151; coverage of AFV activities, 31, 118
New York Times Magazine, 20, 22, 71
Ngo Dinh Can, 55, 99, 193 (n. 38)
Ngo Dinh Diem, ix–xiii, 120, 128, 151, 153, 160, 167 (nn. 3, 15)
—American supporters and: early contacts, 3–8; influence, 10–11, 27–29; expectations, 11–14, 29–30, 158; relationship with AFV, 32, 42, 51–52, 72–76, 206–7 (n. 21); in 1957 state visit to United States, 50–51
—early life and exile: background, 1–2; trips to Japan, United States, and Europe, 2–3
—as leader of RVN: appointment by Bao Dai, 9–11; domestic opposition, 15–16, 23–24, 55–56, 62–63, 67, 68, 82, 84, 93, 94–95; elections as president, 27, 71; investment policies, 49, 59–60; establishment of dictatorship, 54–55; overthrow and assassination, 98–99. *See also* American Friends of Vietnam (AFV); Bao Dai; Ngo Dinh Nhu; Tran Van Chuong; *individual AFV members*
Ngo Dinh Kha, 1
Ngo Dinh Khoi, 2
Ngo Dinh Luyen, 9, 55, 99
Ngo Dinh Nhu, 10, 20, 50, 62, 185 (n. 2); influence in Diem regime, 55, 66, 73, 82, 83–84, 92, 94–95; assassination, 99
Ngo Dinh Nhu, Mme., 20, 50, 55, 62, 73, 93, 97, 99, 101, 185 (n. 2)
Ngo Dinh Thuc, 1–3, 5, 11, 54–55, 99
Nguyen Cao Ky, 118, 129
Nguyen Dinh Quat, 71
Nguyen Huu Chi, 146
Nguyen Khanh, 105
Nguyen Ngoc Tho, 58, 65, 72, 105
Nguyen Phu Duc, 128, 139, 157, 158, 206 (n. 21)
Nguyen Thanh Phuong, 71
Nguyen The Truyen, 71
Nguyen Ton Hoan, 91–92, 191 (n. 1)
Nguyen Van Thieu, 118, 126, 129, 146–47, 148–49, 151; and message from AFV members, 144–45
Nitze, Paul, 149
Nixon, Richard M., 26, 58, 67, 137, 140, 141, 143, 144, 145, 147
Nixon administration, 128, 147; Vietnam policy of, 140, 141–42, 144, 145; relationship with AFV, 140–41, 142, 145, 155
Nolting, Frederick, 81, 83, 84

O'Daniel, Lt. Gen. John W., x, 67, 85, 156, 182 (n. 51); background, 34; as AFV chairman, 34–35, 39, 86–87, 102–3, 176 (nn. 16, 24), 180 (n. 13);

contacts with Eisenhower administration, 35, 40–41, 43, 184 (n. 85); support for Diem, 35, 52, 57–58, 70, 71, 72, 74, 78, 79, 88, 94, 189 (n. 32), 190 (n. 48); AFV investment program and, 47, 48–49, 59; resignation from AFV, 96–97, 100–101
O'Melia, Thomas, 5–6
O'Neill, Hugh, 126, 127, 129, 130–31, 135–36, 138, 139
OPLAN 34-A, 106
Oram, Harold L., 75, 84, 153, 154, 155, 158; as AFV officer, x, 33, 39, 46, 79, 86, 96, 102; background, 21; assistance to Buttinger, 21–22; establishment of AFV, 24–26, 35, 176 (n. 16); public relations contract with RVN, 26–27, 51, 65, 156–57, 186 (n. 29), 188 (n. 15), 206 (n. 15); AFV investment programs and, 47–48, 59; support for Diem, 56–57, 67; termination of public relations contract with RVN, 80–82, 128
Ortiz, Jorge, 206–7 (n. 21)

Paris, 134, 140, 144
Paris accords, 145, 149
Parmer, Norman, 113
Parsons, J. Graham, 54
Pathet Lao, 141
Paulding, Gouverneur, 6
Personalism, 6
Persons, Wilton B., 43, 178 (n. 58)
Pew Foundation, 130–31
Pham Cong Tac, 27
Philippines, 13, 107
Pleiku, 108, 109
Powell, Adam Clayton, 54
Price, Hoyt, 48
Public Information Office (PIO), 39

Quiet American (novel and film), 34, 52–53

Ramparts, 27, 44, 120
Reader's Digest, 131, 201 (n. 47)

Refugees: Hungarian, 51
Refugees: Vietnamese, 126, 128, 200 (n. 32); influence on U.S. public opinion, 16, 29, 175 (n. 89)
Reinhardt, G. Frederick, 32, 40, 43
Reisin, Seymour, 116
Reporter, 6, 12, 22
Republic of Vietnam (RVN), xi–xiii, 41, 125, 137; elections in, 27, 71, 126, 199 (n. 16); relationship with AFV, 44, 128–29, 138–39, 146, 202 (n. 8); U.S. aid to, 50, 57–60, 98, 147; communist insurgency in, 62–63, 82, 108, 115; political weakness of, 105, 123, 147, 160; collapse of, 148–49, 150–51. *See also* American Friends of Vietnam (AFV); Democratic Republic of Vietnam (DRV); Jonas, Gilbert A.; Ngo Dinh Diem; Oram, Harold L.
Research Institute of America (RIA), 17, 65
Revolutionary Socialists, 18
Richards, James P., 54
Roberts, James C., 147
Robertson, Walter S., 40, 41–42, 44, 54
Roche, John P., 132–33
Rockefeller, David, 132, 197 (n. 64)
ROLLING THUNDER, 108, 114
Rooney, John J., 54
Roosevelt, Eleanor, 83
Rostow, Eugene, 149
Rostow, Walt W., 77
Rothman, Stanley, 117, 118, 198 (n. 82)
Rowan, Carl, 112
Royal Lao Government (RLG), 141
Rusk, Dean, 3, 77, 83
Ryan, William Fitts, 115

Sacks, I. Milton, 7, 33, 38, 40, 56, 104, 133, 149, 168 (n. 28)
Saigon, 9, 17, 24, 68, 98–99, 146, 149, 151
Saltonstall, Leverett, 133
Salzmann, Richard, 25, 51
Sanders, Sol W., 51, 187 (n. 64); back-

Index   227

ground and early support for Diem, 6–7; as AFV member, 25, 33; protest to Diem, 56; resignation from AFV, 100
Sarris, Lewis G., 109
Scheer, Robert, 119–21, 132
Scheuer, James, 110
Schlesinger, Arthur M., Jr., 13, 101
Schneider, William, 147
Scripps-Howard papers, 57, 60
Serong, F. P., 146
Shaplen, Robert, 104, 107, 115, 151
Sihanouk, Norodom, Prince, 141
Southeast Asian Perspectives, 144, 145, 146
Southeast Asia Treaty Organization (SEATO), 19
Soviet Union, 2, 12, 37, 64, 114, 115
Spellman, Francis Cardinal, ix, 10, 21, 51; relationship with Diem, 5, 168 (nn. 17, 18); relationship with AFV, 179 (n. 5)
Stassen, Harold, 18
State Department (U.S), 2–3, 4, 8, 21, 102, 128, 173 (n. 53); relationship with AFV, 35, 40–41, 48, 77–78, 90, 107, 109
State of Vietnam (SVN), 1, 9
Steibel, Gerald, 115
Steinbeck, John, 126, 131
Stevenson, Adlai, 112
Stone, Walker, 57, 58
Stringfellow, William, 127
Student Committee for Victory in Vietnam, 130
Student Coordinating Committee for Freedom in Vietnam, 130, 200–201 (n. 42)
Sun Myung Moon, 150
Sussman, Leonard R., 148

Tanham, George K., 123, 125, 134, 137, 155
Taylor, Maxwell, 82, 89, 101, 130
Teach-ins, 110–11, 113
Teller, Edward, 149

Temple, Mary, 147–48
Tet Offensive, 134–35, 137
Thailand, 33, 37, 134, 137
"Third Force" theories, 13–14
Thomas, Norman M., x, 58, 83, 127; as AFV member, 25, 180 (n. 13); criticisms of Diem, 56, 182 (n. 56)
Thomson, James C., 107
Time, 19–20, 118
Times of Vietnam, 48, 185 (n. 2), 187 (n. 52)
Trager, Frank N., 78, 88, 125, 133, 155; as AFV officer, 47, 79, 113, 114, 115, 116–17, 123–24, 140–41, 144, 148, 149–50
Tran Kim Phuong, 49
Tran Van Chuong, 26, 39, 52, 80, 102, 158; relationship with AFV, 40, 69, 157, 206–7 (n. 21); hostility toward Diem, 74–75, 95, 97, 187 (n. 64); role in Diem's break with Oram, 81–82
Tran Van Chuong, Mme., 52, 75, 192 (n. 29)
Tran Van Huong, 151
Truman, Harry S., 2, 133, 143
Truman administration, 2, 25

United Nations, 48, 83, 139, 146
United States Information Agency (USIA), 112
United States Information Service (USIS), 8, 48
United States Operation Mission (USOM), 20
United States Youth Council, 118, 155
University of Hanoi, 1
University of Hue, 33, 97; AFV aid to, 53, 85, 95–96
University of Michigan, 111
U.S. News and World Report, 20

Valenti, Jack, 111–12, 135
Vanden Heuvel, William, 33
Viet Minh, 2, 5, 9, 10, 12, 15, 62; popular appeal of, 20, 35–36

Vietnam, South. *See* Republic of Vietnam (RVN)
Vietnamese National Army (VNA), 23, 24, 27
Vietnam Perspectives, 117, 118, 127, 128, 143
Vietnam Presse, 32
Viet Nam Report, 117
Vo Van Hai, 69
Vu Van Mau, 50, 95
Vu Van Thai, 50; discontent and break with Diem regime, 63, 65, 82–83, 189 (n. 32); relationship with AFV, 74, 128–29, 158

Wallace, DeWitt, 131
Wallace, Lila Acheson, 131
Ward, William F., 128; as AFV officer, 123–24; as AFV chairman, 137–45 passim; resignation of, 146–47
Washington, D.C., 23, 49, 50, 128, 149–50
Washington Post, 31, 56, 83, 149, 189 (n. 32)
Watergate scandal, 147

Weinberg, Sidney, 112, 118, 135, 196 (n. 39)
Weisl, Edwin, Sr., 116–17, 118, 197 (n. 67)
Westmoreland, Gen. William C., 108, 115, 132
White, Peter, 4, 6, 11–12
Wicker, Tom, 143
Williams, Harrison A., 150
Williams, Lt. Gen. Samuel T., 35, 52, 81, 204 (n. 38)
Woolard, Frazier T., 155
Wright, Quincy, 7, 168 (n. 29)
Wurfel, David, 113

Xuan Loc: battle, 151

Young, Kenneth T., 21–22, 24, 40, 48, 115; support of Diem, 70, 71; as AFV officer, 104, 107, 110, 113, 186 (n. 39)
Young Americans for Freedom (YAF), 130

Zablocki, Clement, 57–58, 110
Zumwalt, Adm. Elmo R., Jr., 149

www.ingramcontent.com/pod-product-compliance
Lightning Source LLC
Chambersburg PA
CBHW021400290426
44108CB00010B/320